Women and Evacuation in the Second World War

Women and Evacuation in the Second World War

Femininity, Domesticity and Motherhood

Maggie Andrews

BLOOMSBURY ACADEMIC
LONDON • NEW YORK • OXFORD • NEW DELHI • SYDNEY

BLOOMSBURY ACADEMIC
Bloomsbury Publishing Plc
50 Bedford Square, London, WC1B 3DP, UK
1385 Broadway, New York, NY 10018, USA
29 Earlsfort Terrace, Dublin 2, Ireland

BLOOMSBURY, BLOOMSBURY ACADEMIC and the Diana logo
are trademarks of Bloomsbury Publishing Plc

First published in Great Britain 2019
Paperback edition first published 2021

Cover image: Schoolchildern evacuated from London during WW" air raids 1939.
(© Trinity Mirror / Mirrorpix / Alamy Stock Photo)

A catalogue record for this book is available from the British Library.

A catalog record for this book is available from the Library of Congress.

ISBN: HB: 978-1-4411-4068-5
PB: 978-1-3501-9616-2
ePDF: 978-1-4411-6411-7
eBook: 978-1-4411-7643-1

Typeset by Newgen KnowledgeWorks Pvt. Ltd., Chennai, India

To find out more about our authors and books visit
www.bloomsbury.com and sign up for our newsletters.

This book is for my children, four very special people
Lynton, Oli, Dom and Annie.
And for all mums who find motherhood an endless mixture of emotions,
joy, insecurity, regret, pride, doubt and love.

Contents

Abbreviations

ARP	Air Raid Precautions
BBC	British Broadcasting Corporation
CORB	Children's Overseas Reception Board
LCC	London County Council
LEA	local education authority
MOI	Ministry of Information
NFWI	National Federation of Women's Institute
WI	Women's Institute
WVS	Women's Voluntary Service

Acknowledgements

This book has taken rather longer than it should have to write and during that time I have had assistance from sources too numerous to mention but it would not have been finished without the support, help and forbearance of many people in both my private and professional life, to whom I owe a debt of gratitude. A huge thank you has to go first to the Staffordshire Archives and Museum Service and those who were involved in Heritage Lottery Funded *Children on the Move Project*: Matthew Blake, Chris Copp and Louise Price. A huge thank you also goes to the interviewees on this project and other oral history and memory projects who have, like the writers of autobiographies, shared and recorded their memories. I have also had the benefit of the help and support at numerous other archives over many years, including Mass Observation Archive, Worcestershire Country Archive and Archeological Service, the National Archives, BBC People's War website, the Women's Library and local and national Women's Institute and Women's Voluntary Service Archives.

Friends and colleagues in the Women's History Network in my workplace and beyond have provided support, encouragement and patience: thank you to Paula Bartley, Neil Fleming, Paddy McNally, Sallie McNamara, Alyzn Johnson, Lesley Spiers, Gill Thorn and first and foremost Janis Lomas who so kindly read this manuscript and provided many helpful suggestions. The University of Worcester also provided practical support by allocating me Research Leave in 2018 and a Vacation Research Assistant in 2014 who worked on the project; thanks also need to go to postgraduate and undergraduate students in the university's History department who have been tolerant in listening to me rabbiting on about evacuation for many years. I would also like to take this opportunity to express my appreciation to my publisher Bloomsbury, for their forbearance with my endless delays in completing this task and also the excellent anonymous reviewer who made a number of really helpful suggestions. Any omissions, mistakes and oversights are of course my own.

Finally, my thanks go to my children and grandchildren for the forbearance about my preoccupation with the past – Lynton, Oliver, Dominic, Annie, and the next generation – Lucia, Erin, Edu, Florence, Stanley and Remi. As always, my special thanks has to go to my partner Neil Eldred for his unflinching emotional support and practical assistance without which I wouldn't ever finish anything.

Introduction

The small child with a label on, carrying a gas mask and a cardboard suitcase waiting at an urban railway station to be evacuated to the countryside has become one of the iconic images of the Second World War. Children removed from city homes to places of safety among the green fields of the British countryside are symbolic of the disruption of the total war, the resilience of the British and the importance of the rural as the heart of the nation. This emphasis on histories of children who were evacuated has however inadvertently silenced many other histories of evacuation – particular those of the ordinary women whose domestic lives and families were turned upside down, many of them destroyed beyond repair, by the political failures that led to war.

This book is an attempt to tell some of these other stories of evacuation – women's stories. It is a book about motherhood, about the lives, sacrifices and experiences of mothering in wartime. It explores the decisions that women had to make in caring for their own children but equally in caring for the children of others. As ever with the care of the young and vulnerable the stakes were high. Children who had not been evacuated were among the approximately sixty thousand people who died as a result of bombing in Britain during the Second World War; about the same number as were killed when the allies bombed Dresden between 13 and 15 February 1945; every British and German death was a consequence of governmental policies of waging industrial-style aerial warfare. The decisions made by those looking after other people's children carried equally dire consequences. Unknowingly or without thinking, harassed and hard-working foster mothers allowed children to roam in unfamiliar rural surroundings. Eight-year-old Eileen Hill, from Margate, was evacuated to Kings Bromley in Staffordshire only to drown in the River Trent on 20 November 1940 while playing with friends. It was later noted by the coroner that she was the third evacuee to die in the river.

That women were 'natural' carers of children was presumed in the Second World War; it was unquestioned that women had a biological imperative to 'mother' whether in homes or schools and hostels. But any natural caring instinct women might have had was shaped and reshaped, pushed this way and that by the 'oughts' and 'shoulds' and 'cans' and 'cant's' of social, community and governmental pressures and prohibitions. During the conflict, the sense that motherhood was a public concern that numerous external groups had a stake in or an opinion on grew. Biological, foster and social mothering were overlaid with a complex web of expectations. Individual women's lives were constrained by tiny gossamer threads, which restrained their being: duty, doing the right thing, guilt, supporting the war effort, patriotism, empathy and sympathy for others, forces and causes which seemed so very much bigger than women were themselves. Wartime accelerated the degree to which motherhood and domesticity were public issues.

War, like peace, is a gendered experience,[1] which shapes the everyday lives of women in a multitude of small or significant ways, according to their class, age, ethnicity, marital status, the region in which they lived and their own individual circumstances. Indeed, at an individual level, the Second World War in Britain may have at various points been experienced by some women as either invigorating, crushing, liberating, exhilarating, soul-destroying, even a time of independence; it is often remembered as having offered new experiences, been the heyday of some women's life but also as a source of grief, boredom, opportunity, insecurity, humour, romance or all or none of these things. For historians seeking to explore and explain the complex interplay of gendered power relations, the scripts that women may perform[2] in wartime are often contradictory, containing both change and continuity. Too often in historians' analyses there has been a desire to see in the horror of war a sharp break with the past, a change of direction, to identify forces of social change. Far too frequently historians have looked for signs of change through the prism of contemporary Western values which equate progress for women with paid work; forgetting that the majority of women in Britain were housewives in both the First and Second World Wars.[3]

This book suggests that during the Second World War the practices and discourses of motherhood and domesticity were stretched, sometimes challenged or reworked, as the local and national governments, voluntary organizations, teachers and, most importantly, housewives and mothers sought to negotiate the multifarious experience of wartime evacuation. For those caught up in it, evacuation changed lives, fractured families and led to a more complex shifting relationship between the public and private spheres. The decision to billet the vast majority of children and their mothers evacuated from danger in private homes in supposedly safe areas, despite much advice to the contrary, meant evacuation was both a public and a private, personal event. Perhaps never before had private domestic relationships and public policy been so entangled.

This book is grounded in the traditions of women's, feminist and people's history in which women are not passive victims – rather, they exert agency; women make their own history but not in circumstances of their own choosing. Women were not merely victims of wartime attentiveness on domestic and family life, so this book is also about resistance and resentment, about women who do not always do and say the right things or follow advice, but who struggle and exploit the spaces and places where they can exert a little autonomy. Women too were war profiteers; although not necessarily spivs or industrialists with lucrative government contracts; instead some women relished the power and influence volunteering for wartime organizations offered, and kept their cars on the road by taking on voluntary war work. Other women sought to expand their areas of influence and expertise via the new opportunities opened up by wartime evacuation; organizing, commentating on, analysing, judging, advising and inspecting the lives of other women.

Academic work undertaken in the 1960s and 1970s focused upon the potential contribution of evacuation to the introduction of the post-war welfare state,[4] in the last thirty years there has been a strong impetus to rediscover the history of evacuation, to gain an understanding beyond this iconic image, focusing on the experiences of those whose families were disrupted and fractured by what might be described as a mass social experiment. The increasing popularity of social history beyond schools and universities, in oral history collections, autobiographies, museums and on television, has facilitated this, as has the work since 1995 of the Evacuees' Reunion Association, so that evacuees now walk in parades on Remembrance Sunday and there is a closer engagement with the emotional impact of evacuation on the children involved.[5] The memories they recall and the stories that are told about evacuation in numerous autobiographies and books are structured by three interwoven and overlapping paradigms of childhood history in post-war Britain. The first of these was concerned with the physical circumstances in which childhood was lived: housing, food, warmth, clothing, poverty and affluence. The second explores the history of welfare, the shifting and competing responsibilities of home and parents, government and local authorities, schools and teachers, health and social workers, who all had responsibility for the welfare of children. In recent years a third approach focusing on childhood as socially constructed has emerged; that is the suggestion that as a society Britain has changed its ideas about what childhood is and how long it lasts, as expectations of children's behaviour and emotions have shifted.

This study seeks to move the terrain of historical studies of evacuation again by placing attention on the mundane and often forgotten histories of the experiences and emotions of the very many women for whom evacuation was an intimate, predominantly domestic experience, about making sandwiches and mending clothes, nature walks and Christmas parties. However, although evacuation is very much part of the national narrative of Britain's experience of the Second World War, understanding how what can be described as a mass social experiment was experienced and responded to by women is not easy. The voices of wartime children, whether evacuees or from host families are still accessible, but the histories of their hosts, the hundreds and thousands of women who looked after evacuees or waved goodbye to their children, can only be glimpsed at, along with the harassed local government workers, billeting officers, and volunteers who with police and teachers organized the practical details of evacuation. Finding ordinary women's voices among the mass of officials, commentators and experts involves what one of my postgraduate students describes as 'grubbing around in the archives' to find traces and snippets of the past.

This research for this book has involved many years of trawling through a mass of personal sources, the letters and diaries, memoirs and biographies of those who lived through this tumultuous time. It also draws upon material produced for Mass Observation, the social research organization founded in 1937, which attempted to record everyday life and through its observers and diarists from across country.[6] At its heart however is a Heritage Lottery Funded project 'Children On the Move: Evacuation in Staffordshire'[7] carried out with Staffordshire Archive and Museum Service between 2010 and 2012 which has been an important foundation for the research for this book. Over ninety oral history interviews were undertaken for the project and examined alongside autobiographies, memoirs and diaries related to Staffordshire. Personal accounts of evacuation were complemented by the study of local government and voluntary organizations written records, newspapers and contemporary writing on evacuation in wartime. The project was one of the first studies to focus on a reception area for evacuees in the Second World War and has provided the foundation for wider research, but the county of Staffordshire and the West Midlands nevertheless lie at the heart of this book. The circumstances that shaped the narratives of these evacuees are regionally specific, in many respects very English stories of evacuation; it should therefore be remembered that women living in Wales, Scotland or Northern Ireland did not necessarily share the particularities of their experiences.

No historical event or crisis happens in a vacuum, even one as tumultuous as the Second World War, evacuation only occurred in the way that it did because of the very particular circumstances of the time, attitudes to children, to housewives, to the education of working-class children and to mothers. To the contemporary critic, the very idea of evacuation may seem absurd, bizarre, cruel, careless of children's and their families' emotions. Every time I talk about the Second World War evacuation, someone inevitably says that they could not possibly have had their children evacuated. But the mindset of someone in the twenty-first century is not that of someone living eighty years ago. The hopes and fears, the practical problems and challenges were very different. As a grandmother I like to imagine I would have welcomed my grandchildren from the danger zones of London and the South Coast to the relative safety of the rural areas of the West Midlands. But I wonder how I would have coped financially, how soon would I have got harassed and tired. Would I by 1942, when many expected the war to last for ten years, willingly agreed to their returning home despite the dangers? This book begins in Chapter 1, by seeking to interrogate the context in which evacuation took place, the fears and the anxieties of people at the time in relation to the threats of bombing before and during the conflict. Chapter 2, 'Nationalizing Hundreds and Thousands of Women', traces external influences on homes and on the women in them, brought about by the government policy of evacuating children in private homes and in particular the work of billeting officers and child psychologists.

The chapters that follow look at the diverse narratives and experiences of the different groups of women who were involved in evacuation: birth mothers whose children were evacuated without them, women who were evacuated with their children, foster mothers, the paid and then the voluntary carers of evacuees. The histories in these chapters, their perspectives are not consistent with one another, rather they convey very different narratives of evacuation. A snippet from a Barnett House survey of London children evacuated to Oxfordshire explaining very different attitudes to evacuee clothing serves to illuminate this:

> On the one hand were Oxford people with 'respectable' standards of a child's minimum requirements and on the other mother's who had 'managed' as long as they had their children with them by purchases from jumble sales and street

markets or by the handing down of garments from child to child, but found things difficult when the child was away.[8]

These perspectives were irreconcilable, as are the narratives examined in the different chapters, and so this is a book that embraces 'messy history', the acceptance that the past which we now have access to does not produce simple or linear narratives, clearly identifiable cause and effect. It is not possible to construct the truth, but rather through the serendipity of chance by which traces of the past have survived, multiple narratives can be written, often overlapping, contradictory, complex, messy histories. What all of these narratives share is that they provide evidence to support the words of Catherine Marshall, suffrage and peace campaigner who argued, '[W]ar is predominantly an outrage on motherhood, all that motherhood means, the destruction of life and the breaking up of homes, it is the undoing of women's work as life-givers and home-makers.'[9]

Chapter 8 seeks to unpick some of the myths, memories and memorials of evacuation, which have airbrushed women and mothers in cultural memory since the Second World War ended. Finally, the afterword will briefly consider how evacuation contributed towards the stretching, challenging and reworking of discourses of motherhood in the post-war era – a heyday of domesticity. For if evacuees became a symbol of wartime, so in contrast, an idealized physically and emotionally close relationship between mother and child in their own homes became a symbol of peace and 'normality' shaping women's lives in the post-war era and indeed memories of evacuation.

1

Setting the scene

This chapter aims to shed some understanding on the multitude of shifting and changing factors, which provided a backdrop for seemingly incomprehensible decisions and emotions that evacuation evoked. It sets the scene for the competing narratives of evacuation explored in later chapters. The attitudes and motivations of mothers, foster mothers, teachers and volunteers were not static but complex, contradictory and liable to change. Mothers' decisions about whether, when or how their families might or might not be involved in evacuation entailed weighing up a variety of factors shaped by assumptions, understandings and anxieties at particular moments of time. Most significantly the fears the civilian population faced as they came to understand themselves as victims of war, in years before and during the conflict. The Second World War was not a homogeneous experience although the first wave of evacuation in 1939 has received a disproportionate amount of attention in academic and popular histories of the conflict.[1] The national and local circumstances of war on the home front constantly altered, and perceived dangers shifted at various junctures in the six years of the conflict; hence this chapter outlines both the planning and the different waves and types of evacuation that occurred. Those who designed the evacuation scheme had as their primary concern the physical care, safety and survival of children, in an era which was not subject to the moral panics about child abuse or 'stranger danger' that emerged in the latter decades of the twentieth century. Decisions about evacuation took place within the private space of the domestic home, shaped by private circumstances and the unstable and contested discourses of motherhood and childhood which prevailed at the time and are the starting point for this chapter.

Shifting discourses of childhood and motherhood

Patterns of childcare, discourses of family life, attitudes to young people and indeed the very notion of who are children is culturally and historically specific, shaped by class and region, personal necessity and parental priorities.[2] In Britain since the beginning of the twentieth century, increasing economic wealth, financial security, improvements in health care and decreasing child mortality, greater access to family planning and the reduction of family size have all contributed to shifting ideas of both childhood and motherhood. Viviana Zelizer argues that 'a major shift in the value of children took place at the turn of the [twentieth] century: from "object of utility" to object of sentiment and from producer asset to consumer good'.[3] Alternatively, Anna Davin suggests that it was the Children's Act in 1908 that fixed the 'reality of dependence' that lies beneath the rhetoric of childhood as a joyful and carefree time. It is adults who thus defined and organized and have responsibility for those in 'childhood'.[4] Attention quickly turned to the training of mothers, Eileen Ross has described early attempts to provide domestic education to urban mothers in the St Pancras School for Mothers, founded in 1907 in Somers Town, a poor district of London near Euston Station.[5] Infant mortality among the working classes in Edwardian Britain was alarmingly high; 20 per cent of children did not live to see their fifth birthday, but it would be wrong to assume that the frequency of infant death meant that parents were less attached to their children. It was rather that they had very different cultural patterns of mourning and different ways of coping with grief.[6] The daughter of working-class suffragist Selena Cooper recalled that her mother rarely mentioned her second child who died as a toddler, but she kept a scrapbook of images of babies she cut out of newspapers.[7] The discovery that there was lower infant mortality among breastfed babies led not only to disapproval of mothers who went out to work but assertions of neglect from middle-class observers with little understanding of the pressures and the poverty that working-class women endured.

Moves to support, monitor and 'educate' urban mothers which included grants for milk depots, medical inspections and an increase in the number of health visitors[8] were further accelerated by the First World War when infant welfare increasingly became a national issue. The poor health of the working class recruits, the need to replace the young men killed on the battlefield and the plight of many mothers gave impetus to numerous individuals and groups from across the political spectrum to become involved in infant and child welfare. The Bishop of London pointed out in 1915 that it was more dangerous to be a child in the slums of London than a soldier on the Western Front.[9] Suffrage campaigners, including the East London Federation of Suffragettes[10] and the Women's Freedom League, set up infant welfare clinics, and by the end of the conflict, National Baby Week, baby shows and infant welfare clinics had been instigated across the country. In the interwar years, Tory grandees established the National Birthday Fund, but as the infant mortality rate continued its steady decline, the maternal mortality rate rose.[11]

Much of this growing attention was on infants while as Davin points out, opinion was divided and confused over how much care, interference and support the state should provide for children and what risks were entailed in them doing so, nevertheless a number of voluntary and government agencies made the health and welfare of children, and particularly working-class children, their concern,[12] including the BBC which through the new medium of radio, regularly broadcast on child welfare.[13] In the interwar years, Ruth Davidson suggests, some of those worried about infant and child welfare used such concerns to argue that local and national government needed to introduce a range other welfare services: improved housing and refuse collection, nurseries, birth control[14] and family allowances. For example, Eleanor Rathbone suggested, 'Children are not simply a private luxury. They are an asset to the community, and the community can no longer afford to leave the provision for their welfare solely to the accident of individual incomes.'[15] Evacuation accelerated the degree to which childhood was a public concern.

In the interwar years, there was a shared assumption that within the home, children were women's responsibility. Widowers with children, like my own grandfather, were quick to remarry to fill the job vacancy their wife's death created and although married women made up 16 per cent of the inmates of workhouses in 1931,[16] women were defined by domesticity. Mothers were predominantly housewives and Judy Giles has pointed out that 'debates about how homes could and should be run, the decline in domestic service and the growing emphasis on housing, household finances, family hygiene and nutrition'[17] could be found in government surveys and political discourse, while the media, including women's magazines, foregrounded discussion about the efficient running of the home. Elizabeth Roberts' oral history research revealed that domestic management, being a 'good manager' and allocating scarce resources defined women as good housewives and mothers in the 1920s and 1930s.[18] 'Managing' was achieved by urban and rural housewives through utilizing very different resources; home-grown carrots and beetroot in the countryside, the chip shop in some urban areas. In on-going debates about housewifery and infant welfare, rural housewives identified themselves as the heart of the nation and their domestic practices as the ideal to which others should aspire[19] and the countryside was perceived to be the healthiest environment for children to grow up in.[20] This assumption made the idea of wartime evacuation more palatable.

Despite the increasing national focus on children and the raising of the school leaving age to 14 in 1918, many working-class children were still expected to contribute to their families' economic survival by helping in parents' businesses, farms or smallholdings, or doing odd jobs. They were also relied upon to look after siblings, or cousins when parents who were busy and in a world with few cars and poor housing, children did so in public spaces, playing in streets and fields. Biological mothers were not necessarily assumed to be the most suitable carers for children. Mothers, who could afford to, used the vast army of 1.3 million domestic servants and maids to assist in the day-to-day care of their childcare.[21] Alternatively, between the 1930s and the 1960s, charities, local authorities and church groups forcibly transported children from deprived backgrounds to Commonwealth countries, often telling the youngsters their parents were dead.[22] Poverty and economic necessity forced many women to hand over their children to others, within the family or beyond. Kathleen Dayus's autobiography charts her struggles as a working-class widow with four young children in Birmingham in the 1930s, who ill and desperate placed her children temporarily in the care of Dr Barnado's homes. She recalled later, 'I returned in a trance to my mother's house, overwhelmed by feelings of loss and loneliness, Just how much I'd given up I realized when I went to the kitchen, empty now with no grubby little faces … for I had no idea, how many years'.[23] It took several years to get her children back, just after the outbreak of war. Her youngest, frightened by the bombing in Birmingham, was evacuated the following year.

Steve Humphries has estimated that in 'the first half of the twentieth century as many as one in ten of all children were partly or wholly brought up by someone other than their natural parents: foster mothers, housemothers in institutions, relatives, siblings, step-parents and nannies'.[24] When the parents were unable to care for their children, private foster arrangements were sometimes made and informal adoptions often took place within families when a girl had an illegitimate child. The Adoption of Children Act 1926 in England and Wales attempted to regulate informal adoptions, but there was 'no compulsion on adopters to legally adopt their child' and informal arrangements continued.[25] The singer Eric Clapton's discovery at 9 years old that the woman, he thought was his elder sister was his mother,[26] was by no mean an isolated occurrence.[27] On the eve of the Second World War, when the Adoption of Children (Regulation)

Act in 1939 was introduced,[28] magazines still carried stories of baby sales and adoption societies rarely interviewed prospective parents or inspected their homes. Cultural concerns about the suitability of prospective parents did not seem to elicit the acute sense of anxiety that aerial warfare did.

Civilians as victims of war: Fears and anxieties

The movement of women, children and the weak, vulnerable or ill from conflict zones became an established practice during the twentieth century. In the First World War, approximately a quarter of a million refugees from Belgium flocked temporarily to Britain, to escape the fighting as the German army advanced across their country, in Autumn 1914.[29] On 16 December 1914, the shelling of the coastal areas of Hartlepool, Whitby and Scarborough by German gunboats led to 592 casualties, and 137 deaths included children, such as the 14-year-old boy who was blown to pieces walking to the shop in Hartlepool.[30] As Susan Grayzel has argued, this and the Zeppelin and bomber raids that followed defined 'women and children as targets of war, rather than a group shielded from its impact'.[31] Hence the term, home front entered the language for the first time, as those in their homes were like those in the trenches or on the battlefield in danger from enemy fire, even when a country had not been invaded by a foreign power.

From January 1915, Zeppelin bombing raids on towns and cities became a regular occurrence creating, as Freedman argues, both fear and fascination.[32] As the huge airships were spotted lumbering across the coast from the channel, air raid warnings led to blackouts across Britain and major cities halted trams and other public transport. Nevertheless, the bombs caused death and injury; during the conflict approximately fifteen hundred civilians died on home soil, as a result of enemy action. When compared with the overall death toll of the conflict, this may seem small, but the devastation bombs left in their wake was a physical manifestation of the threat that the enemy posed to everyday life, written onto the landscape of towns and cities. Although initially images of the destroyed or damaged buildings were suppressed, they slowly began to appear in the uncensored local papers. These pictures have survived and with the photographic collections in the Imperial War Museum provide numerous images of buildings reduced to rubble. In the areas where bombs were dropped, the memories and stories of the bombing remained strong, told and retold through generations.[33]

In 1917 the Gotha bombers, who dropped their deadly cargo on London and the South Coast, provided a foretaste of the horrors of twentieth-century warfare. The raid on London on 13 June 1917 made an impact on the minds of both officials and parents and convinced many that in the event of another war London would have to be evacuated. Fourteen bombers dropped high-explosive bombs on East Ham, Stratford, Bermondsey and Southwark. The raid killed 145 Londoners and injured 382 more, among this tally, were children in the Upper North Street London County Council School in Poplar. Eighteen were killed and a further thirty-four children were injured when the bomb entered the roof of the Girls' Department, passed through the Boys' Department and exploded in the Infants' Department. Further raids were more deadly, but a raid on a school and the death of so many young children changed forever the understanding of what war could mean.[34] When bombers shifted their raids to the night-time, as a precaution, crowds regularly sought safety in tube stations and other shelters even before sirens had been sounded or planes sighted. By early October 1917, as Jerry White points out there was 'an impromptu evacuation of London, all classes of Londoner took part, Waterloo station was crowded with families, poor mothers and children who are leaving London … people were sleeping out in Richmond Park and others moved as far away as Devon if they could'.[35] A fundamental change to the experience and response to war had occurred, the Second World War evacuation was the result of this.

In the twenty years between the signing of the Versailles Peace Treaty in 1919, which formally ended the First World War, and the outbreak of the Second World War, the capacities of planes and mechanized warfare did not stand still. If air transport had not perhaps completed its transition from spectacle to the mundane, the size, range, capacity and reliability of planes had manifestly multiplied. The work of historians such as Tami Davis Biddle has shed light on how 'visionaries, enthusiasts, disarmers, civil defence and pulp fiction' all contributed to the fear of aerial attack and the debate about how the civilian population should be protected from these dangers.[36] But despite pressure group campaigns against aerial warfare and political negotiations, the dangers of civilian bombing became an increasing concern in the 1930s.

Such concerns were the backdrop to what Brett Holman describes as the political issues of the 1930s, 'collective security, disarmament, rearmament and appeasement'.[37] In the view of much of the press and aviation writers, any future conflict would begin with a full-scale bombing seeking to inflict a 'knock out blow' on urban areas and London in particular to avoid the stalemate of the First World War trench warfare. Holman argues that there were three suggestions of how to combat this, resistance by air defence or counter-bombing, which was the preferred option of the Royal Air Force (RAF) and those who argued for rearmament. The second involved adaption, bomb shelters and evacuation and civil defence. Finally, there were those who argued for agreements to limit bombing and negotiations to encourage disarmament.[38] There were campaigns, conferences and some political will during the interwar years to create an embargo on the bombing of civilians but to no avail.[39] Baldwin's statement that there was nothing that could be done to prevent the bombers from getting through[40] had more truth in it that many politicians and civilians were keen to admit to themselves or others. The 1930s, was increasingly overshadowed by a genuine, and it turned out justified, fear that another war was looming despite the Women's Co-operative Guild's introduction of the white poppy as a symbol of the wearer's commitment to peace and the Oxford Union strong support of a 1933 motion 'that this House will in no circumstances fight for its King and Country'. In 1934 Dick Shepherd, the Canon of St Paul's Cathedral, wrote a letter to the *Guardian* asking men to pledge never to support war, which led to the formation of the Peace Pledge Union.[41] Nevertheless, as the 1930s wore on, as Michel Shapira argues, a new level of anxiety over aerial bombing was ushered in.[42] Thus, Richard Overy has observed fears of bombing and gas attacks were all pervading in the minds of the British population.[43]

Government spending on civil defence cannot be seen as wholeheartedly seeking to allay these anxieties, although in 1935 the Home Office did issue a circular on Air Raid Precautions to local authorities. Michele Haapamaki has pointed out the climate of anticipation and fear led to a reappraisal of ideas about citizenship. Debates about who should be responsible for providing the planning, preparations, equipment and infrastructure needs for civil defence raised questions about the relationship between local and central government and between government and individuals. There was controversy as whether the large-scale building of air raid shelters was the responsibility of government, as many on the political left suggested or was the responsibility of individuals, a controversy Haapamaki suggests which indicates that the social change and the reworking of the relationship between citizens and state associated with the 'people's war', began much earlier.[44] Arguably, a renegotiated of the relationship between individuals and government was a necessary precursor for the organization of the wartime government evacuation scheme. Thus alongside increasing German aircraft construction, the Committee for Imperial Defence set up an evacuation subcommittee in 1934, to plan possible evacuation schemes under the chairmanship of Sir John Anderson.

For the general public who watched newsreels, on their frequent visits to the cinema, the bombing carried out by supporters of Franco's Nationalist Army during the Spanish Civil War (1936–9) provided ample evidence of how devastating aerial warfare could be. The images of German bombing, initially of Madrid and then of Guernica on 23 April 1937, convinced many of the British population that if another war came, radical steps would need to be taken to avoid the consequences on the civilian population. The Duchess of Atholl, president of the National Joint Committee for Spanish Relief, campaigned with much public support, for Britain to respond to the Basque government's appeal for temporary asylum for the children of the region. Despite initial resistance from the British government, on 23 May 1937, 3,840 children, 80 teachers, 120 helpers, 15 Catholic priests and 2 doctors from the region arrived in Southampton, on board the steamship the *Habana*. Controversy surrounded the children's arrival and their eventual return, many to live in fascist orphanages as their parents had been killed.[45]

Over the following two years, ten thousand, predominantly Jewish, children came to Britain from counties under Nazi control, as part of the Kindertransport. The decision to send them was taken by parents who feared for their children's lives, and although some parents followed their children, many were uncertain if or when they would see their children again. As Anthony Grenville argues, 'It is hard to convey the distress of parents forced to send their children away as the only means of saving their lives, or that of the children separated from their parents.'[46] Arguably, however much historiographical controversy now surrounds the Kindertransport,[47] the starkness of the fate that awaited these children, internment and possible death in a concentration camp, is usually regarded as a justification for the traumatic separation of parents and children. The trauma many of these children suffered was, as Edward Timms points out, of a different level to that experienced by most evacuees[48] but those involved in both schemes shared fears of large civilian death tolls.

In January 1938, the government passed the Air Raid Precautions (ARP) Act putting onto local authorities the responsibility to prepare air raid precaution schemes and a legal obligation to prepare ARP schemes, albeit with heavy reliance on 'dispersal' and 'self-reliance' rather than 'total' protection.[49] Householders received a leaflet on *The Protection of Your Home against Air Raids*, and Professor J. B. S. Haldane published a small volume entitled *Air Raid Precautions* intended for, as he explained in the preface, 'the ordinary citizen, the sort of man and woman who is going to be killed if Britain is raided again from the air'.[50] Drawing on his experience of visiting Spain during the Spanish Civil War, he discussed in details how civilians could die not just from bombs but also panic or gas attacks. He advocated various government and individual strategies that needed to be put in place to protect the civilian population. Evacuation according to Haldane was 'a comfortable word for a process which is at best uncomfortable, at worst appalling'.[51] He painted a gruesome picture of evacuation once war had begun, which included a mother with a small child being killed when Paddington station is bombed as she embarks on her journey. He remarked that 'a woman must be in a state bordering on panic if she is to leave her home and husband at a moment's notice for an unknown destination'.[52] He argues for plans to be drawn up to evacuate all young children, then pregnant women and then other mothers and children speedily to rural areas.

Others continued to seek an embargo on the aerial bombing of civilians. On 2 February 1938, the Labour MP for Caerphilly, Morgan Jones, put the following motion to the House of Commons:

> That, in the opinion of this House, the growing horror of aerial bombardment of defenseless civilians should be expressed in an international agreement to co-operate in its prohibition, and urges His Majesty's Government to exert its influence to this end.

He explained,

> I think it is desirable that the British House of Commons, speaking as it is entitled to do on behalf of the British people, should give utterance to its detestation of the horrible massacres, which accompany aerial bombing. I am sure that the unanimous view of the House is that it is a crime against humanity and a reproach to civilization that these outrages should continue. Almost every day brings further news of these ghastly and fiendish attacks upon defenseless and innocent people. It is surely time that the peoples of the world should cry a halt to this horrible business, for let us be perfectly clear about it, unless we do abolish it, the disastrous events which we have witnessed in the last year or two are but a feeble foretaste of what is in store for the world if by some unfortunate chance the most powerful nations become engaged in a life and death struggle.[53]

In fiction and film, documentary and newspapers, public and political discourse, the fear of aerial bombing was reaching fever pitch when Germany annexed Austria in February 1938. In this climate of growing anxiety and public and political pressure, what became known as the Anderson committee finally published their proposals for evacuation in July that same year.

Preparation, planning and practising

As Richard Titmuss has pointed out, 'The idea of evacuation, of a planned and orderly transfer of people from vulnerable cities to safer areas of the country, grew out of contemporary theories about the character of the future war.'[54] Nevertheless, both the government and the evacuation subcommittee wavered between the benefits of persuasion or compulsion in relation to evacuation, but Edward Timms explains that when the recommendations for the evacuation of schoolchildren, mothers with infants and the elderly to safe areas were decided, the government adhered to the following guidelines:

1. Evacuation would not be compulsory, but arrangements should be made to organize facilities to move substantial numbers away from industrial cities.
2. In the reception areas, evacuees should be mainly accommodated in private houses under powers of compulsory billeting.
3. The initial costs should be borne by the government, but families that could afford to contribute to maintenance costs should be expected to do so.
4. Priority arrangements should be made for groups of schoolchildren to travel with their teachers.[55]

The plans sought 'to protect all civilians even those women and children who could make no useful contribution to the war effort,'[56] and the elderly, infirm, mentally and physically disabled were also identified as needing to be removed from areas liable to be bombed, on the eve of war or soon after. Children under five were considered too young to be evacuated without their mothers; therefore, plans were put in place for their mothers and pregnant women also to be evacuated.

The atmosphere of fear and impending, almost inevitable, warfare continued to grow during the Munich crisis, when gas masks were issued to the civilian population, the Women's Voluntary Service (WVS) was set up and over 150,000 people apparently migrated to Wales in a steady stream of cars rushing out of London. Some schools and their pupils were evacuated in September, when war seemed imminent. Colin Ryder Richardson recalled his school moved from St John's Wood to Scotland:

> We were told to pack some food and clothes and that we would be getting the night train. It was an enormous shock to me, my parents packed me off. We

arrived in Scotland and went to a hotel on an estate. We stayed there a week while the school tried to carry on – turning a day school into a boarding school in a temporary location. Then Munich was resolved and we came back. But it left an impression on me and indicated to me that the political situation wasn't very stable.[57]

Despite the rhetoric of 'Peace in our time', government preparations ground on, the country was categorized by civil servants into danger areas from where evacuation would take place. Those areas considered safe would become reception areas for evacuees while neutral zones were held in reserve, considered at least at this point as unsuitable to receive evacuees but not in danger from bombing. The rationale for the categorization was not always obvious and met with local resistance. The description of the county as a safe area, suitable as a reception area, mystified the Clerk of the Council in Stone, Staffordshire who questioned the wisdom of sending evacuees to the area that it was 'fast becoming a vulnerable zone, as it is bounded on the north by the potteries, aerodromes, aerodrome factories, on north-east by another aircraft factory, on the west by an ammunition depot, on the south by further aircraft factories, and also on the north west in the centre of the district, it is proposed to erect a super power station'.[58] Many saw London as a target and also ports, industrial areas such as Birmingham or military bases such as Portsmouth, but initially, Plymouth and Bristol were considered to be neutral areas; in 1941 they were extensively bombed. Some local areas challenged the decisions, with limited success.

Reception areas were often in rural regions, but not necessarily. The image of children playing contentedly in the countryside has some credibility but is only part of the narrative of evacuation; children were evacuated, for example, to Stafford and Stoke-on-Trent, both industrial areas of Staffordshire. Nor should it be imagined that evacuees were placed in areas that were sheltered from all bombing or air-raid sirens. For some in a remote part of rural Wales, Cornwall, or the Scottish Highlands this might have been the case. Others were evacuated to areas close enough to home to hear the sound of bombers overhead, and of bombs dropping, or to be able to see the sky lit up by their hometown burning in the distance. In retrospect some of the categorization may seem bizarre and in practical terms this was also the case. In one part of the Midlands, the residents of one street were surprised to discover that those on one side of the street were considered to be a danger zone while those on their side were apparently living in a reception area. The categorizations did, however, shift as the progress of the war unfolded.

A billeting survey of potential accommodation was undertaken in reception areas in Spring 1939 as the government made plans for nearly five million vulnerable children and adults to be evacuated at speed with minimal expense. Proposals and suggestions of how to best organize evacuation poured into the government who decided that the care of evacuees should be a predominantly domestic affair, reliant on the goodwill and the unpaid service of women. This decision went against the advice of the Women's Institute Movement, then the largest organization of the rural women, but it mimicked and scaled up the care of many evacuees during the Spanish Civil War or children who came over with the Kindertransport. In the months that followed the survey and before the outbreak of war, friends and relations 'privately' reserved one-sixth of the available accommodation in safe areas.

The planning for evacuation required a complex interaction between central and local government, the Ministry of Health and the Ministry of Education, paid local and national government, employees and unpaid volunteers. The London County Council (LCC) requisitioned buses and trains in preparation for mass evacuation; some rural reception areas began to line up volunteers with cars to transport children to outlying farms. In July 1939 Air Raid Precautions issued a leaflet entitled *Some Things You Should Know* which provided guidance on gas masks, air raid warning and evacuation while the government passed the Civil Defence bill setting out payments to be given to the hosts of evacuees. Both the government and the population as a whole expected war to begin with immediate full-scale bombing of British cities and gas attacks. My grandmother recounted how she was visiting friends on the day that war was declared. Their hostess, after hearing the announcement that the country was at war on the radio, immediately jumped up and covered the budgerigar. German bombers with their fateful cargo were expected to arrive immediately, and the poor creature it was felt needed protecting. Indeed, twenty-seven minutes after the declaration of war the sirens were heard for the first time; the false alarm caused by a French plane drifting into British airspace.[59] Psychologists had warned that the population's response to bombing was likely to be panic and mass hysteria and there was a grave concern that cities like London would grind to a halt. Civil defence planners were eager to ensure that even after an air raid, cities functioned efficiently and hysterical civilians would not hamper the rescue efforts of emergency services. Arguments were given some credibility when in the first week of the war, London traffic was brought to a standstill for several hours after air-raid sirens went off.[60]

Evacuation began two days before war broke out and continued in waves throughout the six years of the conflict. The evacuation had many phases, and was as varied as the number of people involved; for all the experience was shaped by class and financial resources. Some evacuees stayed in places of safety for a few days others for several years. Children could be billeted in one home for all of their stay in a safe area, many more changed billets; Reg Walsh had thirteen different sets of foster parents during his time in Staffordshire.[61] Some were billeted in first one area of the county and then another, others to-ed and fro-ed between reception areas and danger zones during the war. So, for example, Oxfordshire had 4,500 unaccompanied child evacuees in September 1939, 75 per cent of these remained in January 1940 although the vast majority of mothers and young children under five had returned home. LCC figures for children in Oxfordshire fluctuated even more; there were 3,250 in September 1939, declining to 1,962 in March 1940 and peaking at 5,099 in October 1940 during the Blitz. As the bombing reduced, these figures declined to only 1,187 in February 1944.[62] As Titmuss points out, 'not until the fifth year of the war … did the Health Department know that whereas they had evacuated nearly 1,500,000 million mothers and children, about 2,000,000 had evacuated themselves.'[63] If figures for movement within Scotland are added in the total figure is closer to 4 million people evacuated at some point during the conflict.

The initial phase of the government evacuation scheme known as Operation Pied Piper began as the German army marched into Poland. It initially involved 826,950 unaccompanied children, 523,670 mothers with preschool children and 12,705 expectant mothers, far less than the government had originally planned for and varied tremendously from one part of the country to another. In Manchester and Liverpool, just under half of the school-age children were evacuated while Birmingham and Walsall had low rates of participation, just over 20 per cent of Birmingham schoolchildren and only 18 per cent from Walsall. Evacuation has been deemed by some historians an administrative success and by others to be a failure, or even a good practice run for later waves of evacuation.[64] It was not an unmitigated disaster, but it was in many ways unsuccessful and administratively clumsy. Despite the months of planning the actual situation was impossible to predict and fluid. Civil Servants and administrators keen to get evacuees out of danger zones as quickly as possible re-allocated transport and destinations rather than have trains and buses leaving half full. Without the benefit of mobile phones and the internet, the communication between central and local government left something to be desired and reception areas became thoroughly flummoxed. Some planned for mothers and young children, only to find unaccompanied children turned up; others expected young boys and received pregnant mothers. Juliet Gardiner has recounted how 'Anglesey was awaiting 625 children, but 2,468 arrived. Pwllheli, North Wales, was expecting none, but received about 400'.[65]

Despite the expectation of mass bombing and the occasional air-raid siren going off, during the first months of the war, a period that became known as the 'phoney war', no bombs dropped. By Christmas 1939, the vast majority of mothers and young children and many unaccompanied children had returned home, or visited for Christmas and never returned to the reception areas. Closer proximity between homes of origin and foster homes and coming from an area with low initial rates of evacuation seems to have increased the likelihood of return. Titmus suggests that 89 per cent of those evacuated from Birmingham to various parts of the country had returned to their homes by January 1940.[66] In Staffordshire, the majority of the 8,605 unaccompanied children evacuated in 1939 were from cities a relatively short train ride away: Birmingham, Manchester and Liverpool and its retention compared unfavourably with other reception areas which retained more than half of their evacuees in January 1940.[67] Indeed, Padley and Cole suggest that Staffordshire was 'strikingly unsuccessful' with initial evacuation.[68]

By early February 1940 questions were beginning to be asked in the House of Commons about how many children had returned home. Mr Elliot, minister for health, whose ministry had responsibility for the evacuation scheme, stated on 8 February that 'As near as can be estimated, the numbers of unaccompanied schoolchildren originally evacuated from each of the 29 evacuating county boroughs and the numbers who have since returned are as follows':[69]

Evacuation area	Number of unaccompanied children evacuated	Number returned to evacuation area
Birkenhead	9,350	4,600
Birmingham	25,241	11,000
Bootle	7,123	3,500
Bradford	7,484	3,400
Coventry	3,082	1,700
Croydon	12,241	3,500
Derby	3,438	2,400
Gateshead	10,598	7,000

Grimsby	1,246	450
Hull	16,389	5,200
Leeds	18,935	8,500
Liverpool	60,795	23,000
Manchester	66,300	41,000
Middlesbrough	5,171	2,800
Newcastle	28,300	14,000
Nottingham	4,763	2,300
Portsmouth	11,970	6,000
Rotherham	332	180
Salford	18,043	9,500
Sheffield	5,338	3,500
Smethwick	2,219	1,000
Southampton	11,175	4,200
South Shields	3,826	2,000
Sunderland	8,289	2,900
Tynemouth	1,481	800
Wallasey	2,622	1,700
Walsall	360	250
West Bromwich	1,786	900
West Hartlepool	2,881	1,900

Within months of Mr Elliot's speech in Parliament the situation had changed significantly – the war in Europe took a dramatic turn for the worse; the fall of Holland on 14 May and then France were compounded by the retreat from Dunkirk between 27 May and 4 June 1940. The government gave approval for the bombing not just of military targets but German towns on 15 May,[70] and fears of reprisals and German invasion reached fever pitch. Both the newspapers and the government began to urge those who were not essential workers to leave London, evacuation was back on the agenda, with a renewed urgency.

Homes in the line of fire

In contemplating the change, May 1940 brought to the experience of those on the home front, Vera Brittain noted,

> Only when the summer is well advanced will civilian groups who have not,
> hitherto, met the direct cost of war, contribute their quota of casualties – the
> men past their prime, the wives and mothers, the children born from no fault of
> their own into a grievous era of peril and pain.[71]

In spring and summer of 1940 some 300,000 moved from coastal regions in the
South or London as a second more extensive phase of longer-term evacuation
began. Approximately twenty-five thousand children and women arrived from
the Chanel Islands, including Jersey, Alderney and around half the population
of Guernsey, 17,000 evacuees, escaped to Britain from before the German
occupation began in June 1940. Gillian Mawson's research has drawn attention
to the number of Channel Island evacuees were billeted in industrial areas that
had been vacated by English evacuees just a few months earlier.[72]

The re-categorization of the South Coast as a danger area required children
evacuated there in 1939, to be re-evacuated as those from Kent or Sussex were
evacuated for the first time. The second tranche of government evacuation was
for unaccompanied children, each allowed to carry only one piece of hand
luggage as they were transported to South Wales and areas of the Midlands
originally defined as neutral areas, which had become reception areas. In the
summer of 1940, Staffordshire with its excellent railway links, geographical
proximity to a number of large industrial towns and satisfactory distance from
the South Coast, had evacuees pouring in from Kent, Birmingham, Liverpool,
Manchester and London, in a process that was often more organized and less
rushed than the first phase of evacuation. Host areas and schools often knew
who to expect and could plan accordingly. Importantly in 1940, the government
changed its policy and agreed to pay billeting allowance and assist with the cost
of travel for children who were privately evacuated. This enabled numerous
individuals to arrange for their children to stay with friends or relations, who
saw hosting privately evacuated children with or without their mothers as
infinitely preferable to taking-in 'strangers'.

Fears of invasion fuelled calls for overseas evacuation. Colonel Wedgwood,
MP for Newcastle-upon-Tyne was one of the strongest advocates, in a speech in
the House of Commons, he asked people to

> [i]magine for one moment that this country is invaded. Every man who is worth
> his salt will be engaged either in the field, or in some munitions factory far
> from his family. All the time, they will be desperately anxious about what is
> happening to their wives and children and parents. I do not blame the Belgians
> for surrendering, and I should not blame the French if they had surrendered.

What is an Army to do when they see those dismal columns of helpless women and children and when they think that their own women and children may be among such crowds, being mercilessly machine-gunned while starving and dropping and dying of exhaustion by the roadside? If that is the fate of their womankind, you cannot expect an Army to fight. Therefore, this problem of evacuation is a very real one and does not apply solely to children. It applies to all the useless mouths in every country, which is meeting this new form of gangster warfare.[73]

There had been offers from other countries to look after British evacuees, within days of the outbreak of war, firms and organizations with connections abroad began to provide their employees with assistance to send their children to another country, including General Electric Company (GEC) and several universities. Some children were evacuated abroad from areas such Staffordshire as other children were being evacuated into the county. Criticism that overseas evacuation was a privilege only available to the wealthy led to the setting up of a Children's Overseas Reception Board (CORB) which assisted 15,000–20,000 children to evacuate to Canada, South Africa, the United States and Australia. However safe, the evacuees' destinations may have been their journey carried its own dangers as convoys of ships zigzagged across the Atlantic. SS *Volendam* was torpedoed on 30 August 1940 with two fatalities. Many children returned to Liverpool and waited for next ship to sail out of port, the SS *City of Benares,* which on 17 September 1940 was torpedoed and sunk by a German U-boat. Out of a hundred evacuees only seventeen survived, the CORB scheme did not; no further children were subsidized by the government to travel overseas.

By Autumn 1940, the government was engrossed in trying to take action against the waves of bombers coming across the channel, heading for Britain's towns, cities and military bases. There were 460,000 children and 60,000 adults billeted under the government evacuation scheme, by August 1940, as bombing raids on London and major cities such as Birmingham were becoming more common. By the first anniversary of Britain's entry into the war, 4,000 civilians had been killed or seriously injured.[74] The threat posed by aerial warfare was beginning to be understood and was eloquently summarized by Vera Brittain:

We realise now that not London only, but all England, is the first line of defence. The front is no distant battlefield to which a small contingent of men and women go forth … Today the front line is part of our daily lives; its dugouts and encampments are in every street; its trenches and encampments occupy sections of every city park and every village green.

Not only regiments, air squadrons, and crews of ships are holding that line, but
the whole nation, its families and households.[75]

This came home to the people of London on 7 September 1940, the first of fifty-
seven days of consecutive heavy bombing, and what is known as the Blitz had
begun. It lasted until Summer 1941. Anti-aircraft guns were generally futile, not
only did they fail to hit their target, estimates suggest less than 1 in one or two
thousand shots fired reached their goal, but as shrapnel fell to the ground it
caused injury to the civilian population. The giant searchlights that shone into
the sky were equally ineffective and may have assisted enemy bombers to find
their targets.

Preventing the bombing was not easily achieved and nor was providing
sufficient shelters for maintaining the safety of civilians. The government began
distributing Anderson shelters before the outbreak of war. They were erected in
the garden and comprised of six corrugated iron sheets bolted together at the
top, with steel plates at either end and at only 6 feet 6 inches by 4 feet 6 inches
(1.95 metres by 1.35 metres) were rather snug inside. These shelters were of
little use to the thousands of working-class people living in poorly constructed
back-to-back houses and tenements, near factories and docks, the target of
enemy bombs. It was not until March 1941 that Ellen Wilkinson and Herbert
Morrison were instrumental in introducing what became known as Morrison
shelters. They were flat-topped table-like shelters which could be erected inside
the house, and their steel frames were supposed to keep two adults and two
children safe inside even if a house was bombed. They were issued free to those
who earned less than £350 a year.[76]

The people's unorganized evacuation

Evacuation tends to ebb and flow with the severity of bombing, as Julia Torrie's
work looking at evacuation in France and Germany also demonstrates, even
when these countries sought to ensure evacuation was centrally controlled and
compulsory individuals took matters into their own hands. As Torrie points
out the threat to family ties undermines people's compliance in evacuation
schemes as does any lack of confidence in the safety of the arrangements made
for civilians.[77] In September 1940, approximately sixty thousand children left
London in organized groups; despite the severity of the raids this represented
only 15 per cent of the number who had left in 1939 and is often referred to as

the trickle evacuation.[78] The low numbers in the face of real danger represent a critique of the government scheme, but mothers and children did not wait passively for the bombs to drop. Even according to government records, in Autumn 1940 the number of evacuees billeted outside London peaked at 1,250,000, but figures for unofficial evacuees, mothers who took matters into their own hands, what I refer to as the People's Evacuation, are hard to gauge.

The Blitz was most severe, but not restricted to London; Bristol, Plymouth, Portsmouth, Hull, Clydebank, Belfast, Manchester, Liverpool, Sheffield, Southampton were all subjected to heavy raids, as was Coventry on 14 and 15 November 1940. The bombing in other places may have seemed more random, the small industrial town of Clydebank with a population of approximately 47,000 was hit by 236 enemy bombers on 13 March 1941, leaving approximately five hundred people dead including seventy children.[79] A second heavy night of bombing left only seven of the 1,945 houses in the area undamaged.[80] Approximately 60,000 civilians lost their lives in the bombing, one in ten of those killed in the Blitz was a child, and nearly four times as many were injured or slightly injured. Bombing did not just cause injury and death; it also destroyed infrastructure, electricity and telephone wires and gas pipes making the tasks of everyday home life, such as cooking and washing, difficult or even impossible.[81]

Mothers sought to keep their children safe, in whatever way they could, but for those in danger areas who had no shelter of their own, evenings or the sound of the air-raid siren signalled a trek to find a place in one of the larger crowded public shelters. Unlike other cities, London had the advantage of the underground but space was limited. A family member was sometimes allocated to remain below during the day to keep a place for the others in the evening. Documentary films such as *London Can Take It* (1940) portray smiling people settling down to sleep, sometimes with their children snuggled up to them on station platforms, but oral histories and eye witness accounts relay the unsavoury conditions and the smell that greeted people as they descended the steps towards the platform. Alf Morris recalled,

> It was very dirty down there. At night, when it was quiet, rats used to come out and crawl over you. It was horrible, but what can you do? Better to suffer that than be upstairs, We'd see them crawling about. That was how we lived – it was part of life.[82]

As the Blitz continued, it was noted that at night the East End became deserted. Some mothers, with their children, joined the trekkers who nightly climbed onto the coaches that drove out of the cities to park up in pub car parks and other places, considered to be safe from bombing. After their night of relative calm, the trekkers returned home. Many cities or areas of cities were bereft of people in the aftermath of bombing raids, and an observer for Mass Observation noted as September turned into October that in the East End

> a fairly large number of people are leaving, many in families but more women and children than men. People that stay envy them, or don't blame them for the most part. Evacuation is mainly unplanned. People seemed shaken and worried, they don't like the thought of this bombardment lasting a long time.[83]

Relentless bombing wore people down: the lack of sleep, and insanitary conditions which they had to inhabit to try and mitigate the danger of bombs. Rumours and urban myths reassured some but amplified the panic of others; apparently the people of Winchester held firm to the notion that their city was safe from bombing because Hitler wanted to be crowned in Winchester Cathedral.[84] Some left the cities for a few days, others for weeks or longer. On 30 September 1940, friends, who wanted a rest from the bombing, visited Francis Partridge, at her home in rural Sussex. She recorded in her diary that 'they talked most of the evening about the raids, and Londoners talked about nothing else. Janetta with the most remarkable candor and realism said she felt more terrified than she would have believed possible, and flung herself on the floor trembling all over'.[85] Having friends with a suitably generous sized house, so that they could put you up for a rest or a short period of time was often restricted to the better off, others found their flight from London less amenable. As with so much of what has often been termed a 'people's war', wealth, class, financial resources dictated the circumstances by which people could avoid the worst consequences of the aerial warfare.

Much has been written about the trauma of children separated from their parents through evacuation, but there was genuine danger and also trauma for those who stayed in London as Sean Longdon has recorded in *Blitz Kids*.[86] The 7-year-old Fred Rowe was sheltering in the cellar when a bomb nearby resulted in the collapse of his family's house on top of him and a long, frightening wait to be dug out of the rubble. Scenes of death and destruction were all too familiar and traumatic for a young boy:

> There was a bloke next door lived in the basement. A bomb had dropped on the house behind him, and he was blown out of his basement on to the railings outside. The railings had ripped him in half. All his guts and gunge were hanging

out of him. And his son, fifteen years old was killed. He was lying in the road with no head, no arm and a bit of his shoulder was gone, I didn't recognise him. And I saw a body all blown apart, mixed into another body. It was a young girl blown into her mum or her dad, blasted together.[87]

Likewise, the young Fred Rowe living in Battersea with his mum and sister while his father was in the army was shocked by what he saw after a heavy night of bombing:

There were fuckin' body parts everywhere. The first thing I saw was a shoulder and arm on the street, people had been blown up into trees. There were legs and heads around, I saw a torso in a tree with all the blood dripping down. The worst thing, the thing that really got me – was seeing dead babies.[88]

Uncertain that they could guarantee accommodation for the homeless in the reception areas, the government did not organize evacuation for mothers with children in 1940 and 1941. Instead they helped with travel and billeting costs for those who found their own place to stay in safe areas of the country. Many women took matters into their own hands, and with children in tow went to stations and boarded the first train they could find which took them away from danger, or drove their cars till the petrol ran out and even commandeered lorries to escape. An observer for Mass Observation recorded that a friend, who lived in Reading, had relayed to him on 20 September 1940:

that freelance as opposed to organised evacuees have arrived in Reading by the hundred. Many are jittery and shell shocked. They are herded into some large hall to live as best they can. He knows of one cinema thus occupied, and says the dirt and stench there are appalling as there are no adequate sanitary arrangements.[89]

Those involved in this people's freelance evacuation had varying degrees of help and success in finding accommodation in reception areas and variable levels of sympathy or warmth of welcome from the local residents, as will be discussed in Chapter 5. There was, as investigators for Mass Observation noted, much class resentment about the appalling conditions that many working-class unofficial evacuees found themselves in, sleeping in church halls or requisitioned cinemas, with poor sanitary conditions and sparse food while the wealthier were eating three meals a day in local hotels.

For those whose homes had been bombed, or who were excluded from their homes because of unexploded bombs nearby, finding accommodation in war-torn London was a problem. Rest centres provided some temporary relief but were very crowded and depressing; they had temporary sanitary arrangements and were often sited in areas close to where the homeless had come from, with the danger of being bombed again. According to Richard Titmuss, 2,250,000 people became homeless as a result of the bombing in 1940–1, about 'one person in every six ... in the London civil defence region'.[90] Temporary accommodation was provided in rest centres, which were located in schools, halls or similar public buildings, where blankets, tea, and basic food – bread and margarine, soup and potted meat – were supplied. Washing facilities were minimal. One such centre in Stepney was described as being full of people 'lying on blankets, mattresses and bundles of clothing' with only ten buckets to serve as toilets for the two hundred to three hundred people sheltering there. According to one observer, the buckets: 'over flow so that as the night advances, urine and faeces spread in ever-increasing volume over the flow. The space is narrow so that whoever enters inevitably steps in the sewage and carries it on his shoes all over the building ... by dawn, I leave to your imagination'.[91]

Such centres were intended to be temporary, but many families found they were stuck in them for more than ten days. The housing crisis in London and many other cities was acute. The problem could not be abated without significant expenditure on housing, despite improvements in local and national government's management of the homeless and determined attempts to repair houses in the latter part of the war. There was an indomitable upbeat message in government propaganda. Margery Scott discussing her work for a local council on the radio in 1942 claimed to have housed a family, which included numerous children, lodgers and pets within a day. Despite her skills, or luck, in finding lodgings for this family of fourteen, most found locating suitable accommodation challenging.[92] Many families were forced to move from London and other areas that were bombed as housing became hard to find.

By 1942 air raids were less frequent but the danger for evacuees in returning home was by no means over, the Baedeker raids on places of cultural significance saw Canterbury and Bath bombed, many of the population continued to take flight when danger seemed acute. Writing in 1943, an investigator for Mass Observation noted that,

> We are still faced by the fact that every time there is a serious blitz a pell-mell evacuation, wholly spontaneous and unorganised, takes place. What have the authorities done to meet this situation? Has anybody in authority realised that the fact that this manifestation of defeatism takes place, every time there is a blitz shows there is something wrong with the measures taken by authorities

themselves? It is no good just abusing the unorganised evacuees, calling them unpatriotic of un-English or anything like that. They have been let down by the very people who they elected to take adequate precautions about this sort of thing. It is something to take such steps as organising field kitchens and communal kitchens and communal feeding places in the country for the people when they have felt the blitz-town, though really it is closing the stable-door after the horse has gone.[93]

On 13 March 1943, after a raid by allied bombers on Berlin, the day before, retaliation was expected. Bethnal Green tube station accommodated more than ten thousand people with beds for three thousand but only one entrance. As the siren wailed out and people were on their way to the shelter, rocket guns started firing and there was a rush for safety underground; a situation exasperated by the pubs emptying and the arrival of two buses of people who also sought shelter. Someone tripped, others fell and those at the bottom of the steps to the station platforms were crushed by the weight of those behind. Alf Morris, then a 13-year-old boy, who was squashed against the wall calling for his mum and his aunt, later recalled, 'I could move my arms but not my legs. I couldn't get out. In the commotion – the screaming, the hollering, the shouting – I could see a lady Air Raid Warden at the bottom.'[94] A total of 173 people died; sixty of them were children: 'Mothers were buried alongside their children, some of whom had been crushed to death in the arms of a protective parent.'[95] Nevertheless by the end of 1943 many evacuees had returned to their homes in 'danger' areas in Midland and North towns, Liverpool, Birmingham and Manchester particularly.

In the summer of 1944 the V1 and V2 flying bombs, doodlebugs as they were known, began to land on London and the bomb alley of Sussex and Kent necessitating further evacuation. Estimates suggest that between one million and one and half million mothers and children once again left London and the South for the reception areas such as Staffordshire, Derbyshire and Warwickshire. In North Staffordshire, the Billeting Officer in Leek warned of the imminent arrival of an unspecified number of evacuees to the town in July 1944 and reported on the successful billeting of 776 mothers and children the following week.[96] The doodlebugs were the last significant external impetus contributing to the ever-changing number of evacuees in reception areas. In Staffordshire, Cheadle Evacuation Committee Minute Books charted numbers that swung between just under two hundred and nearly three thousand.[97] But by April 1945, the danger from doodlebugs was reduced by the reallocation of anti-aircraft guns to the south coast, where they had more success than they had firing at planes. Later in 1945 the return of all evacuees to their homes required another complex organizational process, involving police, voluntary organizations, escorts to accompany children on their journey, light refreshments provided at stations and an intricate system of different coloured labels to ensure children went back to the right place.

Conclusion

Evacuation during the Second World War was shaped by a multitude of factors: practical, cultural and emotional. Local and central government made decisions and plans, sought to manage and organize, but evacuation was an acutely emotional experience for the mothers, teachers for the multiplicity of women across the country who in one way or another cared for evacuees. Women responded to the fears and anxieties evoked by the threat of aerial bombing and government attempts and failures in organizing evacuation in a legion of different unorganized ways, as the need arose. Their decisions and actions were inevitably contingent, shifting as circumstances changed over the course of the war, but always shaped by the unstable and contested discourses of motherhood and childhood, practical circumstances and the appalling threat to civilians' lives and bodies that aerial warfare has posed since the beginning of the twentieth century.[98]

2

Nationalizing hundreds and thousands of women

The decision taken to billet the majority of evacuees in private homes was a domestic response to a national problem which instigated 'an experiment in government intervention into private life'[1] on an unparalleled scale. The Fabian writer Margaret Cole described the scheme as akin to 'nationalising hundreds of thousands of women' but optimistically suggested evacuation 'sought to combine the compulsion of national need with as much as could be retained, in emergency, of the voluntary principle'.[2] The examination of the billeting process and the work of many women employed as billeting officers in this chapter seeks to draw attention to the increasing government interference in the home, to legal and discursive control over the domestic spaces and housewives lives that evacuation brought about. Children's welfare played a central role in the wartime project of defending the country from the foe; evacuation made the care and protection of the young national concerns. Consequently, a multitude of social reformers, psychologists, psychoanalysts, child guidance and child welfare experts used evacuation to promote their own political or intellectual projects and the significance of their profession. An unfortunate and unforeseen consequence of this was to accelerate the degree to which rights, responsibilities and expertise about children's welfare, once private issues for families, became public concerns. Various theories about the organization of society, education, mothering and children's upbringing were articulated in response to the problems evacuation exposed. The home, even the intimate space of the bedroom, became a government concern when, for example, the problems and consequences of evacuees' bed-wetting were considered. The provision of rubber sheets became a national rather than domestic issue, while practically and discursively mothers and motherhood increasingly came under surveillance.

Identifying and allocating billets

The billeting survey, undertaken under the auspices of the Ministry of Health in January and February of 1939, was a precursor for the new wartime relationship between the nation and domestic homes. Local volunteers were persuaded, or sometimes pressured, to undertake the survey, many of whom later became billeting officers. They were members of women's organizations, clergy of all denominations and their wives, local gentry, teachers, social workers and 'the great and the good' in reception areas. The survey necessitated undertaking a visit to each house in an allocated neighbourhood and completing an extensive questionnaire with the householder. The survey explored physical and resource issues which would affect the householder's ability to host evacuees in the event of war, including bedding, the proximity of local schools, the number of rooms and residents in the house. In Cheltenham, the local newspaper reminded residents that local women would be visiting and that the Government circular had stipulated that where 'a householder expresses unwillingness to afford accommodation; the Visitor must record his or her opinion of whether the reason given was sufficient to justify exemption of a house and if not the billeting officer's assessment of how many evacuees could be accommodated.'[3] It was also pointed out that an inspection and appraisal of bedrooms was required to identify any need for extra blankets or mattresses. Thus state representatives were empowered to physically enter the private domestic space of the home, to size it up, comment and critique on everything including bed linen. There was no appraisal of the suitability of hosts to look after children; surveillance was initially concerned only with physical, rather than the emotional, capacity of households.

Potential billets were calculated by subtracting the number of people in the house from the number of rooms. All rooms, upstairs or down, were included, whatever purpose they were serving and no adjustment was made for the size of the room. Homes were deemed to be able to accommodate one person for every room, although it was assumed children would share bedrooms leaving other rooms free for living and eating, an approach that advantaged those in larger houses with bigger rooms. Local newspapers announced the numbers of billets various communities had offered and how these matched central government expectations. A degree of truculence began to creep into areas, which fell short of their targets. Mr F. P. Cottey, chairman of the Air Raid Precautions Committee in Exeter warned, '[W]here you have people, as we have had who say "We don't want them, we may be going away" it may be necessary to take over the house', adding, 'Our job is to see that every citizen takes his or her fair share of the responsibility in the billeting of these children.'[4]

It had been hoped that people would volunteer to host evacuees, as they had during the Kindertransport and canvassers or visitors recorded from each housewife the number of evacuees they would be prepared to host. However, with potentially five million evacuees to be billeted, the first hints that the government would create powers, which would enable them to force householders to accept evacuees reached local newspapers in April 1939.[5] In the months that followed many people, particularly the middle and upper classes went to great lengths to fill up their spare rooms with friends, family, private evacuees, paying guests or anyone they could find to ensure that they would not have evacuees billeted upon them. As early as April 1939, Sir George Chrystal, permanent secretary to the Ministry of Health, said that he thought there were already 800,000 such arrangements in place.[6] The Clerk to West Riding Council noted the problem being created by the number of private billets[7] while in Cheshire it was pointed out that 'military billeting would cut across accommodation intended for children'.[8] The situation in many households, by the time evacuation took place at the beginning of September, was very different from that suggested by the billeting survey. Government powers had also increased and the Emergency Powers (defence) act passed in August 1939 gave local authorities the ability to requisition residential and other buildings, whether unoccupied or not, for evacuees.

A significant level of 'womanpower', tact and care was required, by many billeting officers and their helpers, when evacuation actually began, to manage the uncertainty and varying degrees of enthusiasm of potential hosts for the scheme. A Mass Observation Investigator reported,

> In the last week about 20 women in this areas have worked the whole day to find enough homes. In the opinion of three helpers about a quarter of families who were asked to take children did not want to take them. Of course they could not refuse under the new act, but as it would be very unpleasant for the children they tried not to put children in such homes … There were a great many lady helpers many more than needed. They made a principle in billeting, not to force people to take children but to persuade them that it would be their duty.[9]

A 48-year-old teacher in Chepstow, who like so many teachers took on the role of billeting officer, carried it out with care, diligence, and it seems some degree of pride. She was aware of all the regulations and had carefully interviewed all the potential hosts on her billeting list and carefully put together her planned allocations of evacuees in August 1939. The woman with a large house, who had just been ill, was to have only teachers placed in her home as she felt children would be too much of a handful for her. Families with girls, she had decided, should have more girls so as to make sharing bedrooms easier. When she waited on Friday, 1 September 1939, for the children to arrive, she mused with pleasure 'that they had not had to bring pressure to bear in a single case'. There was both excitement and momentary panic when the buses arrive – with the evacuees who all turned out to be boys. She recorded in her Mass Observation diary,

> We started off with brothers and got them placed together. I found two chubby rosy cheeked brothers for the women who had spoken to me at the whist drive last night. I am sure she will be pleased with them. Then we took pairs who would like to stay together. The only one instance was a child billeted by himself and as he was an only child he preferred it. All the rest in twos, threes or fours.[10]

With almost clockwork precision, 450 children from Birmingham were distributed across four districts in the town and foster parents were soon seen at church or out walking, accompanied by their evacuees.[11] In smaller villages, local billeting officers knew the community and were aware of wholly unsuitable hosts, but no such luxury was afforded to large communities or towns and, consequently, problems did occur. Juliet Gardiner has pointed out that 'the evacuation scheme was prepared centrally but the main burden of detailed planning and execution fell upon local authorities ... the matter was a complex one involving many services and the co-operation of many authorities'.[12] Jean Wilks, who was 5 when evacuated, recalled the billeting officers trying to persuade householders to accept evacuees, which was 'absolutely horrendous'.[13] In the rush and confusion of trying to get children housed in appropriate billets, it was not just the billeting officers who assessed private homes. One teacher, evacuated with her school, was asked to inspect the bedrooms in potential homes for her charges. She noted in her diary, 'Never before had this unusual inspection been my lot and I regret to say that a hasty observation was not as thorough as I would have liked but, as time proved, the truth will out.'[14]

Had bombs, as expected, fallen in Autumn 1939, then all the efforts to billet children, sometimes with their mothers, the inspections and impositions into domestic spaces, would have been justified. However, this first wave of evacuation did not save children or their mothers from maiming and death. The vacuum of the phoney war was filled with a cacophony of voices carping, criticizing and undermining the decisions of both the government and many parents to send children to safety and the organization of the billeting. An anonymous report on evacuation in a small market town, published the following year, stated,

> Within 24 hours of the arrival of evacuees, the Billeting Officer was overwhelmed with complaints from billetors and evacuees. Adult evacuees complained they were without washing facilities; that their rooms were damp or inconveniently furnished. Billetors said the adult evacuees were unadaptable; they behaved as if they owned the house; that they were communists; that their manners were deplorable. They complained the children wet the beds; their clothes were completely inadequate; that they would not eat the food provided for them.[15]

As Margaret Cole and Richard Padley pointed out, people's understanding of how the evacuation scheme was working relied upon anecdote: '[E]vacuation, like other problems of domestic life' lent itself 'to gossip and to newspaper stories magnified out of all proportion.'[16] The carping and complaints, which voiced a mixture of class prejudice and towneyism,[17] quickly reached the House of Commons where a debate on 14 September 1939 got rather heated. Captain Colin Thornton-Kemsley, the Conservative MP for Kincardine and Western Aberdeenshire, caused an uproar by derogatory accusations about evacuees. He claimed to have a letter from a doctor and magistrate who

> says that the children and their mothers arrived in his district mostly in a very filthy and verminous condition and that many were very inadequately clad. Their habits were indescribable, and many cases had come to his notice where carpets, mattresses and bedding had had to be completely destroyed owing to the primitive habits of these evacuees … This is not a pleasant matter for anyone to raise in this House.[18]

Portrayals of evacuees and their mothers as dirty, polluting, diseased with unclean habits, fuelled a discourse of towneyism, which has much in common with the racism of the 1960s and 1970s.[19] The analytical framework offered by anthropologist Mary Douglas in her ground-breaking book *Purity and Danger* is helpful to understanding this phenomenon.[20] She points out that dirt is matter out of place; arguably evacuees and refugees are regarded in this way, as not belonging in rural villages, and hence are sometimes described as polluting the countryside.[21] Despite government propaganda, a not-in-my-backyard nimbyism suggested that evacuees did not belong in the reception areas; that those women who were evacuated with their children whose husbands were left at home or those that sent their children away unaccompanied had contravened the perceived order of things. As Douglas explains,

> Dirt then, is never a unique, isolated event. Where there is dirt, there is a system. Dirt is the by-product of a systematic ordering and classification of matter, in so far as ordering involves rejecting inappropriate elements.[22]
>
> If uncleanliness is matter out of place, we must approach it through order.[23]

The problem of dirt can be addressed by removal and cleaning; order can be created out of chaos. Hence a plethora of narratives and myths refer to evacuees being cleaned, given new clothes, retrained, educated and brought into a newly established order and categorization of things. In reception areas, the myth that children's health, welfare and manners enhanced as a result of their stay in the idyllic countryside was quickly established.[24]

The widely circulating rumours and myths had emotional and practical consequences for the billeting officers who discovered that things were not so ideal as the teacher who was a billeting officer in Chepstow initially hoped when she noted in her diary that 'bringing the industrial type and the agricultural type more together' would result in a new social order as 'half of England is learning how the other half lives'.[25] As Padley noted, '[E]vacuation was both an effort of national government and an operation which gravely affected social institutions as well as the lives of individuals'.[26] Billeting officers were on the sharp end of both press and political pundits, virulently repeated myths and gossip, with the assumption that it was up to the local and national governments to address them rather than parents. Thus evacuation placed the private world of the home and the care of children and the vulnerable in the public sphere. Up and down the country billeting officers, government officials and voluntary workers found themselves increasingly involved in concerns of the everyday domestic life, from rubber sheets to nit combs.

Increasing intervention

The responses of various government departments to the issues raised about evacuation can be grouped under three categories. Firstly, they sought increased input from local authority employees, volunteers and voluntary organizations, as will be explored in Chapter 8. Secondly, there was a multitude of platitudes and policies. Malcolm McDonald, minister of health, expressed the view, 'The family life of both hostess and guest are disturbed and all should try to ensure that there is mutual give and take'.[27] It is unlikely that this cut much ice with those actually experiencing the difficulties of evacuation themselves. There was also the production of endless policy documents and government circulars, which were not necessarily, and possibly could not have been, followed through on the ground. Local authorities received numerous memos and circulars on all manner of issues in relation to evacuation from unmarried mothers to deaths in reception areas. Circular 1897 dealt with compensation for damage to property, other than fair wear and tear, when evacuees were billeted. This resulted in lengthy correspondence often between local authority officials and householders over what and when damage had occurred and who was responsible for it.[28] The tendency of stressed and anxious children, scared to visit outside loos and in unfamiliar rural environments, to wet their beds led to a scheme for compensation for damage to bedding. This was covered in circular 1871 para 22 and necessitated time-consuming inspections of mattresses and bedding. Alternatively the need for arrangements for husbands to visit their evacuated wives or for mothers to visit their children led to other government circulars, trying to address the issue of how often was reasonable, who should cover the cost of hospitality and how many vouchers for cheap day travel should be allocated.[29] Finally, the government increased their provision of finance and resources for the evacuation scheme. The operation of all these measures, the work of investigating, recording and dealing with complaints, meant that the state became involved in the minutiae of its citizens' private domestic lives to a hitherto unprecedented extent. For example, a government circular on 25 March 1940 discussed the role of billeting officers in providing mackintosh overlays for beds to householders.[30] Thus evacuation made the intimate domestic space of the bedroom a central government concern in wartime, alongside the armed forces and bomb shelters.

By Spring 1940, a government circular confirmed that in the next phase of evacuation 'children who are to be evacuated will be medically examined before evacuation takes place'.[31] The medical inspections sought to ensure that children arrived in their billets without infectious diseases or nits. The effectiveness of this policy is put in question by reports that health inspectors, who went into schools, apparently inspected 480 students in one hour. Mrs Mann recalled being employed by the London County Council for weeks to prepare children for evacuation in 1940: 'I was responsible for seeing that the children to be evacuated were clean in every way and healthy ... [children] were examined by doctors at their schools and if found with dirty heads they were sent to Cleaning Stations all over London'.[32] In May 1940, the local newspaper in Bedfordshire was able to report that 'arrangements have been made, in the event of the new evacuation scheme being put into operation, to place the children who are in a dirty venomous state in special hostels until they are fit to be billeted'.[33] Infirmaries were set up for children who were ill whose foster parents could not look after them and children's homes to care for children considered to be unmanageable. Ensuring that children's heads were checked for nits was now added to the provision of rubber sheets as part of the war effort as the government became increasingly entwined in children's lives and took responsibility for the domestic care and mothering of disadvantaged children from danger areas.

A veritable army of experts emerged with suggestions and criticisms of the public policies, analysing evacuation through the prism of their own particular political and ideological agendas or prejudices. They sought to commandeer the great social experiment of evacuation for their own causes. Campaigns for family allowances, health care, nursery provision and welfare services as ways of addressing deprivation and social problems had been gaining support since the late nineteenth century and had brought about some new provision. Many who sought to dominate public agendas considered governments should continue to undertake greater responsibility for children and that in wartime more school camps should have been set up to house evacuees. Joan Simeon Clarke suggested that 'the more private billets that are used, the less chance there is of eventual success'.[34] The Fabian Society, proponents of a democratic route to socialism, saw in evacuation evidence of the need for greater social welfare and collective or communal activities. But in wartime expenditure by the government prioritized military objectives. The Fabian society pamphlet entitled *Evacuation Failure or Reform* argued for 'a well-designed experiment in social reform' which would 'leave the country a heritage of camp schools, village halls, clubs, nursery hostels and the like such as had never experienced before'[35] had limited immediate impact but an increasing range of services and responsibilities for evacuee children, which had predominantly resided with mothers were taken over by national and local government or the voluntary sector.

Evacuation revealed the uncertainty, even fluidity about exactly which adults should organize, which parts of childhood. The financial burden of children, concerns for their health and welfare, the provision of shoes and clothes and the consequences of children's sometimes troublesome behaviour all became issues of public concern. This met with criticism in some quarters and mutterings of speeches explaining the new policies by counsellors were accused of being socialist.[36] If social-welfare reformers wanted more public provision, a bevy of psychologists began to critique the emotional impact of evacuation on children and argued for the importance of the home and domestic care of children. Bowlby suggested that a child sent away from home, even for their own safety would feel unwanted and that 'whether this is really so or only in his imagination'. Children would apparently find this very difficult and 'miserable and insecure' they would apparently hold a grudge against their 'parents and society in general and for a long while'.[37]

A growing number of welfare services were introduced to provide psychological support for children; a cottage industry of psychologists analysed and attempted to cure psychological problems. As John Stewart has convincingly argued, a network of Child Guidance clinics was already becoming established across Britain by the outbreak of war. These often acted as a hub for the work and activities of a variety of child-focused professionals, including psychiatric social workers, psychologists, psychoanalysts, all of whom took a role in both commenting upon and providing assistance and support for evacuees. The clinics were often linked to hospitals and local authority funding supported some, as in Birmingham. In wartime the approaches of different centres and experts in the field varied but as some clinics in urban areas closed and the needs of evacuees became an issue of public concern, there was a greater dissemination of child guidance across the country. Staff from the Manchester centre, for example, visited patients in the reception areas, while at Cambridge, a centre was set up to train child welfare staff.[38]

A flurry of academics from Oxford, Cambridge and Liverpool universities, social commentators and psychologists investigated evacuation and in time produced reports on this first phase which overwhelming found that evacuation was in the vast majority of cases successful. In many of the 320 cases examined in the Cambridge Evacuation Survey, only a handful indicated poor relationships between the child and foster mother, and it pointed out,

> [F]or the very small number of unbillatable children, who themselves came from families where relationships were bad, small hostels proved to be a success. The careful choosing of foster-homes is the nearest we can get in wartime to give children the stability and the emotional sustenance they would have got from their own families.[39]

Contrary to the anecdotes of Captain Colin Thornton-Kemsley, a survey undertaken by Liverpool University, similarly found that 86 per cent foster parents had no complaints about their evacuees while 7 per cent had problems that were easily overcome.[40] Likewise, the survey by Barnett House Study Group on children evacuated to Oxford not only praised the work of foster mothers but expressed the view that 'future educational and social policy should lay greater emphasis on boarding-out'.[41] As the war ground on over six years, the financial

burden of children, concerns for their health and welfare and the consequences
of children's sometimes troublesome behaviour become issues for the state. In
time the government efforts paid off as the Mass Observation annual surveys
on wartime inconveniences carried out between 1939 and 1945 indicated. In
1939–40 evacuation was listed in sixth place as an irritation, annoyance and
inconvenience of war, following for example prices and blackout. It had slipped to
fifteenth place in 1940–1 and only rose a little in 1941–2.[42] Nevertheless, billeting
officers found that offers of accommodation for evacuees in the summer of 1940
were rather unforthcoming.

Struggles to find billets when really needed

The class prejudice expressed in the anecdotes that Captain Colin Thornton-
Kemsley and others about evacuees were reflected in attitudes to hosting
evacuees. The perception emerged, and has remained, that many of the better
off avoided having children or families evacuated through the government
scheme in their homes. Desiree Moore recalled the challenging time her
mother had:

> She was a Billeting Officer right from the word go … , it was all volunteer work
> and you had to go around and visit all the families and find out who would have
> people, who wouldn't … it was very strange that all the smaller houses would
> have children and there seemed to be an awful anathema as far as some of the
> larger houses were concerned about having 'those awful children' as some of
> them referred to them. The children came from South East London … parts of
> which were quite reasonable areas, parts of which weren't.[43]

It appeared to many of the working class in the reception areas that the social
background and networks, from which the billeting officers came, made them
more sympathetic to the resistance of the better off to housing evacuees, than
they were to the working classes. It was ironically suggested in Evelyn Waugh's
novel *Put Out More Flags* (1942) that the wealthy bribed billeting officers to avoid
taking evacuees.[44] Arguably pressure could be brought to bear on working-class
householders to host evacuees in smaller hierarchically structured villages when
the billeting officers came from a wealthier class. This pressure was magnified, if
the billeting officer was related to, or themselves perhaps, a property owner who
rented out a house or employed the cottage people. In Staffordshire, Michael
Whitebrook recalled, '[I]t was a strange situation the billeting officers who were

the ones with the best properties in the village ... but they didn't put on their own ... they didn't have any at all.'[45]

Certainly by May 1940 when the threat of invasion and bombing was becoming more severe, in many areas billeting officers were faced with genuine difficulty in finding enough billets. The Evacuation Committee Minutes from Cheadle in Staffordshire reported that an appeal for billets only produced 192 offers of accommodation and that billeting officers and voluntary agencies would be going house to house to try and obtain further volunteers.[46] Government policies did not always help their pursuit of suitable billets, which were not supposed to be within 1,000 yards of military. Police were also barred from taking evacuee and others tried to get themselves excluded on the basis of their jobs, for example, some members of the Church of England clergy, and only a desperate billeting officer billeted a child where they were not welcome. As the survey of evacuation carried out by the University of Liverpool, noted although, 'Undoubtedly it was a source of irritation that a neighbour should refuse her share in a common duty, but damage would have been done to children compulsorily thrust into homes where they were emphatically not wanted, cannot be overlooked.'[47] Resentment grew, questions were asked in the House of Commons, including one wanting to know why 150 mothers and children had to sleep in a draughty hall when the Duke of Argyll's large house was almost unused nearby.[48]

Some shared the views of the Fabian Society that the government should take more responsibility for evacuees, and one respondent explained to a Mass Observation investigator, 'I consider it an outrage. Proper shelters should be provided in London or else the people could live together in village halls, houses etc.'[49] In Derbyshire, the teacher May Smith, who was a billeting officer, noted in her diary in May 1940 that she was engaged in

> a house-to-house visitation of Belmont Street, Stanley Street, and Drayton Street about the billeting of children in wartime. Oh dear! A thankless job though most people very decent. Everyone I approach refused ... The only one who volunteered to have a child was a boy whose mother was out – and I don't think he dared refuse me. But I bet his mother will have something to say when she returns.[50]

She finished off her visits the following Saturday.[51] But within a couple of months recorded in her diary: 'Launched myself upon another billeting campaign with the utmost reluctance, to ensure billets for the additional 1200 B'ham children who are to come. All my potential clients exclaimed in horror when I told them where the children were from.'[52] May's experience was repeated across the country, in E. M. Delafield's fictionalized autobiography *Diary of a Provincial Lady* – she describes how the role of Billeting officer has destroyed one poor women's social interaction as people scuttled off in the opposite direction at the sight of her, scared of being asked to look after more evacuees.[53] In August 1940 Constance Miles noted in her diary: 'I saw the billeting officer, Mrs L., looking very determined, driving rapidly along to enforce some householder possibly to take children from Portsmouth.'[54]

Despite the challenges faced by the billeting officers, once the effects of bombing were actually seen, some argued that in danger areas the government should introduce compulsory evacuation of children. The *Sunderland Daily Echo and Shipping Gazette* pointed out, 'Large scale movements of children from dangerous areas are in progress now: but it is idle to mask the fact that there remain many hundreds of thousands of the young generation, our most precious possession, still lodged in vulnerable areas.'[55] The government baulked at this level of imposition into parental responsibility and control, even after the bombing of Coventry in November 1940 again raised the question of people whose stayed in exposed areas when it was not essential. Newspapers suggested, '[C]ompulsory removal must come within the realm of practical politics.'[56] The government could not, however, introduce compulsory evacuation, when it was so difficult to accommodate those who were evacuated voluntarily.

Local authorities had powers to force householders to take evacuees but as a 33-year-old housewife explained to a Mass Observation Investigator in Burford, Oxfordshire, 'No-one knows exactly the rights and powers of the billeting officers. And no one challenges them because they seem to be rigorously exercised on the poor people rather than on the rich.'[57] The use of legal powers varied widely but local newspapers carried reports of cases of people who were prosecuted. As early as 1939, the full force of the law was used against a couple in North Claines, Worcestershire, who had refused to take in evacuees. It seems that the authorities were keen to make 'an example of someone in order that a similar attitude might not be adopted in future'.[58] Recourse to legal action seems to have increased throughout the war as households became evacuee-weary. In 1944 *The Leek Post and Times* in Staffordshire reported that three people were charged in the Police Court for failing to comply with billeting notices. Mrs Bowcock who lived in a three-bedroom house had been asked to take a woman and her three children in although she had had two operations recently herself which had left her in poor health, despite this the court ordered her to pay fines and costs.[59]

The state or at least representatives of the state were making decisions that were once the prerogative of mothers and housewives, about who should sleep in their house. Not only could householders be fined for their unwillingness to take evacuees, but billeting officers and their representatives were expected to regularly visit and inspect private homes in order to monitor evacuees' welfare throughout the war. Ivy Wilson recalled that after only about three to six weeks she was removed from the home of a 'nasty lady' who had 'shaved her hair right off'.[60] The billeting officer had it appeared, regarded this rather aggressive approach to nits as an indication that little Ivy was not receiving appropriate care. Many harassed billeting officers found their time and energy so entirely taken up with finding new billets for children rejected in one home and dealing with immediate crises that they had little time or inclination to go looking for difficulties and surveying the foster mothers' homes. Instead volunteer visitors were expected to inspect children and the homes they were in. The Ministry of Health's 1942 *Handbook on Billeting and Welfare for the Use by Chief Billeting Officers* in districts explained,

> It is essential that arrangements should be made for responsible persons to make regular visits to billets occupied by unaccompanied children. These arrangements should ordinarily be organised by the Authority's Welfare Committee (see paragraph 119). It is suggested that all billets should be systematically visited by a person qualified to form an opinion on the health and wellbeing of the child and the care, which it is receiving.[61]

The booklet goes on to suggest the focus should be on the provision of friendly advice and ascertaining the need for out of school activities, holiday camps. This army of volunteer visitors entering domestic homes to provide guidance to foster mothers were themselves given advice by professionals in child welfare such as Lucy Faithfull who was a regional welfare officer in the Midlands.[62] Evidence suggests that for many householders that when and if these women visited, they were regarded as middle-class busybodies. Middle-class interference in the lives of working-class mothers was something that was not entirely novel, but what was new was the level to which this was licensed by the state.

Social reformers psychologists and psycho-analysts take centre stage

Those foster mothers, who did not face too many physical inspections of their homes, parenting or domestic skills, did not escape surveillance. The challenges of billeting, the myths, anecdotes and rumours that evacuation gave rise to, placed a spotlight onto issues of dirt, infectious disease, nits, personal habits and childhood anxieties. Some took the issues at face value; others saw them as symptomatic of the evacuation scheme, urban deprivation or poor childrearing. Joan Simeon Clarke of Girton College, Cambridge, warned in 1940, 'Family life cannot be artificially created' and evacuation required not just competent household management but caring and mothering.[63] She was not alone in emphasizing the importance of maternal responsibilities and everyday practices of domesticity. The intimate spaces within which family relationships were played out were increasing the focus of discussion and debate by politicians, women's organizations, teachers and the newly developing army of childcare experts who unleashed a range of criticisms upon mothers. All concerns were, as Geoffrey Field argues, focused on the notion of the working-class family in crisis.[64] Likewise, John Welshman has drawn attention to how those politicians and social workers with eugenicist leanings saw inherited inadequacies at the root of child neglect, deprivation and poverty.[65] Such assumptions, in the interwar years, led to calls to limit working-class reproduction, which motivated birth-control campaigners and even led to calls for compulsory sterilization.[66] Many of the problems of evacuation were utilized to confirm such views that a 'social problem group' at the bottom of society was responsible for vagrancy, criminality and unemployment.[67]

Alternatively, some social reformers argued that social conditions, lack of education and economic circumstances were the cause of deprivation and that social welfare and economic support were the route to solve the problems. The widespread provision of school meals and milk in the early 1940s can be seen in this light.[68] However, as Pat Starkey suggests, concerned social workers and reformers shifted their emphases from problem families to the 'feckless mother'.[69] Issues with the health or cleanliness of working-class evacuees were sometimes the result of the inadequacy of their mothers, who were 'unfortunate enough to be at the intersection of eugenic, class and social anxieties'.[70] A number of women from parliament and women's organizations aligned to the *Women's Group on Problems arising from Evacuation* produced the *Our Towns* report in 1943,[71] and likewise, as Welshman suggests, '[W]restled with the question of whether improvements in education, or progress on environmental factors, were more likely to solve the problem of poverty'.[72] There remains some debate among historians about how influential any of the arguments put forward in this or other writing about evacuation was to social policy and welfare reform.[73] To Welshman, evacuation and the wider problems it revealed in relation to disease, footwear, clothing and nutrition led to 'significant policy changes'.[74] While this might be overstating the case, evacuation did bring about an unparalleled public interference into what had previously been considered to be the private space of the home, and the experience was used by a number of individuals and groups, such as the Fabian Society, to legitimate their arguments for social change. The progress of reform, they had been already advocating in the interwar years, was perhaps accelerated. Discourses were nudged away from eugenics, as a range of competing public discourses about motherhood gained greater visibility in the public sphere.

Michal Shapira has argued that psychoanalytic approaches to childcare, influenced by Melanie Klein, and her emphasis on children's relationship to the mother's breast, had established a place in popular and professional discourse in the interwar era. Furthermore, 'because women were viewed as natural care-givers,' it was easier for women 'to carve out a place for themselves as female experts. Their work positioned women psychologists as equal to male experts'[75] as the professionalization of childcare occurred. Nursery nurses and nannies' training incorporated a more scientific approach in their curricula and Susan Isaacs writing under the pseudonym of Ursula Wise in the popular journal *Nursery World* from 1929–36 'taught British parents and child caregivers to "speak Kleinian"'.[76] There was an increasing focus on the child's perspective and an acknowledgement that children were 'independent subjects and future democratic citizens'.[77] Isaacs and other psychoanalysts also broadcast on radio in the 1930s; the BBC saw educating the housewife and mother as one element of their public service remit.[78] An approach the audience did not always receive positively. The *Daily Herald* critiqued presenters who talked 'endlessly of child psychology and isms'.[79] In 1937 the BBC introduced Margaret McCook Weir, a mother of four boys from Suffolk to the airwaves. She described herself as 'living a peasant's life in isolated East Anglia' and explained, '[H]aving four babies I feel I've been washing napkins all my life, and I can scarcely imagine a morning without washing, drying, airing and adjusting, pinning or inspecting napkins.'[80] She also admitted, '[S]ometimes in fact I loathe them and their ever pressing demands threaten to overwhelm me.'[81] It would be many years before such refreshing honesty would appear again or mothers would be seen as the experts.

War precipitated a greater focus on children's psychological development in the period from birth to 5 years, and the central role of the mother in this, as Angela Davis points out. She also argues evacuation offered new opportunities for research, for example, that undertaken by Anna Freud running the Hampstead War Nurseries intended for 'bombed-out' children in London or Susan Isaacs work on the *Cambridge Evacuation Survey*.[82] Many psychologists, including

John Bowlby and Donald Winnicott, explored the significance of evacuation in relation to their own pre-existing concerns about motherhood and maternal attachment. Although there was a grudging admission that 'children over 5 can stand separation from home, and even benefit from it.'[83] Bowbly and Winnicott were adamant in their opposition to any under-fives being separated from their mothers even if the children appeared to be quite happy. They asserted, '[T]he evacuation of small children between 2 and 5 introduces major psychological problems.'[84] Few under-fives were evacuated and the government circular in Spring 1940 confirmed that evacuation would 'be limited to school children from 5-year-old upwards together with a very small number of under-fives who were already attending school last summer and 'it will only be carried out if it is clear that air attack on a substantial scale is developing.'[85]

To Anna Freud and Dorothy Burlingham successful fostering was almost unattainable. They suggested, '[W]ithout the primitive possessiveness and overestimation at the bottom of the mother love', it would be impossible for women to cope with the strain of looking after children without feeling abused.[86] They argued 'foster mothers can either adopt a position of indifference, in which case the children suffer, or treat an evacuee child as if they were their own children, in which case the children will become alienated from their birth family.'[87] Initially, Burlingham and Freud also argued that for children, the anxiety and stress of living through air raids was a direct result of their mother's inability to control her own fears and anxieties.[88] Mothers, justifiably anxious about air raids, found themselves criticized for lacking emotional restraint; a perspective linked perhaps something to psychoanalytic associations between femininity and hysteria.[89] Burlingham and Freud reappraised their position when the Blitz actually began and even noted that 'the air raids on London demonstrated against all possible objection the practical need for the children's evacuation'.[90]

Susan Isaacs was already an established psychologist, broadcaster, writer and pioneer of child-centred education when on returning to Cambridge, she chaired the group, which included John Bowlby, investigating the effects of family separation on evacuated children. The researchers interviewed children and got them to write compositions to reveal their feelings about their separation from parents and communities. The results were published in 1941 as the *Cambridge Evacuation Survey*, which discussed the effects of separation anxiety.[91] Jenny Willan has suggested that much of this research 'focussed on separation from mothers because fathers were already separated by virtue of being absent in war or in work'.[92] Psychologist's focus on separation from the mother was arguably a consequence of their own pre-conceived interests and cultural assumptions about the sexual division of labour within families at the time. The call up of men into the forces was slow to put into operation but by 1942 of approximately fifteen million males between the ages of 14 and 64 who were British subjects only 3,784,000 were in the armed and auxiliary services – obviously those between 18 and 40 were disproportionately represented in this group. However many men in the engineering, building trades, transportation, mining, shipping and the railways remained at home during the conflict.

The opinions of intellectual experts about motherhood, whether they were sociologists, psychologists and psychoanalysts, welfare and social workers or members of the Fabian society, were increasingly foregrounded in public discourse. As their voices gained traction, they flexed their muscles seeking to become not just an expert or voice on the issues around the welfare of children but the expert and the voice for the post-war world. In doing so the everyday lives of mothers and motherhood itself increasing came under surveillance – mother's expertise was in danger of being marginalized or silenced by experts.

Mythical good mothers

When Susan Isaacs and John Bowlby were recruited to look into the reasons that so few parents were complying with the need for evacuation in 1940, they argued that what was required was for the 'psychologically informed state to create homely environments to minimise children's anxieties'.[93] A consensus grew among many of the child guidance experts that the individual attention and affection provided in a home by mothers was indispensable to children's physical and emotional development. Thus it was argued,

> Now that the social conditions have greatly improved compared with forty years ago, the child who has boarded out with foster parents usually has a far better chance of becoming a normal member of society than a child who is kept in an orphanage or a public assistance home.[94]

Thus billeting officers, social workers, field workers, many psychologists and psychoanalysts seemed to agree that evacuee-children should be in the care of a 'good mother'.[95] A non-working, affectionate, child-focused mother was seen as the ideal, but this was not linked to biological motherhood, as John Bowlby explained when discussing only children and children from broken homes: 'The prospects for successful development for children experiencing stronger personal affection in their foster-families than in their own homes were better if the unsatisfactory relationships at home were due to external factors like poverty and unemployment.[96]

The myth of positive evacuation surfaced in stories of the beneficial influence of sympathetic, understanding foster mothers who, taking advice from psychologists, social or welfare workers, were able to address a range of behavioural issues among evacuees which included: screaming fits, faecal incontinence, bad temper and a penchant for swallowing marbles. Runaways were also to be sorted out within a family environment where home life and schooling were not interrupted by bombing raids. Thus the Barnett House Study Group were able to argue,

> Whatever may be said against evacuation, it not only saved many children's lives but also took them away from conditions, which would have led them into delinquency. In the reception area they enjoyed an almost continuous school-life, often with the advantage of smaller classes, and in the majority of cases, a happy home life, under the care of a foster-mother who devoted her whole time to domestic duties.[97]

All of the surveys, reports and commentaries by psychologists and psychoanalysts carried numerous case studies of individual problem children whose behaviour was transformed. Each such narrative carried an implicit sense of how the ideal mother should behave. Many experts had a clear sense of home and what was an appropriate upbringing for children in their minds – arguably a class-specific one which swallowed wholeheartedly the interwar cult of domesticity.[98] First and foremost, they most emphatically were domestic not working mothers. The Barnett House Survey argued,

> Employment of the mother was another important factor influencing the atmosphere of the household ... [it] must be accepted with some reservation, for not all jobs mean leaving the home and not all home workers can supervise the children constantly. For many children, however, a chance of unimpaired family life was offered by evacuation, which thus offset to some extent the less desirable effects of widespread female employment in wartime.[99]

When women undertook paid work alongside domestic responsibilities it was conceived as putting a strain upon mothers, for which the children suffered. Thus in reviewing the case of a young lad of 13 in Oxfordshire where the school considered the parents showed little interest: '[T]he field worker attributed mother's attitude in part to the twofold burden of factory and domestic duties.'[100]

Experts built their arguments on how a good mother should behave, with references to case studies of children. Mrs St Loe Strachey's *Borrowed Children*, written for the everyday reader and with an eye on the American market, included the story of a boy she called Leslie. He was described as 'a lively, red haired urchin, always fighting apparently very tough, but also sensitive to criticism and anxious to please'. Veiled criticism of his biological parents referred to their quarrelling and 'violent tempers' and implied that his 'aggressive and unmanageable behaviour' in his first billet with a quiet elderly couple was to some degree learnt from his own parents. His problems were solved when the

> billeting officer transferred him to a remote farmhouse with a young, easy going hostess with one child. She would have liked a large family of her own, was fond of children, very tolerant, and slightly amused at the failure of other people to deal with this child. At the same time she could see he was a child who easily became unhappy through his tempers, and was glad to talk over his problems with the social worker who visited regularly. He settled down quickly.'[101]

After a change to a nearby school all it seems was well, yet there are a number of telling and familiar references in this extract. The good foster mother not only wants a large family but is willing to take advice from a social worker, the expert. Patience, willingness to take advice, and accepting that the children's problems were psychological not to do with inherited 'badness' or social background were key qualities for the good mother. Quoting Dr Moodle, Mrs St Loe Strachey's argues that what children need is comfort, warmth, affection, things to do, security and safety.[102]

The discourses that emerged and debates that took place about motherhood during the evacuation process arguably contributed to legitimating 'common sense' about the significance of a mother's role in child development. Evacuation laid bare the uncertainty and fluidity around exactly which adults should organize what parts of childhood, and whether the state and the parents should be responsible for. The ideal and devoted mother was increasingly expected to provide unconditional, emotional support, be self-sacrificing, but to provide safety and security for a child she also required a certain level of social welfare. Social reformers argued that she needed appropriate housing and some financial security for the family and of course an absence of threat from bombing to provide this idealized maternal care. The merging of both welfare and psychological support for mothers contributed to the Fabian Society politics which Bowlby and Isaacs supported and ideas of the New Jerusalem that it was hoped the 1945 election would usher in.[103]

Conclusion

The Government evacuation scheme blurred the boundaries of public and private spheres in new ways, as the domestic home and the homemaker was requisitioned for unpaid war work. It also unleashed a plethora of advice, expectation and interference into homes. Inevitably perhaps, a slippage and stretching of the discursive construction of housewifery and women's domestic role took place during evacuation. Whereas the interwar period prioritized women's role as household managers, in the post-war period motherhood became housewives' primary responsibility. Perhaps even more importantly, mothers increasingly became 'objects for the regulatory discourse of experts'[104] during discussions about wartime evacuation. Mothers' confidence in their motherhood was undermined in the first half of the twentieth century, not through force but by almost unintended multiple tiny subtle exercises of hegemony. Responses to evacuation played a role in accelerating this, giving a new impetus to a whole plethora of experts and professionals to become involved in formulating ideas about what 'good mothering might be'. This placed further strain on both biological and foster mothers who were already encountering the fears, dangers and trauma of warfare and the emotions and practical upheaval of evacuation, as the next chapters demonstrate.

3

Mothers who waved goodbye

Mothering, and motherhood, is perhaps one of the first casualties of aerial warfare. A mother's desire to physically and emotionally protect their child becomes impossible in modern warfare. As Vera Brittain noted, bombs ensured that non-combatants, women and children, who had taken no decision to take part in war, found themselves on the front line. Vera Brittain chose to have her children evacuated to the United States, where they remained for three years. In the first months of the war, horrified by the threat to her children that bombing presented, she lamented, 'Such an effort' I think in spite of myself, 'to bring up a child through its first ten years of life – and now, for what?'[1] She echoes Olive Schreiner's description of the horrors of the Boer war battlefields when she suggests 'no woman, whether she has borne children, or is merely potentially a child bearer, could look down upon the battlefield covered with the slain, but the thought would rise in her. So many mothers' sons! So many bodies brought into the world to lie there!'[2] The horror of a mother looking upon a battlefield is extended to all mothers when civilian populations are bombed.

During the Second World War many mothers decided to have their children evacuated, hoping they were doing the right thing and keeping their children safe. The decision about whether to do so robbed many women of the joys of motherhood, Margaret Kennedy who chose not evacuate her children but recorded that whereas in times of difficulty, trouble or anxiety, her children had always 'been an unfailing source of consolation. Now I can hardly bear to look at them. They are a sword in my heart.'[3] It was a tortuous decision, to send children away from their home, their neighbourhood and their family, that led to guilt and recrimination. Whatever decision a mother made for her offspring, it could be compared to an idealized version of childhood that a son or daughter might have had, if a different decision had been made. Mothers, who allowed their children to become unaccompanied evacuees, gave up both day-to-day responsibility and knowledge for their children's welfare and happiness. Cole and Padley, echoing prevailing assumptions that mothering was women's 'natural role', suggested, 'Suddenly to ask these women to give up their children is like asking a physician to give up his practice or a naval captain to give up his ship. They will feel bored and miserable.'[4] Mothers, however, found ways to continue to care for their children, even if their children were away for a prolonged period of time, they wrote letters and visited. Some determinedly battled to retain intimacy with, and control of, their offspring. Others were more ambivalent or defeated by difficulties, weighed down by numerous day-to-day worries and anxieties of wartime. Ultimately they gave up, feeling inadequate in comparison with the new life that evacuation had given their children.

The first heart-rending decision in 1939

Ruth Inglis argues that it was the government decision that 'evacuation should be voluntary … [that] … left parents with the critical decision about whether to keep their children where they would be loved and cared for, or to send them away where they would be safe but might not be as happy as they would be at home.'[5] Inglis' argument and most of the post-war writing on evacuation make assumptions about the homes from which children came. Families were very varied, shaped by multiple forces that could limit a mother's ability to care for and love her offspring. Children's physical safety was assumed but not assured by evacuation, their capacity for happiness, as in their own homes, was subject to numerous influences.

Mothers, in choosing whether or not to have their children evacuated, weighed up numerous competing, uncertain, shifting factors and the potential to regret their decision. Joyce Sidebotham who, aged six and a half, was evacuated to Staffordshire for only a few weeks in 1939 had a strong sense that her mother was 'upset that we went … when I asked her about it, she said that they were brainwashed into believing that they were doing the *wrong* thing if they didn't let the children go'.[6] Women might ignore or bow to pressure from other members of their family, but any decision they made was always contingent, reevaluated if circumstances changed. They considered the proximity and intensity of bombing, made assessments of the relative safety and potential risks of different places at different points during the six years of war. Rosalie Diamondstone recalled being brought home, '[W]hen Anderson shelters were installed in the cellars' of the back-to-back houses in Leeds where her family lived.[7] Many mothers shifted their children to-and-fro between danger areas and places of safety several times, always weighing up guilt, the pain of separation and potential regret. Public and private discourses of what was for the best, economic necessities and personal circumstances were entwined with messages from propaganda posters and films encouraging women in danger areas to allow their children to be evacuated, and once evacuated to leave them there. In August 1939, at the commencement of Operation Pied Piper many preparing for evacuation clung to the hope that, as in 1938, war would be averted at the last minute, and evacuation was only temporary. Secrecy about the destination for children evacuated under the government scheme added to the uncertainty about the length of time a mother might be separated from their children. A mother's almost impossible quandaries and traumas, as they made the decision to have their children evacuated to places thought to be safe, was predicated upon hopes and fears, anxieties and insecurities.

The idea of evacuation had been established in parents' minds well before September 1939, during the Munich crisis in 1938 some wealthier families had shipped their children off to relatives in the countryside. Nevertheless, many evacuees describe slowly becoming aware of private parental discussions taking place in their homes. As one evacuee recalled, 'I did notice my mother looking more worried and my parents seemed to do a lot of quiet talking.'[8] In encouraging women to evacuate their children, the government asked them to do something that in other circumstances would signify their failure as a mother. Oral testimonies, memoirs and the reports of observers provide ample evidence of how difficult the decision was for women. Pam Hobbs recalled,

> As the only family members of school age, Iris and I were prospective evacuees. On reading the letter from the school, my mother wept for the first time since war began. Evacuation was not compulsory, but advisable in view of our vulnerable location, and she said it was right that we should live in safety.[9]

Some parents invited their children to be part of the decision-making process; some evacuees remember being asked about whether they wanted to go abroad or to the camp schools when they opened. Some children were enthusiastic about evacuation, particularly if their friends were going, but for most children evacuation was not voluntary and oral histories suggest that parents sometimes gave the impression they were forced to evacuate children by the government. Initially those under 5 were only supposed to be evacuated if accompanied by their mothers, however this was not always the case and in 1945 Manchester parents wrote gratefully to the *Leek Post and Times* about their daughter who was due to return after 5 years in Leek, having been initially evacuated when 'she was not quite 4 ... with her haversack nearly as big as herself and a determination to carry her own like the older ones'.[10] Some nurseries and children's homes were also evacuated. One lady recalled over seventy years later, the lovely time she had had when evacuated with her nursery in Birmingham to a stately home in Shropshire.[11]

The process of speedily preparing children for evacuation was not straightforward, local authorities and schools provided lists of required items for each child but the poverty and deprivation in which many families in the inner cities lived made collecting the necessary garments challenging. Some proudly showed the clothes they had purchased to the teachers; others got themselves into debt acquiring extra underwear, toothpaste, soap and socks so that their children would not be a bother to those who were going to look after them.[12] For some mothers such diligence was not an option. A Liverpool mother of six children who shared her only towel between them, faced with packing their belongings 'had to cut it into pieces so that every child had a bit of toweling to go with, nothing more than a facecloth really, just a strip'.[13] The preparations could become a displacement activity for mothers; Irene Weller, evacuated from Small Heath in Birmingham, recalled her mother kept polishing her and her siblings' shoes and saying,

> We must get these polished; it's very important ... I suppose it gave her something to do, to stop crying. And she kept going over the list of things we had to take. Toothpaste, toothbrushes, but, being poor, we only had one tube between the three of us, and she kept saying, 'I don't know how you are going to manage if you're split up. I just don't know.'[14]

Mothers expressed their concern over their children's well-being in a number of ways, seeking to ensure the welfare of their youngsters even if they were far from home, by proxy. Where siblings were evacuated together, parents' parting message to the elder children was frequently to look after their younger siblings. Asked to hand responsibility for their children to strangers, they instead handed it over to older siblings. This would not have been an unfamiliar responsibility to children from larger families and children in families with several siblings were more likely to be evacuated in 1939 than only children or those from smaller families. Mothers' instinctive requests caused anxiety for elder children who could not prevent their siblings from being placed in different billets and consequently were unable to keep an eye on them. Some mothers seeking to reassure their children had painted a rosy picture of the countryside for their offspring, hoping to ensure they looked forward to their new homes. Mrs St Loe Strachey recalled, 'One little girl whom I had driven to another billet, on the first day, had been full of what she wanted: "Oh I do hope it's a farm! I do hope there's a pig. Would there be a calf do you think?" [15] Alternatively, Terence Frisby's mum instructed her two sons to let her know what their billet was like via a secret code on a postcard she had prepared for them to send on their arrival in their foster home. She explained,

'When you get there ... you find out the address of the place where they take you write it on the card there.' She looked at us both. She had left a space ...

'Now this is the code. Our secret. You know you write kisses don't you?' We agreed with 'earg' 'yuck' noises to brandish our distaste for such things. She waited for the ritual to subside. 'You put one kiss if its horrible and I'll come straight there and bring you back home. D'you see? You put two kisses if it's alright. And three kisses if it's nice. Really nice. Then I'll know.' [16]

A postcard that arrived soon after they were evacuated, covered in kisses reassured her; the carefully thought through system provided her with some peace of mind.

Concern about how mothers would react to seeing their children leave for an unknown destination and unspecified period of time led to a degree of caution over the arrangements at railway stations as children departed. A number of mothers had taken matters into their own hands, aware that they would struggle to control their emotions, they commandeered neighbours, siblings and husbands to manage the last moments of the send-off and the delivery of their children into the care of someone else. Pam Hobbs recalled, 'My Mother looked on the point of collapse as Dad walked us determinedly down the path ... When we turned the corner of Kent Avenue I looked back for one last wave, but she had buried her head in her pinny.' [17] Lily Nye, evacuated to Staffordshire remembered going on a tram with her sisters, her mother left standing at the gate with her youngest child in her arms. [18] Families were kept back from the immediate embarkation areas in case of hysteria or civil unrest. The *Birkenhead News* described how '[p]arents were not allowed inside the station and police officers were on duty to restrain any who found the parting too hard and attempted to follow the children.' [19] Mass Observation investigators went to many of the big London stations to record events. On 1 September 1939 it was noted that only those in the school party were allowed onto the platform and that

[w]omen are quiet and all gaze towards the platform, some mopping their eyes with handkerchiefs. The children are about 50 yards away down the platform. People smile at the singing, a good many cry ... We can't do any more says

one woman. Thank God they've gone … About one in three of the women are weeping unobtrusively into their handkerchiefs, wiping eyes quickly from time to time and keeping handkerchiefs, screwed up and wet in their hands.[20]

Many tried to suppress their own emotions, held back their tears as they waved their children off stoically. Terence Frisby's mother, having walked him to the station, stood in a crowd of smiling mums waving children off, but later admitted she went home and sobbed.[21] Children's naive willingness to cheerfully set off with their friends or siblings cut many mothers to the core. Others seem to have been more upbeat, and Mass Observation investigators overheard mothers express their relief that their children were safely away,[22] they expected the full force of German Luftwaffe bombers at any day, but no bombers delivered their lethal load during those first months of the phoney war.

When children were evacuated within a reasonable distance of their home, parents made an early initial visit to appraise the foster home and sometimes moved their children's billet, finding an alternative within the area to enable children to remain with their school. These moves were not necessarily in response to a request from their children or even to a billet that their children considered preferable. But moving a child, finding a new billet was a way mothers could still exert some control over their children's welfare and place their priorities and values in their child's lives. They were also exerting the rights that those who could afford to privately evacuate their children had; they had chosen friends, relations or friends of friends to host their children, making an effort to ensure their children's welfare. However, when later in the war a mother whose home had been demolished and who had herself been machine-gunned visited Rudyard in Staffordshire and found her children new billets, she caused much consternation and difficulty for the billeting officers as the correct paperwork had not been completed.[23]

The phoney war gives way to threats of invasion and the Blitz

As the phoney war dragged on, and there was little sign of the expected bombing, mothers reappraised their initial decision to have their children evacuated, particularly if they had reservations about their children's billet, had other younger children at home, were not themselves working or coping with other pressures. Many chose to bring their children home and even when danger loomed in 1940 did not let them return to areas of safety. Tom Harrisson suggested that the fear of bombing, and evacuation, 'introduced a new insecurity into women's lives' which was 'often felt only most privately and not healed by holding onto their children'.[24] Women missed their children acutely, a survey carried out on mothers in Liverpool indicated that '38% of women with some children away are definitely made unhappy' thereby and '54% of women with all their children away are definitely made unhappy' while 'only 11% are glad their children are evacuated although 94% specifically say their evacuated children are very happy'.[25] This was however in the early months of the war, before Liverpool became the second most bombed area outside London and four thousand people were killed in Merseyside.

In 1940, propaganda posters and films encouraged women, in areas where the civilian population was considered to be in danger, to allow their children to be evacuated. One wartime poster portrayed a ghostly cartoon of Hitler whispering into a mother's ear, 'Take them Back', and an instruction underneath which read, 'Don't do it mother leave the children where they are.'[26] Women's magazines also supported evacuation, reassuring and encouraging mothers that it was for the best. Rosita Forbes in *Woman's Own* used interesting language suggesting mothers energies should be focused elsewhere instructing that they '[d]on't fight the evacuation plans. They are wholly for the benefit of your children ... if you can bear to let your children go for a while you will give them a better chance'.[27] For those on the South Coast, the need for evacuation became more acute as countries in Europe, fell under German rule and the British Expeditionary Force beat a hasty retreat from France via Dunkirk. The threat of an invasion became very real, and newspapers conveyed the government's message again advising parents in danger areas to register their children to be evacuated. The threat to children who lived on the South Coast and particularly Kent was emphasized in a Government Information film *Westward Ho* (1940). Initially, the film portrayed images from 1939 showing children being evacuated to Torquay who were happily settled in their seaside billets, delivered by a 'nice car' that had been waiting for them. A child's voice explained they were welcomed and that 'our auntie is ever so nice and kind'. They were seen sitting down to a hearty meal. The 'voice of God' narration pointed out that as these children were being transferred to safety in plenty of time, there was no danger of the train they travelled in being machine-gunned from the air. This was compared favourably with the situation of refugees in Norway, Holland, Belgium and France. It was explained that the mothers of France knew the horrors of invasion and then the film featured a direct appeal from mothers in France, Belgium, Holland to the mothers of Britain, telling them to evacuate their children before it was too late. For the women in the South of England this must have had a particular poignancy.

As bombs began to drop in 1940, culminating at the beginning of the Blitz in September, women reappraised their decisions about evacuating their children or bringing them home. Jean Cruichshank's mother shipped her off from her Everton home to Wales rather speedily after a nearby bomb lifted the table she was playing under, while Bill Turnstall and his siblings were dispatched after a bullet from a German plane went right through the house.[28] For some parents seeing the emotional trauma and anxiety that children experienced during bombing raids changed their minds as Jennifer Purcell noted; in Birmingham the increasing ferocity and danger of raids led mothers to rethink their resistance to their children being evacuated. An eleven-hour raid across 23–24 November 1940, the largest of the Birmingham Blitz, killed eight hundred and injured two thousand, while a further twenty thousand were rendered homeless. Alice Bridges, who had previously been reluctant to send her child away, questioned the wisdom of keeping her child in an urban area in wartime. When during another raid on 3 December her daughter turned white with fear and was unable to sleep, she sought a billet in the comparative safety of the countryside.[29] Nevertheless, Dicky Blood recalled many years after, the anguished expression in his mother's eyes as the buses drove away from his school in Birmingham taking him and his school to the railway station in February 1941 when the Blitz was underway.[30]

The decision was for many parents a much clearer and easier one; they had to get their children to safety, but then it was a question of where, how and to whom? Personal circumstances played a part in the decision-making process, not all children were necessarily living with their parents, Ann Ridout's father had died when she was 6 months old and her mother when she was 3, so that when war broke out, she was living with her elderly granny. After her school was bombed her grandmother decided to send her to an aunt and uncle living near Tamworth:

> Well granny had just lost her son and her daughter-in-law and she didn't want to lose me at that point but she thought of that then, she thought I don't want her to go to anybody I don't know where she's going to go or who she's going to go to, so she wrote to them and said would they take me, just for while the war was on? And they agreed to do that.[31]

The evacuations, which took place from 1940 onwards, still involved tortuous decisions for many mothers; made worse by the rumours and stories they had heard of the difficulties of the 1939 evacuation. Sonya Brett's mother allowed her two daughters to be evacuated from London to Cornwall during the London Blitz, but not having heard from them for about three to four weeks, as Sonya recalled, '[M]y mother came down to see what was happening. She said afterwards that she cried all night when she saw our condition. It took my mother a week to get our heads completely clean, and that was with washing every 2 or 3 hours.'[32] The girls and their mother stayed on a neighbouring farm until another billet was identified. Sonya's mother inspected her daughter's new foster home and got the girls settled; reassured her daughters would be well looked after and safe she returned to London.[33] Many mothers sought to avoid sending their children to complete strangers, as Margaret Lee in Brighton explained in a letter to prospective foster parents, who were friends of friends. Her daughter was living in fear of invasion but too scared to be evacuated to strangers with her school friends. Her mother expounded,

> After much thought and feeling that that it must be for the best we have decided to send Olive to you – we note all you say … It is a heart breaking decision to make and I could never send her to strangers – but your letter has made all the difference and somehow I feel that is a direct answer to our prayers. The children who were not evacuated have had so much drilled into their little heads as to how it may come (this invasion business) and what they must or must not do, that it is making them ill with nerves.
>
> She is a good girl and helps me so much that I am sure she will not give you any trouble, there is only one thing about her she is at present in a nervous state and should you have any raids, with a little love and kindness and patience and she's quickly re-assured and gets very brave.[34]

As she was looking after invalid parents, she arranged for her husband to deliver her daughter to her new home. In letters she asked, as her daughter apparently had a passion for flowers, if she may be allowed to arrange the flowers as she does at home and after a bad raid explained how grateful she was that her daughter was away from Brighton.[35]

A much bigger decision: Sending children abroad

The decision to send children abroad for the duration of the war, whether undertaken privately or under a government or company scheme, was a momentous one for any mother. It is very easy from the safety of western countries in the twenty-first century to underestimate the worry and anxiety of mothers of children, as invasion seemed likely, and rumours of German parachutists abounded, many had the sense that nowhere in Britain was safe. Bombing was not restricted to London or urban cities, nowhere was immune to the random bomb dropped by a German pilot heading for home after a mission and keen to ensure that his plane was as light as possible so his fuel would be sufficient to get him back to his aerodrome. A Mass Observation Investigator recorded the 'bewilderment and anxiety' of one mother trying to make her mind up in the Summer of 1940 with her husband away in the forces:

> So Cruel. I don't know what's going to happen now, I really don't. It seems all up. You don't know what do for the best. I don't know whether to send my children away or not. I'll never see them again if I send them abroad, I don't know whether to apply for a shelter or not ... I wish I had someone to discuss it with.[36]

Many families saw foreign evacuation as a way of protecting their children from the deprivations of war and the anxiety, fear, uncertainty and upheaval that families would go through. Hindsight and myth gloss over the fear and despondency of those mothers who sent their children abroad in 1940. Films such as *Finest Hour* (2018) suggest that no one doubted the ultimate victory of Britain and the Commonwealth, but it did not feel that way to people in 1940. A woman whose daughter went to Canada with her boarding school in 1940 explained,

> It is difficult today to understand the feeling of the average inhabitant of England after the horrors of Dunkirk, the fall of France, the knowledge the whole of Europe was in the hands of Hitler. Great Britain stood isolated, with only the narrow breadth of the Channel to protect us. Anyone could see for themselves the inadequacy of our defenses – a few road blocks, old motor cars, small concrete blocks on the roadside, no signposts, blackout as far as possible, barrage balloons over London, small gun sites spaced over the country and a few elderly gentlemen patrolling villages and seashore and keeping watch from the church towers! Even early in 1940 enemy aircraft would make hit and run raids anywhere within reach of the coast. A bomb was dropped in the fields of Dorset. It seemed impossible that the Germans, sooner or later, should not successfully invade England.[37]

Some parents felt that if they were to die in a war, then they wanted their children at least to be safe. Others, because of their own or their relations' politics or ethnicity, were particularly anxious. For Jewish mothers the fear of invasion was acute, some had themselves escaped from Nazi Germany in the 1930s and were determined that their children would not be put in danger from an invasion. Jessica Mann's parents sent her and her brother, aged 2 and 4, to Canada, having escaped Nazi Germany they were keenly aware of the dangers of a German invasion. There were rumours that the Germans had blacklists of people who would be rounded up after an invasion, with Jewish émigrés among them.[38] Those who chose to evacuate their children abroad came from all walks of life as Vera Brittain noted,

> The moment that the Children's Overseas Reception Board – to be known familiarly as 'CORB' is established in the Berkeley Street offices of Messrs Cook and Son … a queue of parents and children begins to stretch from the office door into Piccadilly. The opportunity of safeguarding the children's future appeals equally to the small households of Mayfair and the large dockland families from Bermondsey and Chatham.[39]

The government paid the fares for children travelling under the CORB scheme and parents initially paid 5s. (25 pence) a week (which rose to 6s. – 30 pence). The government handled to process of ensuring this went to foster mothers abroad, to cover the cost of their children's keep. There was quite a bit of resentment towards those parents who paid to send their children abroad, although many of these parents, like Vera Brittain, saw themselves as having freed up space which could go to those unable to pay the fares themselves.

Once Vera Brittain had made the decision and put into motion the train of official and financial procedures to have her children evacuated to the United States, she was gripped by the fear that she could neither bear the separation nor subject her children to the danger of being torpedoed at sea. She looked towards the date of their sailing with dread and worried about how long it would be until she would see her children again. She recounted the anguish of her children's departure:

> Now that the moment has come, my legs suddenly feel as though they will no longer sustain me. Oh my darling children is there time to call you back from salvation even now … Beyond the enclosure we see now the grey – painted hulk of the anonymous liner, waiting to carry away from us the dearest possessions that are ours on earth.[40]

Intense anxiety followed children's departure, would they safety arrive in their destination or be torpedoed on the way? Molly Bond delivered her children to her Canadian cousin herself, to ensure they arrived safely, and then returned to Britain. She believed that her children should have the 'best chance of living their life' and that she had a duty to return to do her bit for the war effort.[41] For others the wait for news that their children had arrived safely was excruciating. Ten days after waving goodbye to her daughters, a telegram told Joan Matthews, 'Your lovely girls arrived safely. We will guard them and cherish them.'[42] Relief that flooded through Joan Matthews and other mothers when the phone call, telegram or letter arrived confirming the safe arrival of their children in a foreign country, far away from bombing, rationing and fears of invasion. Even more unimaginable is the pain and misery of those who had very different news. The Grimmond family from Brixton in East London lost five of their eleven children when the SS *Benares* was torpedoed; their mother initially unwilling to let them go had relented when the family home was bombed.[43]

In sending their children abroad, mothers had relinquished the responsibility, privilege and pleasure of so many of the maternal moments. If wealthier parents were used to handing over the day-to-day care of their children to nannies and boarding schools, many working-class families lived in very close proximity to one another and had never spent a night away from their children. Mothers in choosing overseas evacuation had made an irrevocable decision. It was very difficult for adults to get exit visas, or to take money out of the country, so visiting their children was almost impossible. They could not swoop down upon their children in their foster home and bring them home if they changed their mind or considered things were unsatisfactory. Having sent her children to the United States, Vera Brittain discovered that she would be unable to visit them, as a pacifist she was not allowed to travel abroad. Only a few months after they have gone she records in her diary, 'My darling shall I ever see you again I speculate for the hundredth time as I walk past the smoldering walls of Maple's store at the corner of Tottenham Court Road.'[44] In this and other notes in her diary she refers to places and buildings where her children would have gone on a day-to-day basis, which had been bombed since they went. A reminder of why she made her decision – justification for what might be seen as an 'unnatural' act for a mother – to relinquish her children to the care of others, out of her reach. In making this decision mothers sought to find ways of continuing to look after and care for their children who were physically separated from them, sometimes giving multiple instructions to those who cared they for them on the trip, about everything from cleaning teeth to how they liked to go to sleep at night. Margaret Sharp wrote to her children's foster mother in Canada, giving her authority to make decisions but also with some advice about how her eldest son might feel it was his duty to look after his siblings.[45] Colin Ryder Richardson recalled how his mother bought clothes to ensure he would be properly equipped when he arrived in America and took him by train to Liverpool, from where the SS *Benares* was to sail. His care was entrusted to Hungarian journalist who was on his way to America and agreed to take him under his wing. His mother, continuing her caring of him even though he would be far away, insisted that night and day he wore his red kapok life jacket, she provided, making him rather distinctive.[46] A number of factors made him one of only thirteen of the ninety children who survived when the ship sank, including the location of his cabin, but he was wearing the life jacket provided by his mother when he was picked up.

Ways of mothering during a prolonged evacuation

In 1940, when the bombing started in earnest, the devastation, injury and loss of life that it brought affirmed the decision of many mothers who had sent their children to safety, but how long they would be separated from their children remained indeterminate. After the Blitz and in areas outside London, fears and anxieties about bombing and invasion came in waves and views about the length of time the war would last also varied. Many freely admitted that they had never imagined it would last more than three years, and yet in 1941 and 1942 others talked of the war lasting for ten years. The challenge for mothers was to maintain their relationship with their children, something many found practically and emotionally very difficult. From the moment that children were evacuated mothers sought to adapt and adopt a range of ways of continuing to care for their children when apart. Kathleen Thomas's mother ensured that at least one member of the family regularly made the journey to see her children evacuated to Wales and sent them a Christmas parcel of 'sweets, cake, storybooks, clothes whatever she could lay her hands on'.[47] Mothers were able to obtain clothing coupons for their children who were abroad, but parcels were restricted to a total value of £10; Vera Brittain recorded in her diary that she sent a Spanish nightdress case off to her daughter for her birthday in 1941.[48]

The Barnett House survey of evacuation undertaken in Oxfordshire recorded that

> [o]ut of 217 unaccompanied children, 85 (39%) received two or more letters a week and/or a visit once per month, 105 (48%) received one letter per week and /or a visit per quarter, and only 27 (13%) received less than this ... Assessment revealed that only 11 per cent, of evacuations with children receiving infrequent

letters and visits were highly successful, as against 44 per cent of those with a high frequency of contacts.[49]

There were a multitude of factors, which influenced the frequency of letters and visits, between children and their parents. Tony Longdon recalled, 'With my mother I used to write. I wrote her a letter and sent it to her in Bexhill and told her the address and everything … we used to write that way.'[50] The government supported the correspondence between children and their parents by providing half-price postage if EVACUEE was written clearly on the left-hand side of the envelope, but parents and grandparents had varied levels of literacy. Ann, an orphan had lived with her granny in London before being evacuated to Tamworth, recalled that she was encouraged to keep in touch with her granny, but

> I did write to her from time to time. She wrote to me a few little letters, yes. But granny's not, you know she wasn't a highly educated person, so she wasn't able to write long and involved letters and she kept her communication to the minimum really, you know about the weather or about various, about how old she was, but she was getting old you see, so. But I wrote and told her what I'd been doing, which she enjoyed I think.[51]

Letters from evacuees could provide reassurance to the mothers at home. Maureen Haslam recalled, '[W]e used to write. My eldest sister always wrote and my mom and dad used to write back and she used to read the letters out or we used to read them.'[52] Many mothers sought to reassure their children that they were safe. Clive Dellino's mother assured him that in her work as a nurse in a First Aid Post, she was deep underground 'the safest place to be in an air raid'.[53] Pam Hobbs's letters from her mum said little about local raids or food shortages that had her queuing at the shops for hours on end. 'When she wrote asking about specific evacuees whose parents were worried by their scrappy little notes home, I would gleefully report on their activities – usually exaggerating about their fun-filled days, which kept them too busy to keep in touch.'[54] Her mother revealed years later that when she received letters '[s]he felt she was loosing me but wasn't unhappy because she knew I was getting a taste of the good life'.[55] For those whose children had been evacuated abroad, the process of keeping in touch via letter was frustratingly difficult – the delays with the post meant that any warnings and advice a mother might attempt to give their children were likely to be irrelevant by the time it arrived.

Margaret and Douglas Sharp were, unusually for this era, divorced when they sent their three boys, Dill, Christopher and Tom to Canada, a privately arranged evacuation, in July 1940. Marie Williamson, who frequently sent letters reassuring Margaret about her children's progress, looked after them. The boys' mother must have been encouraged when a friend who had managed to visit the lads gave her a detailed account of their progress ending by saying, 'I am not going to have time to tell you properly how enormously I liked Mrs Williamson. She has exactly the kind of quietness with the family (a warm quietness) that you would hope … Your family is O.K.'[56] Margaret and many others however found that their children were somewhat lax in their letter writing and this seems to have led to a degree of anxiety, exasperation and even at times despair. One teenage girl from Cannock who travelled with her younger brother to Canada, under a scheme the General Electric Company (GEC) offered its employees, wrote home only intermittently. She was supposed to be staying with the family of GEC employees in Canada but seems to have stayed with two single, wealthy ladies with little experience of teenage girls. In an early letter home she enthused, 'I tried hot dogs … They are long sausages in a roll and taste very good.'[57] She continued to send her parents chatty if rather spasmodic letters throughout her four-year stay which were all about her increasingly active social life, her private school and protestations of disbelief that butter was rationed in England. The teenager started every year of the war announcing that she would write more regularly to her parents, but as the years went by her mother it seems may have expressed concern in her letters (which have not survived) about her teenage daughter growing up in a foreign country. The daughter's letters of stories of dances and out at night would have led her mother in rural Staffordshire, like many others, to have had a sense that she was losing her daughter, to a world that was unfamiliar and a teenage social life she had very little control over. Her daughter steadily adopted a slightly indulgent tone implying that her mother had nothing to worry about, which probably provided little reassurance.

The anxiety over their children, so far away, seemingly beyond their care, for some women was too much. Mrs Muir, a widow from Edinburgh, sent her two sons, Douglas and Harry, to live in Chicago under the CORB scheme in 1940; when three years later she heard that Harry had tuberculosis, her anxiety became acute. Children were evacuated through CORB on the understanding that they would remain in their host country until the end of the war; but Mrs Muir found this hard to accept. Her requests to either visit her son or have him returned home to her met with no success. Attempts to see her son included numerous irate letters to CORB officials and a petition to King George VI. Eventually her boys came home, but it was not a happy reunion; her eldest son refused to live with her and went instead to stay with his grandmother.[58] His mother had protected him from the bombing but still lost him.

For mothers whose children were evacuated in Britain, there was the hope of visiting their children which many parents regularly did, sending siblings and relations if this was difficult. Keeping in contact was like so much of the 'peoples war', framed by class and disposable income, wealthier parents drove to visit their offspring. Kathleen Thomas, as a 17-year-old borrowed money from the local council to go and visit her young brother and sister in Wales when her brother was ill.[59] Managing the situation was easiest for those whose children were evacuated near to them facilitating weekly visits; others did not see their children for years. Those whose children were at County Council boarding schools, like the Birmingham ones set up in Staffordshire could visit regularly. Subsidized travel was introduced for evacuee parents but still the cost and time needed to navigate a journey on wartime trains was challenging for mothers who were working, looking after younger children or elderly relatives. For those whose children had been evacuated several hours train journey away, a visit required overnight accommodation which some hosts provided willingly. Margaret Lee, whose daughter was privately evacuated, from Brighton to the Midlands, used all her powers of persuasion to arrange such a visit. In one letter she wrote,

> I am writing to ask if you can manage to have me for just a day or so. Every letter Olive send she pleads so hard for this & I really feel a day or two away from things would set me going again. I do not wish to give you any trouble. I shall deem it a privilege if I can come and give you a rest, from what Olive tells us poor Auntie is never resting. If I can come the latter end of next week if that is convenient.[60]

When Pam Hobbs' mother and sister came to stay for a week, in the Derbyshire farmhouse where she was billeted, she had not seen her daughters for nearly a year. On her arrival she struggled to recognize Pam, who in floppy shorts and sandals looked more like a boy. It was also the first time she had had a holiday and slept in a bed that was not her own, but importantly she was immensely reassured by how much she had in common with Pam's foster mother with whom she spent the week's visit 'animatedly discussing subjects as diverse as keeping hens and how Violet had a bout of pneumonia as a child' returning to London loaded down with a 'large ham, butter and a dozen eggs'.[61] She also took with her an image in her mind of where her daughter lived and slept and of the women who looked after her. Unfortunately it only lasted a little while, as Pam had to move to another unknown billet when she obtained a place at a grammar school.[62]

Visits could be emotionally mixed experiences; mothers often found interacting with their children in a strange place was uncomfortable, formal and stiff. When the children were well settled into their foster homes, mothers often felt they were losing them, Sydney Cox recalled that when his mother came to visit him in Staffordshire, staying in a nearby farmhouse, he was unbothered and more interested in playing with his friends.[63] James Neville, who loved being evacuated to Colton, Staffordshire remembered 'he used to go and hide when his mother came to see him'.[64] Children were careless with their parent's emotions if they were happy in their billets; they also adopted mannerisms, accents and ways of a community and family, which might be very different from their mothers. When Newcastle-upon-Tyne-born Gwenda Bampton's mother visited her in the Lake District she 'abruptly snapped her head around' at hearing her daughters' accent when she said to her friend, 'Art thou coomin t'play'.[65] Religion, class or rather strata within class, regional accents and diets were all codifiers of identity, signifiers indicating whose family, neighbourhood or community the children belonged to. But they were all ignored in the official evacuation process, which took no notice of parental wishes and often ignored parents' desire for siblings not to be separated. Many mothers were also upset when they discovered their children were not adhering to the religious practices, or in some cases absence of them that their own family followed. A Liverpool mother wrote to her children's foster mother on the 15 September 1941 informing her that her two children 'must not attend any other than their own religion as I said before I would bring them home'. Equally concerned that her children might not be attending a Catholic school she continued, 'Well Mrs Bugh I do not think for one moment that it is fair for the Cannock education to take action like this wen this Free Country of England is at War. Surely the least they can do is to let the Children go the way there Mother and Fathers has brought them up'.[66]

Children often went home to visit their parents in the summer or Christmas holidays, although during the worst of the bombing this was discouraged and in 1940 the school summer holiday was reduced from one month to two weeks. For those with the financial resources, as Gwenda Brady's mother had, there was scope to take the children on a holiday away from their billet.[67] This was not unproblematic. At Easter 1941, Staffordshire Education Committee felt it necessary to point out, 'In view of the difficulty of meeting the demand for billets for various catagories of evacuated persons and transferred workers there can be no assurance that billets if vacated by children in the holiday period will be again available for them.'[68]

There was one final means open to parents to communicate with their children. The new medium of the radio at Christmas broadcast greetings from evacuated children in Great Britain, Canada and the United States, South Africa and Australia. This initially involved messages being read out and then recorded messages. By January 1940 the first live linkup between parents and nine children evacuated to the United States and brought into an American radio studio went on air and the announcer's introduction affirmed the role of radio in reuniting fractured families with the following words, 'Across the Atlantic in London all their parents are assembled and in just a few minutes warm words will be exchanged over land and sea as the magic of radio reunites mothers and fathers with sons and daughters.'[69] For both children and their parents the allotted two minutes of communication, in front of an audience of millions was far from satisfactory as Jessica Mann pointed out. 'Everyone always said, it was lovely to hear your voice. But it was a frustrating exercise,' many children and parents had mike fright.[70] One follow-up memo in 1942 remarked, 'I hope the Richardson's were not too upset by their daughter's tears. She sounded as if she was trying to be brave and finding it difficult. We considered it a good programme though.'[71] The trauma of these broadcasts for mothers is hard to assess. Despite a number of difficulties, including getting parents and children to the studios simultaneously and in different parts of the world or the United States, audiences being offended by British exclamations of horror that their children had acquired American accents, the programmes continued approximately once a month or once every two months until late 1943.[72]

Regrets, traumas and the living with decisions

Vera Brittain suggested, 'For many young evacuees, the choice has lain between nights of terror and days without kindness.'[73] While her assessment underestimates the love and care many children found in their billets, for the children's mothers the choice and consequences of evacuation were even starker. They were about life and death and parents' long-term relationship with their children. George Lock felt his parent's decision to have him evacuated with his brother to Aberdare to Wales had saved his life. He recalled,

> The school in Birmingham which we used to go to; it's name was Ellen Street School, was destroyed just after we were evacuated ...

You could say we got away from there just in time as there were hundreds killed my parents told us when they came to visit.[74]

Other mothers were not so lucky in the choices they made and there was a group of mothers for whom the 'what-ifs' and regrets at the end of the conflict were particularly intense; a small number of evacuated children died from accidents and illness or died in the places they had been sent to keep them safe. Newspapers recounted details of children killed, including 6-year-old Kathleen Smith who was hit by a Burton Co-operative Society lorry.[75] Eileen Hills, evacuated from Margate to Staffordshire drowned in the River Trent at the age of 8 in Autumn 1940. A local newspaper reported,

> It appears that on Saturday afternoon Eileen went out with other girls and entered a field which was fenced and had barbed wire round. They reached the river, which had overflowed its banks and Eileen, who had a pair of Wellington boots on, said she was going to paddle. As part of the field was under water the riverbank could not be seen. Eileen took a few steps forward, lost her foothold, and slipped into several feet of water. The river had a good flow and she was quickly carried away.[76]

Eileen was not the only urban child, naïve about the dangers of the countryside, who met a tragic end. In Staffordshire alone, there were stories of children who were run over by farm horses and carts, accidentally shot playing with farmers' guns or succumbed to childhood diseases. Peter Askins recalled his younger sister dying of diphtheria while they were evacuees.[77] The first person killed by a bomb jettisoned over the Isle of Wight was an evacueee, and in 1944 two young evacuees were killed by an unmarked mine in Gunwalloe Fishing Cove in Cornwall.[78] For these children's mothers their child's death, many miles away, was heartbreaking and a source of infinite regret.

The emotions of women whose children were evacuated fluctuated. The psychologist John Bowlby observed mothers of evacuees complained alternatively that their children were suffering or that they were so well looked after they would not wish to return home.[79] Both fears turned out to have some justification and explain why so many mothers, expressed a preference for their children to be in boarding schools where they were looked after by teachers and teaching assistants, ensuring that there was a professional distance between evacuees and those who cared for them. Mrs St Joe Strachey, who wrote *Borrowed Children*, a title that carried with it a clear message emphasizing the temporary nature of caring for evacuees, strongly objected to the use of the terms 'foster mother' and 'foster homes'. To her, drawing on her own privileged background, perhaps the appropriate term was 'nanny' and evacuees' accommodation should be referred to as billets, so as to emphasize that children's homes were elsewhere. The suggestion that children call their foster parents mum and dad was resented by their biological mothers and seems to have been rare. Oral histories and memoirs overwhelmingly refer to foster parents as auntie and uncle, terms frequently used in this era when children addressed adults who were friends of their parents but unrelated.

Nevertheless, as evacuation and bombing continued, the issue of adoption entered the minds of parents and children as a series of 'what-ifs' in relation to the possibility of parents being killed or reported missing. Although, even some children who had a happy billet felt, in retrospect, that if their parents had been the victims of bombing, they would rather have been killed with them.[80] And this was the rhetoric that many mothers used when they decided against evacuation. The very mention of adoption arguably brought to the fore the ambiguous and contradictory sense of family belonging that evacuation evoked. Exerting the right to remove children from their billets was one of the few areas of control mothers retained, they continually weighed up the dangers of children becoming alienated from them against the dangers of bombing. Lily Nye had spent nearly four years evacuated in Leek in Staffordshire, when to her parents' horror her elder sister's foster parents expressed a wish to adopt her. Both girls were taken home soon after, although the war was far from over.[81]

This was not the response of all parents, where the mother was a widow or careworn by poverty, her own or her husband's illness she might make very different decisions. Marjorie Clowes' mother was a widow who had been struggling to combine looking after her three children and working in a biscuit factory prior to the war. She had relied upon her eldest children to babysit. Marjorie who was evacuated at the age of 9, recalled, 'Ah well I think she thought we'd be safe. That was the only thing.'[82] Marjorie settled very well with her new foster family and recalled good food and a nice home where she was well looked after, but her relationship with her family 'gradually altered'. To her surprise, her mother agreed to the adoption of her 12-year-old daughter in the middle of the war. According to Marjorie, her mother 'later said it was the worst thing she'd ever done' even though she did not lose contact with her daughter who visited occasionally but changed her name and never returned to live in Manchester.[83] Marjorie's mother may have come to the conclusion that her daughter would be safest, healthiest and looked after better by this comfortably off-working class Staffordshire family; if so, she was far from the only single mother to reach this decision during and at the end of the war.

The question of how permanent or temporary foster homes should be was a difficult one for many mothers; they faced both anxiety and criticism when their children were away. The decision about when their children should return home was often a pragmatic one, linked to the need for the youngster to take on more adult responsibilities at home. In February 1944 on the day he reached 14 and could leave school, Dicky Blood's mother made the journey from Birmingham to Yoxall in Staffordshire to bring her son home. She was expecting her sixth child and would soon have to give up her job working nights at the Austin Factory, the wages her son could earn would make an important contribution in the household. He could also help with his younger siblings and ensure they got to school each morning.[84] Sydney Cox also returned, with some reticence to London from Staffordshire as his family found him a job in London with his grandfather.[85] Two years previously, a Barnett House Survey had noted that

> a social worker in South East London,' writing to the *Daily Telegraph* on 2 November 1942, pleaded for the ending of the 'scandal' of evacuation. 'The only children away' she said, 'are the unmanageable and the unwanted. In many cases the parents are paying nothing towards their children's keep and have no intention of doing so while the government will keep them.'[86]

The researchers at Barnett house pointed out the inaccuracy of such an assertion and the criticism of mothers whose children were away for prolonged periods of time. This sort of criticism played down the danger of bombing, which in 1942 was not over. Injury and death occurred well beyond the end of the Blitz. It also made difficult decisions about when to bring their children home even harder for mothers. Both of Vera Brittain's children were back in Britain by the Christmas of 1943 and their journey home was uneventful. But many parents lived with the unintended consequences of their decisions for years to come; decisions that could be life-changing or life-ending.

On 20 January 1943, during a daylight raid on London a bomb was dropped on Sandhurst Road School, Catford killing thirty-eight children and six teachers. The headmistress, her face bleeding from cuts by broken glass, sobbed as she explained to the local newspaper how the teachers had shepherded as many children as they could into school shelters but 'before we could get everyone the bomb had fallen'.[87] The newspaper report went on to explain that 'the school accommodated two hundred pupils, many of whom stayed to lunch'. The bomb fell on the dining hall where children were having their midday meal. Those who were not killed were described as 'not frightened, just stupefied, unable to even say what their names were'. Outside the school 'weeping mothers watched the pitiful bundles which had been their children being dragged from the heap of rubble by Civil Defense workers and soldiers.'[88] Lydia Coxhead who was a child at the school later recalled,

> I do not know what my Mother felt when she saw me coming down the road, my dress spattered with blood and dust, which was also in my hair. She had only just heard that the school had been hit and was on her way. I remember she said 'Oh my baby.' and fainted.[89]

The deaths of these children must have caused their London mothers to question the wisdom of having them in London at this point in the conflict, when the bombing was far less frequent and intense but danger remained. For one mother, the grief and regret were almost too much to bear. Eric Brady and his sister Kitty were both pupils at Sandhurst Road School when the bomb hit; they had been evacuated to Folkestone in September 1939, only to be moved the following year to the mining valleys of South Wales. When awareness of the intensity of the bombing during the Blitz reached Kitty's foster parents, they wrote to suggest that

> they loved Kitty dearly. If 'anything happened' to our mother and father, which they prayed wouldn't of course, to safeguard Kitty's future would our parents be willing to sign Consent to Adopt papers for them to be able to adopt Kitty legally – to be used only the event of our parents demise.[90]

Kitty and Eric's mother was furious and although prevented from bringing Kitty home immediately by her husband, would not sign the papers. Unfortunately a few months later, when the bombing had eased off and her husband was ill with pneumonia, both children were brought back to London. The bomb struck the school at 12.30 am, but it took many hours to dig the children out of the rubble. Their mother's response to the bombing was an immediate sense of guilt; lying on the sofa crying and repeating that it was all her fault as she waited for news. Later that night, she learned that Kitty died soon after she arrived at the hospital and Eric was badly injured.

Eric was left with permanent injuries and spent eighteen months in the hospital, during which time his mother had a nervous breakdown. She became suicidal and was admitted to a psychiatric hospital, after one of her daily visits to Kitty's grave she had a chance meeting Kitty's foster parents. Her mental state deteriorated and she was placed in a padded cell. Although she recovered sufficiently to come home and look after her children, the regrets and the self-blame could not be forgotten. She had been faced with an impossible choice, and her instinctive desire to keep her children near her, to protect her family had been thwarted by the inevitable consequences of aerial warfare.

Sandhurst Road School was not the only or the last school to be bombed, a wing of the Maria Grey High School for Girls was destroyed by a V2 bomb in 1944 when Jan Pollard and the other pupils had returned to London from their evacuation.[91] While in 1945 close to the end of the war, one mother in Kent was brought face to face with the danger in which she and her children lived when a doodlebug unexpectedly went off near her house shattering the windows. She explained,

> I rushed upstairs and found them all covered with glass – ever inch of Billy's cot, it was a mass of glass. It was a miracle he wasn't killed, but he never had a scratch he was right under the clothes you see. My, but it gave me a shock. I still keep trembling when I think of what might of happened.[92]

No happy ending

The vast majority of children returned home safely to their mothers after evacuation and soon slotted back into family life, but oral testimony also indicates that there is some credibility in Burlingham and Freud's concerns that children might become alienated from their birth families through evacuation.[93] Ivy Wilson struggled to recognize her mother when she came to fetch her after six years of evacuation and clung to the leg of the dining table as she did not want to leave the foster home that was familiar.[94] Ivy's mother was not the only woman to find that her longed-for reunion with her children was heartbreaking as their children expressed ambivalence towards their own parents.

A number of children were unable to settle, no longer feeling they belonged with their natural parents or the culture into which they had been born. Accents, which were much stronger and regionally varied in the 1940s further distanced mothers from their children, particularly if the children who had been abroad in the United States, Canada and Australia and returned speaking with an unfamiliar twang. Kathleen Thomas recalled how her mother 'couldn't get over' her little brother's 'strong Welsh accent when he finally came home'. More problematically, Johnny played up, and his misdemeanours included throwing mashed potato at his mother during supper, but with perseverance she sorted him out, laying the blame for his behaviour on the Nazis.[95] Betty Allsop's little sister, Pat, told her mother that her foster parents had prevented her from having any butter while spreading it lavishly on their bread, a year later she admitted concocting this story to harrow her mother.[96] As Rusby has noted, the age at which children were evacuated made a significant difference on whether they had a positive or negative perception of the outcomes of evacuation, alongside a number of other factors such as the length of time evacuated, the organization and the frequency of parental contact.[97]

Some mothers faced the rejection from their children who demanded to return to their foster parents only initially, but for others their bond with their children had sometimes been broken irreparably. Mothers, who had not seen their children for several years, perhaps because they had been sent abroad, sometimes discovered the children who were returned were not the same ones they had sent away, the years had changed them, replaced them with older sisters and brothers to the ones they had said goodbye to.[98] One poor mother wrote to her husband, 'Rosemary & Stephen have come back and I feel no love for them'[99] and another 'that she felt like her children's adoptive parents because she'd missed so much of their development'.[100] These mothers had kept their children alive, the most important task of any mother, but at a tremendous cost to themselves and their children and for some the rift between parents and children was irreparable. George Emptage recalled how he returned home to Margate in 1944, at the age of 13 after four years in Staffordshire:

> there was me father and three of me sisters waiting for me, my mother couldn't come 'cause she was bedridden. So on the way home, showing me all sorts of things where the bombs dropped and shells and what have you. You know, and eventually I got home it was terrible. It was tiny 'cause I'd been used to a great big house although I wasn't allowed to run round in it, 270 acres, it was tiny. He said 'your mother's in the front room, in the parlour' she was, so I went in the parlour and there was this little old wizened lady laying in the bed and they said 'That's your mother' course I was looking at her. She started crying, so did I, and never really got to know her after that because later that year she died.[101]

His father did not cope well after his wife died and George returned to the farm in Staffordshire he had been evacuated to when he was 15. Likewise, Ann Ridout who had been living with her grandmother prior to the war and evacuated to stay with her aunt and uncle in Tamworth could not return to her granny at the end of the war. She later recalled,

> she really couldn't take me back. I mean I'd settled here, I was doing well at school and aunty and uncle were willing to keep me, I think they took me back to London once, and grownups must have had talks about it, I think they sort

of must have agreed with themselves that I should stay. I was never formally adopted, not legally adopted I don't know why … But I think my granny got really old and feeble and she couldn't possibly deal with me again. And her daughter that she'd live with, Aunty Jenny, her daughter was terminally ill with cancer, so she'd got quite enough on her plate and she couldn't manage me, so, so I just stayed and I hope I was a bit of a blessing to my aunt and uncle.[102]

Conclusion

Many mothers made the brave decision to have their children evacuated when faced with the threat of aerial bombardment, their decisions were tortious, contingent, shifting as they tried to weigh up the relative merits and dangers of circumstances they could not control. They were pushed to do one thing and then another, surrounded by a plethora of advice, social, community pressures and governmental guidance and criticism. What it meant to be a good mother was shaped and reshaped, stretched and pulled this way and that, increasingly brought into public focus and scrutiny in wartime. The personal stories of mothers who chose to have their children evacuated suggest that for many there were was not necessarily a happy-ever-after to their quest to keep her children safe in wartime. The path of those mothers who could not bear to be parted from their children was equally fraught, as the next chapter indicates.

4

Mothers who were evacuated
with their children

The government plans for evacuation relied upon persuading, encouraging and occasionally on scare tactics, yet many mothers were not prepared to be parted from their children for more than a very short period of time. Accommodating mothers and children in reception areas, whether through government schemes or in the pell-mell people's evacuation when the bombing began, proved difficult. Many mothers felt under strong pressure to send their schoolchildren to safety through the government evacuation scheme, those with children below the age of 5 were encouraged to accompany their children to safety. Mothers in emotional turmoil tried to weigh up the competing anxieties of remaining in danger areas or leaving with their children. Children's ages could shape for mothers' decisions, one explained to a Mass Observation Investigator, 'I shan't send my little girl. She can't read or write and I'd have to rely on her foster mother to hear about her.'[1] She was not alone in holding the not unreasonable view that a foster mother could not take the same care for their children that their mothers did. Another 'working class mother of two children said, "They's be a lot going, I dare say. I shall keep mine here. You don't know where they'll be sent, thats the trouble. If I could leave here I might take my boy with me." '[2]

The decision was not straightforward; for many mothers, it was a tortuous choice between taking their children to safety or remaining with their husbands. Many women had jobs or supplemented the family income by undertaking outwork at home. Some mothers had elderly relatives to care for or sons and daughters who, having reached the age of 14, were working. Nevertheless, with the fear of saturation bombing uppermost, many mothers did decide to take part in the government evacuation scheme only to find that a torrent of criticism, prejudice, surveillance and scurrilous rumour was added to the practical difficulties they encountered. *Town Children through Country Eyes* published by the National Federation of Women's Institutes articulated these most overtly when it was claimed 'mothers fell into two types (a) the frankly dirty and shiftless mother, (b) the mother who though passably clean or even smart herself yet seemed too indolent, bored or incompetent to train her children or look after her home'.[3] These attitudes, which I have referred to as Towneyism shaped the experiences and emotions of mothers evacuated with their children, such prejudice exasperated accommodation problems and made these poor women feel that they were living under surveillance, always open to criticism.[4]

Into the unknown in 1939

Mothers with young children were only allowed to take one small case as luggage, a small amount of food and no pram when in 1939 they boarded trains to unknown destinations. There were difficulties on long journeys with small children; one London mother described how after a six-hour journey with five changes of train and an hour and twenty minutes standing on the curb at Luton she arrived at Dunstable in Devon, where they faced a humiliating attempt to find a billet.

> We arrived at a skating rink and then were picked out. So you can guess what some poor devils were like, who has four of five children? They were still there on Sunday afternoon and then eight families were put in an empty house and different people gave them bits of furniture. I admit some of them were a bit much with their hair in curlers and overhauls but we are not all the same.[5]

Nevertheless, in the first days of the war a positive spin was placed on women's sojourn into the countryside with their children. The *Worcester Evening News and Times* interviewed Birmingham mothers, reporting their views under the straplines 'More Children Welcomed to Worcester: Everyone has been so Kind', it was explained,

> There were tears of course, as one mother thought of her husband in the services, her other small children evacuated to other places, her home for the moment shut and empty ...
>
> There were smiles too, far more of those than frowns, for the Birmingham woman like her menfolk is gay and of perky humour. 'It will do my old man good to have to get the dinner for himself' said one.[6]

Such good humour did not last as the women faced practical, financial and emotional difficulties in an environment and culture that was unfamiliar to them and where they often had to live in cramped or uncomfortable billets. Dennis Thorn recalled his modest terraced house in Plymouth being literally divided in two when a family was billeted on them in 1939; his family lived upstairs and the evacuee family occupied the downstairs.[7] Families sharing a kitchen, washing facilities and toilets (whether inside the house or not) placed enormous stress on all concerned. Doreen Wilson's mother was in more palatial surroundings when she was billeted in a large house, but felt in an uncomfortable position as she neither fitted in nor felt welcomed by the servants or the owners of the house.[8] Indeed as Richard Titmuss pointed out generally many evacuee mothers were 'not welcomed into the billeting household'.[9]

Muriel Green, writing for Mass Observation from her home in a Norfolk village, recorded rumours of evacuee mothers feeling so uncomfortable in their new environment, that they were starving themselves so they could afford the train fare home. The urban mothers also questioned the safety of their billets after an air-raid warning was heard:

> They decided they were no safer on the East Coast than in London especially as they have air raid shelters in their gardens and in the parks. There are none here. One woman said, 'In our own blocks of flats we have had ARP [Air Raid Precautions] practices and know just what to do, but here there are no shelters and we seem to be in as much danger of passing raiders.'[10]

The diarist went on to note the evacuees' complaints about the high prices in the shops, inconvenience of the transport and lack of cinemas which included the pronouncement from one young mum: 'I'd rather be bombed on my own door step than stay here and die of depression.'[11] Another mother evacuated to Dunstable complained of being treated 'as bits of dirt by the locals'.[12] The housing conditions in rural areas could also come as a shock to those who had lived in the suburbs with full 'mod cons'. George Seward's mother, her friend Ena and their four children obtained a cottage in Deerhurst, Gloucestershire in Autumn of 1939 but 'water had to be pumped up from a well, the lavatory was in a hut down the garden, there was no gas or electricity and paraffin oil provided light and heat. Mum and Ena had to master the art of cooking by paraffin stove.'[13] Unsurprisingly perhaps they only stayed six weeks.

For the mothers of children of both preschool and school age, an added trauma was that they were often separated from their eldest children who might have been evacuated with their school to a completely different part of the county. In September 1939, Evelyn Margaret Fee was living with children in Dulwich in London but aware that her husband who had previously been in the navy would be called up very quickly; she tidied through the house and prepared to leave London. Her two eldest children were evacuated first with their school, but she and her two younger children stood ready to go for a further week, before finally being transported to West Sussex. The organization worked well; she and her children were assisted onto the train by helpers while buses met them in Pulborough and took them to the village hall in the nearby of Bury. Although initially chosen by a 'lady' she explained that she preferred to be with someone her own sort and so was billeted with Mrs Hemmings, the caretakers of the big house in Bury. She and her hostess carried the two children up to their home where she stayed for a week before she and another evacuee were billeted together in a three-bedroom house. However, the two women, who had never even met before, turned out to have very different ideas about children's behaviour and housekeeping and tensions emerged.[14] In the weeks that followed Evelyn was moved into a house of her own and her elder children collected from the other side of the country by friends in the village and she spent the next six years of war in Bury. In this she was a rarity, almost all the other evacuee mothers in the area returned home; many did a midnight flit when their husbands visited.[15]

Key factors in any mother's decision to remain in a place of safety were whether her family was all together and how appropriate the accommodation was. Thus when six Irish women from Liverpool and their fifteen children were billeted all in one room of a large house in Cheshire, with makeshift bedding provided by the village, unsurprisingly they wanted to return home after two days.[16] In Scotland, children were supposed to be evacuated in their families rather than with their schools, but larger families encountered problems. Samuel Mullin recalled being evacuated with his mother, two sisters and three brothers, leaving behind his father who worked as a millwright in the flour mill and ARP warden in Glasgow. The family was separated into three groups, without his mother being given the addresses for his siblings. When his father came to visit, he managed to round them all up and rent half a house for the family to be together where they remained for some time.[17]

There were other factors which weighed on mothers' minds and influenced whether they stayed in safe billets; these included leaving a husband at home in a danger area. The National Service (Armed Forces) Act imposed conscription on all males aged between 18 and 41 but the call up took some time to process, many husbands were outside this age bracket or in protected industries and needed to remain in workplaces that were targets for enemy bombing. The potential expense of maintaining two homes, if circumstances or distance made it difficult for husbands to visit and the problems of communication with few telephones combined with anxieties husbands' affections would wander when left on their own all placed pressure on evacuated mothers. Mass Observation reported one woman saying, 'I'm going back home I can't trust my husband to be left alone.'[18] In 1939 most men were not familiar with the skills of running a household, they worked long hours, many at physically arduous jobs and did not want to come home to an empty home or to cook their own dinner. For most couples, a women's first priority was expected to be her home and husband rather than her children and leaving them led to social criticism. Members of Staffordshire Women Institute commented that 'the best mothers would not have left their household and homes.'[19] The Women's Institute Magazine *Home and Country* included a letter in which one rural housewife remarked, 'If I had a hubby in Lambeth do you think I would leave him to fend for himself in these troublous times? Surely there was no woman on the committee which started (I can't say organized) this hasty and ineffectual scheme.'[20]

Mothers with school-age children who did not want them evacuated to an unknown destination, on their own, could opt to accompany their schools as a paid helpers or volunteers in 1939. For some, particularly if their husband was due to be called up this may have seemed an ideal solution. Diana Morrison recalled that her mother went as a helper with her brother's school to Kirkby Lonsdale as he was 'just five or six'. She was in charge of 'about six evacuees'. However, she was separated from her older daughter, who had been evacuated with her own school, and did not see 'her much for two and a half years nearly'.[21] Others, particularly with husbands languishing in London on their own, or if finances were very tight found that in practice, the role of helper was no easy solution to the challenges of evacuation, as the letters Dick Coomber wrote to his wife Rose make clear. Rose accompanied her boys' London school evacuated to Exmouth, Devon. The conditions and expectations on her as a paid helper do not seem to have been well worked out in advance, and she was unhappy with the work she was asked to do, her accommodation, the financial restraints the couple faced, all of which took their toll on her. Her husband wrote a series of chatty letters, regularly assuring her of his affections and how much he missed their physical intimacy. In October, he wrote delightedly about a planned visit from her:

I am glad to hear that you may have the chance to come home for a weekend Dearest, but make sure that children will be alright before you do, won't you, because I would worry about their being down there by themselves although if Mrs White says she will look after them, then I know that they will be safe.[22]

They share their concern about their children being separated from her, and when he hears from someone else who has returned to London, that his wife is not happy but has hidden it in her letters, he is dismayed. In one of his last letters, he tries to reassure her,

> Rose you said in your last letter that if I wanted you to come home you would but I know that you wouldn't think of leaving the boys down there on their own so I wouldn't suggest it. I love them just as much as you do and whats more I realize that your place is with them and not with me. Mrs Green has come home with her children yet I still think that its best not to come home for a while as things haven't started yet.[23]

Nevertheless, like the vast majority of mothers evacuated with their children, she had returned by November and seems to have remained in London even when her husband was posted abroad in the forces.[24]

For some the experience was more positive, Jean Gibbon's mother was evacuated with her two school-aged children and her youngest son who was only 3 from Dagenham to Great Yarmouth by Paddle Steamer and then to a village near Cromer in Norfolk. Jean recalled, '[T]he four of us shared a very large, comfortable bedroom with our own bathroom. There was a large dining room and lounge on the ground floor. The mothers were expected to help out with chores in the dining room and kitchen.' The family was offered a bungalow in the village, and she recalled that her mother settled down well and made friends.[25] Likewise, Michael Whitebrook remembers how in Hoar Cross in Staffordshire Geoff and Ruth English's mother came up as a helper with the school and then moved on to a job with the local 'lady of the manor which came with a cottage where all her family could settle'.[26] The government provided some financial support for mothers billeted in reception areas, paying householders 5s. (25 pence) a week for the mother and 3s. (15 pence) a week for each child. The cost of maintaining two homes was prohibitive for many couples, and despite the assistance from the government, finance was yet another contributing factor in the return of mothers from evacuation. As Richard Titmuss points out, '[A]t the beginning of the war 46,000 women in reception areas received these payments but within four months the number had fallen to about 4,400, largely because of the return of mothers to towns.'[27]

The second wave of evacuation

As many mothers were returning, others were accompanying their husbands who were employed in government departments and key industries being moved out of London. A number of teachers' wives went with the first wave of evacuation, but as 1939 gave way to 1940 the Bank of England, parts of the BBC and many other organizations also relocated. Nadine Sinyard's family moved from Berkshire to Burton on Trent, Staffordshire where her father was employed in the ordnance depot. She recalls her mother, 'standing on the back doorstep and crying'.[28] Melvyn Jones's father taught in a Catholic school in Margate, and his wife and children were evacuated with him, spending the next four years in Milford in Staffordshire.[29] Similarly, Brenda Bryant's mother took her children when she accompanied her husband's school as a helper in their evacuation from Margate in 1940.[30]

By Spring of 1940, many men had been called up removing the conflict of loyalty between husband and family for some women, just as the dangers of war became more acute. Women were more willing to consider leaving the towns and cities as bombing and the fear of invasion increased, but they were still resistant to being billeted in someone else's home, sharing kitchens and other amenities. Feelings that seem to have been reciprocated. One Cambridgeshire Billeting Officer stated that 'he would refuse to attempt to billet women and children in his district and that if compulsory powers were used, half the people would prefer to go to goal'.[31] Faced with such hostility the government scheme no longer evacuated mothers in Spring 1940. This policy created its own problems, Jean Gibbins's mother had been evacuated to Norfolk; when this area was itself deemed to be at risk due to the threat of invasion, her children were evacuated elsewhere without her.[32]

As the threat of invasion grew worse and intermittent bombing occurred, mothers began to make their own plans, especially once the Ministry of Health confirmed in June 1940 that their accommodation costs would be met and travel vouchers issued if they arranged a billet. Approximately 430,000 mothers took advantage of this scheme over the following months,[33] although for some evacuation was only a brief interlude. Margaret Pryer's mother took her two very small children up to a large country house in Staffordshire but returned when she discovered that her family was referred to as refugees and her husband would not be able to stay the night when he visited.[34] The new policy did make it possible to stay with relations, without being a financial burden. Jean Gibbins' mother took her youngest child to Dundee to Jean's grandfather's house while her teenage daughters resided with an aunt.[35] Margaret Brazier, living in Evesham, recalled 'an aunt and her little boy came to live with us'.[36] Joan Twyman from Margate was initially evacuated to Great Whitely in Staffordshire but rescued by her mother after sending a tear-stained letter home to say how unhappy she was. Instead, in November 1940, her mother moved with her family of three children to Salisbury where they remained with their grandparents for the next two years.[37]

A few women, particularly those with relations abroad, chose to take their children to the safety of another country, for the duration of the war. This was an option only available to those whose families had the resources, not only to fund the voyages but also pay for the families' upkeep when they were away. Mrs Matthews sailed with her three children to Canada in early 1940 living with her sister and brother in Quebec for four years. The government restrictions on sending money abroad placed her in an uncomfortable position, despite taking a job as a teacher she was financially dependent on others.[38] Women who chose this course action were also subject to censure, often regarded as unpatriotic, or even cowards for leaving Britain at a moment of crisis. Likewise, as Gillian Mawson has explained, there was criticism of mothers evacuated from Guernsey to Britain in June 1940 who arrived with little money, few possessions and not knowing where they would live as they disembarked at Weymouth. It appears that the authorities were not expecting any mothers and sometimes initially separated them from their children.[39] Although supported by charities and voluntary donations, for these mothers their time in Britain was a varied experience. If they did not have a husband in the services, they could not rent houses and some were billeted with women who expected them to work for them.[40] Olive Quinn, and her baby daughter, found herself expected to help in a pokey little family shop in Burnley where she was billeted; depressed, she cried herself to sleep at night until her landlady insisted that she be removed.[41] Despite Ministry of Health guidance – leaflets advising women how to behave while billeted in others' houses and how hosts should treat their evacuees – relationships were rarely easy or comfortable. Mass Observation noted in July 1940 that the 'most far-reaching in the effect of the war on home life and social habits, has been evacuation, and this most of the difficulties and failures have been due to the inability of adults to adapt themselves to new conditions, rather than children.'[42] The Mass Observation report went on to point out: the problems of 'feeling out of place away from familiar town surroundings' or 'away from their husbands'.[43]

After the first wave of evacuation, there was a multitude of rumours, anecdotes and urban myths circulating about the poor treatment of child-evacuees. Some women expressed fatalism about the dangers of war; one explained, '[I]t don't do no good going away if that bomb's got your name on it.'[44] Many women were determined not to allow their children to be evacuated without them. Alf Morris's mother was resolute even when the Blitz began that they would be alright, telling her children, 'We'll rough it in the shelters, We're not going to be evacuated.'[45] Some mothers were put off the idea of evacuation by rumours of German parachutists landing in the British countryside; a rumour that was given more credibility when a number of parachutes were found discarded in the Midlands in August of 1941. The nearly seventy parachutes were decorated with large eagles and precipitated an extensive search by the police, troops and home guard but eventually considered to be a dummy drop by the Luftwaffe to undermine morale.[46] Hence many parents did not evacuate their children despite the increasing danger in 1940. A sentiment expressed by many parents was that if anyone in the family died, then it would be better for them all to die together; this feeling, arguably, was born out of their awareness of the inadequacy of social care provision for children without parents or relations to look after them. There was an added poignancy in this response by a mother with one little girl of 6 who explained, 'I'm keeping my little girl here I don't want to leave my husband and we'd rather die together. Who would look after my child? She's delicate and has a club foot?'[47] This poor mother, weighing up of what would be best for her child, was faced with inadequate welfare provision. But the reality of 'all going together' was painful beyond comprehension for some women. Mrs Wade and her two teenage children were buried by rubble in a shelter behind their house in Glasgow for three days, after a bombing raid. Her son died first and then her daughter. She was the only one in the shelter to survive, a girder having kept the brickwork from suffocating her. When a neighbour met her two years later, she was unrecognizable; her red hair had turned snow white.[48]

The Blitz and the people's evacuation

When bombing began in earnest, many mothers changed their minds about staying in London and other cities. Unwilling to let their children be evacuated unaccompanied they set off with their children to find sanctuary in safer parts of the country. A Mass Observation Home Intelligence Report on 10 September 1940 noted, 'Exodus from East End growing rapidly. Taxi Drivers reports taking party after party to Euston or Paddington with their belongings ... Citizens' Advice Bureau inundated with mothers and young children hysterical and asking to be removed from the district.'[49] Ethel Salmon remembers her mother had a premonition that the local school which was supposed to act as a shelter in their area of Canning Town was unsafe. She took her five children to Suffolk in September 1940. The local vicar organized a dilapidated cottage for them where they stayed for two years.[50] Others struggled to decide what would be best. Some whose children had been evacuated in 1939 returned their children to their original billets. In the days after the Blitz began, Mass Observation Investigators noted East End women and children leaving the capital in droves. One Mass Observation Investigator stopped and talked to women at Paddington station and inquired where they were going. He recorded, '[S]ome were going to relatives, some had very vague connections in other parts of the country, one women was just trusting that God will look after us.'[51]

On 22 September 1940 the official government evacuation scheme for parents and children was opened up again, and until March 1942 it organized trainloads of evacuees, including many mothers with their children relocating to places of safety. Betty Pooley was a 31-year-old mother of two young children during the Blitz, her confidence in the protection provided by hiding beneath a reinforced dining table diminished as the bombs exploded nearby. Having received a train fare from the council, she gathered up her children and set off for Kings Cross station, attaching herself to a line of evacuating mothers and children as they boarded a train. She ended up in Poppleton in Yorkshire and later recalled,

> We were the last to be chosen by country people – maybe it was because I kept saying – 'Does anyone have a cottage?' I didn't want to billeted where I'd have to share. The miracle is that someone did have a gardener's cottage on an estate. The gardener had been called up, the lady of the manor explained ... She never interfered ... but would do kind things, like giving my sons six eggs a week to bring back to me.[52]

The local community looked after Betty when she went into labour, called a doctor, comforted her when her third son was born with spina bifida and when he died soon after.

Likewise, Bryan Cogley recalled that his mother took her two sons to live with a local family in Polesworth in Staffordshire, after many nights in neighbours' air-raid shelters or under the stairs when she tried to calm her children as they listened to the drone of bombers overhead during the bombing of Coventry. With a building in the vicinity destroyed and their home near a munitions works considered a target for bombing, evacuation seemed the best solution.[53] By the end of 1940 mothers faced the horrors of intense bombing to their homes or those around them and the difficulties of finding a safe place in the shelters. As mothers poured out of danger areas, seeking safety for their children, the reception areas and towns easily reached by direct trains struggled to cope. Between the 9 and 28 November 1940 approximately 800 people were killed and 2,345 injured in Birmingham and 20,000 civilians rendered homeless.[54] By mid-November, the mayor of Worcester, which was on a direct train line from Birmingham, announced that 'the city had practically reached the limit' of evacuees it could accommodate and sought suggestions of how to limit any more people coming into the city.[55] Despite a communal meal service having been set up for mothers and children, food supplies were in short supply; schools were full to the brim. The problems in Worcester were repeated across the country with far greater intensity: one Oxford don, with a touch of exaggeration, told Vera Brittain, 'We've had half London turned into the city – and a large part of Kent as well.'[56] Thousands had indeed poured into the city, and Brittain herself noted that she

> had thought Oxford station as closely crammed with humanity as any limited space could possibly achieve; but now looking at the High Street, I find that I was wrong. Up and down the great curving thoroughfare, packed almost too close for movement and pushing one another from the pavement into the gutter struggles a crowd which varies from harassed dons in tweeds to weary homeless mothers from Poplar to Plaistow dragging small bewildered children by the hand.[57]

The luckier mothers who were officially evacuated from Kent found temporary accommodation in the numerous colleges, being allocated a student room per family. At Christ Church nappies were hung up to dry in the quad. The Salvation Army provided clothes; the Mayor started a fund for hardship cases to tide people over till they found a billet or work and assisted mothers who needed a pram for their little ones.

The less fortunate informal evacuees were to be found in the Majestic cinema on the Botley Road, not watching a film but residing in an overcrowded, evacuee depot, run by the Public Assistance Board which caused much consternation among the local residents, articulated in the press. The cinema, which had the potential to seat two thousand, had become a clearinghouse for approximately seven hundred mothers and their children who fled from London and who, it was hoped, could be dissipated out from the centre of the city, as billets were found for them. Its small café was converted into a feeding station. There were notices in the toilets informing mothers who were bottle-feeding their infants to turn up at 10.30 in their morning to get bottles sterilized and explaining that fireman and nurses were on call at night. The mothers and children slept on the floor, in corridors or between seats putting their belongings on seats. When she visited Vera Brittain was first struck by the stench and then observed,

> Covering the floor beneath upturned velveteen seats of the cinema chairs, disorderly piles of mattresses, pillows, rugs and cushions indicate 'pitches' staked out by different evacuated families. Many of the women, too dispirited to move, lie wearily on the floor with their children beside them in the fetid air, though the hour is eleven A.M. and a warm sun is shinning cheerfully on the city streets. Between the mattresses and cushions, the customary collection of soiled newspapers and ancient apple cores.[58]

The depot provided space to have a daily wash in the toilets, advice for nursing and pregnant mothers from the sister in charge, milk for the babies and food and cups of tea (criticized as just like dishwater) organized by the Women's Voluntary Service (WVS). According to one helper many of the mothers when they arrived were 'so dazed and quiet after all they had been through that they're grateful for anything'. The shelter was supposed to be temporary, and women tried to look for a more permanent billet, but this was not easy. A Mass Observation Investigator described the plight of a Royal Air Force man who brought his wife to the town after her maternity home was bombed; they spent the day traipsing around looking for rooms, and within hours of finding one, the wife gave birth to twins.[59]

Similarly, Susan Hess has identified how large numbers of mothers and children arrived in Devon at all hours of the night, attempting to escape first the London bombing and then the Plymouth Blitz. This included two destitute women who reached Totness with eleven to twelve children in tow in the middle of the night in late September 1940. Halls were allocated across the county to be used by the homeless who had frequently lost all their clothes, possessions, money and official documentation such as ration cards in the bombing and needed replacements.[60] In Stoke-on-Trent the evacuation committee noted with dismay that there were some families which three weeks after their arrival still had no change of underclothing and no night attire. These were their minimum needs and 'some of them were consequently fearful of becoming lousy especially when sleeping in crowded conditions and dismayed to be told by authorities to sleep in her clothes.'[61] In Barnstable those arriving late at night were allowed to sleep in railway carriages and in Newton Abbot they were directed to the Rest and

Shelter Station in the Congregational Schoolroom.[62] This was a pattern repeated in many towns and villages across the country as mothers fled the bombing, not waiting for official forms or guidance, they caught the first train available and consequently sometimes ended up in industrialized areas, which were also targets for enemy bombing, or within in easy reach of German bombers now that much of France was occupied territory. By 13 November 1940, Exmouth counted 1,373 unofficially evacuated mothers and children among its 4,000 evacuees, but the area was subjected to air raids between 1940 and 1943, one of which killed an evacuee mother and her four children.[63]

The influx of evacuees called for a more systematic approach to their reception where possible in order to give them the support and advice these poor mothers and children needed. Stoke-on-Trent set out to provide a printed sheet to every evacuee-mother on their arrival, containing information including, addresses of all organizations associated with evacuation and their scope and function. In 1940 when the bombing began, they received waves of hop-pickers from Kent, 206 other Londoners, 570 children under five and 906 older children. The authorities tried to help women and their families into billets in the five towns and surrounding villages. Irene Parry's family were on their seasonal hop-picking sojourn to Kent in 1940 when the London Blitz started and chose to be evacuated to Stoke-on-Trent rather than return to their homes in London. After a long train journey and a night in a hostel they were taken out in a charabanc to try and find them accommodation in the surrounding villages. Initially, she and her sister were placed in one billet, her brother across the road and their mother and baby around the corner. Eventually they were rehoused in a shared house. She later recalled, 'I think it'd got four or five bedrooms … we were there the longest, several families came and went you know, and they had two gas stoves in the kitchen.'[64] The Evacuation Reception Committee sought to place officials at reception centres, such as the London Road Hospital, which had a member of the Citizens' Advice Bureau to advise on the rights of the evacuees. Thus one family who arrived in Stoke-on-Trent were sent (with their cat) in a basket to watch a film at the cinema while accommodation, clothes and provisions were found for them.[65] Many others were not so lucky.

Accommodation problems

Prior to the outbreak of war a number of people, including the first women to take up a seat in the House of Commons, Lady Astor, had advocated the construction of purpose-built hostels for mothers and young children who were evacuated. As with so much else in relation to women and children in wartime, the investment needed was not forthcoming and the reception centres and shelters that sprung up in 'safe' areas left much to be desired. They were not purpose built or necessarily appropriate buildings, they were inadequately equipped, overcrowded and often insanitary, like the Majestic Cinema in Oxford. They were intended to provide a short-term temporary solution, but more permanent billets for mothers were not forthcoming. The Chief Billeting Officer in Dorchester, Dorset sent out 5,245 forms asking for volunteers to take evacuees and received only eighty-four offers of help.[66] By the middle of 1940, when billets were really needed, many householders were unwilling to share their home with evacuee families.

What mothers who were evacuated sought was accommodation to rent in which they could create a safe home, albeit a temporary one, for all their family. This however proved challenging to find and placed mothers and their children in danger. Doris Groves recalled that during the Blitz, as her father had joined the army, her mother decided it was no longer safe to remain in London and evacuated the family to Norfolk. However three weeks later, after they spent the night sleeping with many other families on the floor of a hall and were unable to find a billet where they could be together, her mother took them back to risk the bombing in London. A mother of two children who evacuated from Birmingham to Staffordshire in December 1940 found it impossible to obtain a billet for them all together. The mother left her son in the countryside and returned with her daughter to the dangers of wartime Birmingham, where they were both killed in a bombing raid. The young lad was left under the guardianship of his foster parents.[67]

The people's evacuation caused something of a housing crisis, when Jacqueline Pickering's mother finally decided that as her husband was away in the forces, she would leave the bombing in Portsmouth; she was lucky to find a safe billet in the nearby Meon valley where she spent nearly a year. She and her three children, including a 2-month-old baby girl, shared a 'modest house' with their host and her three children.[68] She was one of the lucky ones; others found that those with property to rent took advantage of the shortage of suitable housing stock to line their own pockets. A Mass Observation Report noted,

> Millions of people had redistributed themselves at random, voluntary evacuees from London have penetrated as far at the Highlands of Scotland and the pubs of Cornwall. Profiteering was rampant, our files included records of 16 guineas a

week (£16: 80 pence) asked for a small Cotswold cottage 18/- [90 pence] a week for a small bedroom North of London, 8/6d [42.5 pence] for a fifthly dinner in a West Country Hotel … Billeting officers found their previous surveys and card index system quite useless, as accommodation earmarked for official evacuees was filled up overnight by voluntaries, usually ready to pay more.[69]

The availability of accommodation was influenced by local factors, some safe areas were housing not just evacuees but military personnel, construction staff building new aerodromes or industrial and agricultural workers. In Torquay arrangements for over 300 mothers and children were described as 'most satisfactory' by a Devon woman seeking shelter after the bombing of Plymouth. This was very probably because hotel rooms and holiday accommodation had been requisitioned for them. In Sidmouth 'two houses were hastily requisitioned as hostels for mothers and children and a Ministry of Labour branch opened to render financial assistance'.[70]

There was in some areas strong resentment towards those fleeing from bombing, who were seen as emptying the shops of provisions and making food shortages worse and 'swamping' towns and villages. While billeting officers put pressure on householders to open their doors to the evacuees, they could not ensure that they were treated well. Joy MacRae, her mother and three siblings were sheltering in a bomb shelter when their house received a direct hit, leaving them homeless. They went to St Albans and for many years lived in temporary refuges. Often occupying only one room in which toileting, eating and sleeping had to be undertaken and at one point being accommodated in the Christian Science Reading Room with others in similar circumstances, all of whom were both short of clothes and sufficient food. Despite the efforts of the government propaganda machine, which produced a somewhat condescending public information film *Living with Strangers* (1941) encouraging hosts and evacuees to get along and make compromises, the difficulties of overcrowding and billeting on unwilling householders remained. Joy MacRae recalled an unwelcoming landlord in a dirty house,

> [W]e were 'allotted' an upstairs room, but it was an unhappy stay and we were constantly locked out of this house. He just didn't want us there. The final straw came when he would not let us in to get our possessions, and Mum had to get the police to bring a ladder, which we put to the upstairs windows and got our clothes and meager belongings out.[71]

Later the family went to live with her aunt, where eight children and granny already lived in a modest house in Rowhedge.[72]

As Sonya Rose has pointed out, the fantasy of the nationhood, brought into sharp relief in wartime and articulated through the idea of a 'People's War', carried with it ideas of social responsibility and obligation. However not all individuals and groups engaged with the rhetoric of people's war or saw themselves as part of 'the nation' in the same way, they did not necessarily all pull together for the national good. There were regional and local tensions, well class, racial and gender divisions.[73] Evacuated mothers seeking accommodation came face to face with the limitations of many people's engagement with the idea of a people's war. Evacuee mothers discovered that there was little sense of social obligation towards them. Stella Doy and her sister went with her mother to Buckinghamshire when the family heard of any old lady prepared to share her cottage where they stayed for some time.[74] But the task of housing Mrs Wright and her three children evacuated to Kings Lynn from London in 1941 suggests others found those who lived in safe areas less than welcoming. The hard-pressed billeting officer recounted the difficulties that she faced in February 1941.

> It was four o'clock before I was free to accompany Mrs Wright and her kiddies up to the house that Mrs Dexter had promised us.
>
> We all went up Mrs Brand was prepared to use compulsory powers if necessary, And with us was Father Vaughan, the girl helper, our little family and myself.
>
> We stopped in front of a cheerful modern brick house.
>
> 'I've changed my mind' were her first words, 'I can't take them' ...
>
> Mrs Wright clutched my arm. 'I"ll have to go back to London' she whispered Don't make me go back to that "place" tonight.'
>
> I reassured her, I listened to the pleading of Father Vaughan and the persuading of Mrs Brand.
>
> 'But these people have been bombed! They are the people to whom you owe hospitality!' I said.
>
> 'I don't care' said Mrs Dexter.
>
> 'I won't take them.'
>
> And she shut the door in our faces.
>
> The children were bewildered, unhappy. For the second time the people of Kings Lynn had turned these little souls away.[75]

Alternatively, in Staffordshire Mrs Goldman and her three children were turned out on the street by their landlady, necessitating her spending a night in an institution with her family and a week with a friend before her husband came and fetched her and moved her to North Weald in Essex.[76]

It was in these circumstances with families pouring out of bombed areas that questions began to be asked of the Minister of Health in the House of Parliament about the extent to which rural authorities were exercising their powers to ensure accommodation was available.[77] Local authorities were for obvious reasons unwilling to place evacuees in households where they were unwelcome, but there was some concern that there were still large houses belonging to the wealthy in safe areas, which were being underutilized. Stoke-on-Trent was not the only area in which it was noted that:

> Many houses have been filled more than their capacity and some evacuee families are too large to reasonably be accommodated in private homes. Meanwhile other houses and premises in the city remain vacant. Much comment is being caused by this discrepancy. Immediate steps should be taken to remedy this inconstancy by taking over such premises, furnishing them and making them available for evacuees.[78]

Local authorities and evacuees themselves sought to identify vacant houses, which could be requisitioned and equipped for mothers and their children to move into, however, this was practically challenging, as Martin Parsons's case study of Shaftesbury makes clear. One potential property identified to house two mothers and their four children who were temporarily accommodated in the soup kitchen was requisitioned. However, by the time they had sorted out the furniture and a leaky pipe the two women had fallen out and refused to be billeted together and the owner returned demanding his property back. When the authorities identified another empty property, before the evacuees could move in a member of the Assistance Board had taken up residence with his wife and daughters whose house had been blown down in Weymouth.[79] Evacuee-mothers were expected to take second place behind locals in any search for accommodation. When Mrs Maguire identified potential accommodation in Stoke-on-Trent and informed the agent that she would like to rent it, she was told, 'she could not have it as someone who had been born and bred in the potteries wanted it'.[80] Unsurprisingly, Mrs Maguire considered returning to London and risking the bombs rather than face such prejudice. Local authorities were forced to take a determined approach towards those who resisted taking-in evacuees, using their legal powers to ensure householders accepted evacuees, however unsuitable the billets might be.

For mothers evacuating with their children in tow, their decisions about when to go, how long to stay and when to return were the result of weighing up a number of finely balanced complex and competing factors. The overcrowding and lack of available accommodation were significant issues in whether mothers remained in 'safe' areas with their children. If their husbands were not in the forces and had remained in danger areas, they were more likely to return home as soon as the bombing ceased. By 1942, there seems to have been an acceptance that 'women could not be happy torn between their husband and child loyalties.'[81] For others the destruction of the bombing left them little to return to. Their temporary accommodation turned into a long-term home. When Joy MacRae got the opportunity to rent a condemned cottage to live in with her four children she jumped at it, despite the vermin, insects and lack of water or inside loo, a very common situation in rural homes well into the post-war era. They remained there until they emigrated to Canada in 1958.[82]

New lives and long-term consequences

Mothers who already had older children evacuated to other parts of the country and sought to have them transferred to the areas in which they and their youngest children had found safety were apt to be told, at least by London Councils, that there would be no objection to the transfer but they would be expected to cover the costs of transport. This was yet another area in which the experience of evacuation was shaped by the mother's economic resources and class. Little wonder then that many mothers in fleeing from danger zones sought to follow their children to wherever in the country they had been evacuated. On the 9 September 1940 the Mass Observation Investigator on Paddington station asked a 35-year-old woman whether she was leaving the capital, she replied,

> Yes I'm going to Bridgewater. That's where my little one's evacuated. The woman's kind I'm sure she'll take me in when she knows what's happened. You can't stand it, Miss. You can't really. They are not human what do these things. We don't know what 'll happen but at least we will be away.[83]

The interviewee was not by any means the only mother of evacuated children who responded to the intense bombing during the Blitz by fleeing to the place where their children were. It was probably an area that they had visited, had some familiarity with and felt an emotional pull towards. In a time of crisis and fear, it enabled these women to end their painful separation from their children and keep them close. Vera Brittian found in the Majestic Cinema in Oxford a mother, whose husband on active service had been missing for five weeks, who explained,

After me house was bombed, me and kids was in the schoolhouse, and I says to Miss Rackham – that's the school mistress - I says 'I've got four children evacuated to Cowley' – well looked after they are to miss – 'and if there's any choice it's Oxford for me. So she fixes it form me some'ow and I come down 'ere on the coach.[84]

The welcome that mothers of evacuees received was varied. One arrived at the Staffordshire farmhouse where her children were staying, heavily pregnant. After her baby was born her children's foster mother looked after them all for several weeks and the families remained friends for many years.[85] As a child evacuated to Staffordshire, Maureen Haslam had this to say:

[W]e were woken up early in the morning and there was me mom and dad with the three boys. Four boys sorry. Sitting in the living room. They'd been bombed, well the house had been bombed twice at Dagenham. They lost the roof and the windows so they just packed their cases and they were evacuated to a place called Cheadle. But it came through, to Tamworth so they decided to get off because they knew we was at Wilnecote. And they went to the police station 'cause it was in the early hours of the morning and they spent the night at the police station. And the police took them to where we were lodging. And after that they got lodgings at Belgrave which was about 5 minute walk away from where we were and they gave us a great big old house to live in, which isn't two minutes walk from here, big old farmhouse. Got no heating, only one cold-water tap, bitter cold and when it rained the floor used to flood 'cause it was built over a stream but we were very happy there.[86]

A number of mothers who lived in danger zones negotiated the multiple and contradictory pressures involved in mothering in wartime by allowing their children to be evacuated first and then seeking work close to where they were billeted. For mothers, with children in the Midlands, there was scope to obtain work in industrial areas, for example around Birmingham or the Swynnerton Royal Ordnance Factory near Newcastle-under-Lyme. Evelyn Hurste recalled that in 1940 she was evacuated at the age of four with her elder sister to Rugeley in Staffordshire, and her mother then went to live in Birmingham. There she obtained munitions work in the Lucas Factory and being much closer was able to visit her children regularly.[87] Likewise, Mary Rose Benton's mother who had four children evacuated with their schools from Kent to two different towns in Staffordshire obtained work in Birmingham, so she could visit and take her children out regularly and where Mary Rose eventually went to live with her mother in Balsall Common.[88]

Some mothers' stay in reception areas was incognito, and they lived separately from their children. There were a number of reasons for this, uncertainty about how long they would stay and quandaries about where to locate if their children had been evacuated to different parts of the county. The difficulties of locating somewhere they could house all their family together was always an issue, especially if they were unwilling to move children from schools in which they had settled. Where children were under 5, the government contributed to both the mother's and the child's billeting allowances. However, mothers of children between the ages of 5 and 15 who lived in a reception area were expected to look after their own children and billeting allowances were stopped. The precariousness of some mothers' situation was amplified when the Ministry of Health set up a recovery authority to force mothers living 'illegally' in reception areas to repay the billeting allowances their children were not entitled to, although this would have involved overworked officials in a lot of paperwork.[89] Nevertheless, the files that have survived in Staffordshire archives contain a number of letters connected with the payment of allowances for mothers living in the safe areas. Mrs Ruby Palmer from London had two children billeted in Eccleshall, and after two major operations she was initially unable to visit them. When she did make the trek to see them in September 1941 there were complaints that she should not be getting unaccompanied child allowance. She responded by saying that she would take them back to London. The foster mother confirmed this had happened and explained that she understood the children would be returned to her if the bombing in London got bad again as 'they enjoyed the country life and have been very happy'.[90]

Even for those mothers, who had independent resources, a job, children under 5 or managed to circumnavigate the government's regulations on billeting allowances, settling into a completely new area was challenging. Tony Longdon recalled that after his mother moved to Stoke, the family rented then bought a house and his mother got a job at the Michelin factory.[91] Alternatively, when Jean Dowd's family first arrived in Staffordshire the industrial landscape of mines and the potteries was both unfamiliar and unappealing to her mother whose immediate response at Kidsgrove Station was to exclaim:

> 'Right, what time's the next train back to London? Bombs or no bombs'. So that
> was a good start. Having said that, as I say she was here for, 'til she died. Yeah but
> it'd been all a big upheaval, here, there and everywhere … it wasn't home. And
> I can remember really, for the first time in my life being hungry and being cold in
> bed at night, it wasn't home you were in somebody else's house and, you made do.[92]

Jean Dowd's mother did adapt, integrate. She joined the Mothers' Union and the church, made friends and, like many women, even enjoyed her new life.[93] When a London mother, her two children aged 6 and 10 months, her sister-in-law and another baby of 6 months moved into a house in Gloucestershire in July 1941, the neighbours wrote to the house owner to report how well they had settled in. The mothers were successfully tending the garden and hens and the 'youngest child [6 months old] has entirely lost that frightened look she came with and is pretty looking now [she was in several bad London raids]'.[94]

Other mothers evacuated with their children faced a quandary about when to return home, the intermittent dangers lasted until April 1945. Sally Pincus recalled that in July 1944,

> I was in the bedroom with my baby who was in the cot. The doodlebugs were coming overhead and when you couldn't hear them it meant that they'd dropped their bombs. I was next to the cot and I couldn't get out of the door. It had jammed. All the glass in the windows fell out and fell onto the dining table. The wall collapsed on the back of the cot ... Me and the baby were fine – just shocked.[95]

Little wonder that hundreds of thousands of mothers who had previously returned home, gathered up their children and once again evacuated themselves during the doodlebug raids.

Conclusion

The wartime bombing produced an extreme housing shortage in London and many areas of the South, which led to some families remaining in the areas in which mothers had settled during the war, for them there was little to go back to. Betty Rose recalled 'our house was very badly hit' and so her father found a job in Staffordshire where she and her mother were already evacuated.[96] For other mothers, their attempts to keep their children safe were not so positive. Mrs Harrison was evacuated with her daughter and son Alfred, who was 12 years old, from Essex to Leek in Staffordshire. However, her son died following an illness and a short stay in an isolation hospital, in 1942.[97]

Aerial warfare is in many ways a gendered experience, women's everyday lives were shaped in a multitude of small or significant ways by their class, age, ethnicity, marital status, the region in which they lived and their own individual circumstances. The potential options for women in areas in danger of being bombed who were committed to keeping their children with them in wartime were limited. These mothers embraced multiple practical problems and hardships; they encountered the limitations of local and government provision and care. These mothers faced at first-hand the varying degree to which many people had or had not bought into the rhetoric and implied obligations and responsibilities of the people's war. While some mothers who fled the bombing, seeking safety for their family, experienced support and kindness, enabling them to create a new life, others faced rejection, alienation, loneliness, criticism, scrutiny and condemnation. For all women in danger areas the decisions they made, the course of action that they took in seeking to mother their children and keep them safe in wartime was fraught with guilt, regret and the anxiety that a different decision would maybe have led to another better outcome. For women in reception areas who became foster mothers, wartime was equally challenging as the next chapter will explore.

5

The challenges of enforced intimacy: Looking after evacuees

When the Barnett House *Survey of Social and Educational Results of Evacuation* was published in 1947, the authors proclaimed,

> This Survey might almost be called the war memorial to the 'unknown foster-mother' for it bears abundant witness to the devoted efforts of the Oxford and Oxfordshire housewives who opened their homes to the young Londoners and saw to it that they improved in health and manners. Some of them tried hard to understand difficult or delinquent boys and girls and often succeeded in overcoming their difficulties, despite repeated disappointments and set-backs.[1]

The huge practical, emotional and often financial efforts of hundreds of thousands of foster mothers saved thousands of children's lives but remain an undervalued contribution to the national war effort. The government assumed that the homes and labour of numerous housewives were at their beck and call. Evacuation was a predominantly domestic experience; that it was generally successful was a consequence of the domestic labour of numerous kind-hearted women. Whether they took children into their homes willingly or with reticence, as part of the government scheme or through a multitude of informal networks, of family, friends, churches or employers, the vast majority 'bravely shouldered their responsibilities, and performed their allotted tasks in the spirit of free citizens of a democratic nation'.[2] Yet, in the popular iconography and myth that now surrounds evacuation, the histories of the predominantly rural women whose domestic lives bore the brunt of a government policy that temporarily rehomed several million women and children are all too often forgotten.

Throughout the conflict, government propaganda defined the care of evacuees as part of the war effort. Foster mothers were exempt from conscription when it was introduced at the end of 1941. Posters noted, 'Women wanted for Evacuation Service. Offer your services to your local council' or pronounced, 'She's in the ranks too. Caring for Evacuees is a national service.'[3] Lucy Noakes suggests women in military uniform, challenged traditional ideas of gender, destabilized clear-cut notions of identity, unsettling the ways in which warfare was seen as masculine territory.[4] While the work of foster mothers did not undermine or challenge femininity, it offered scope for it to be reworked, stretched and shifted as domesticity and motherhood became nationally significant and the evacuation scheme put domestic life under the spotlight. The move towards greater surveillance, criticism and potential external interference that occurred in the twentieth century was accelerated by evacuation, adding to the pressures of foster mothers. Most foster mothers coped admirably with the challenge of enforced intimacy and increased domestic labour required to care for evacuees for an indeterminate amount of time. However, other women found fulfilling the expectations of the mythical 'good mother' beyond their emotional, physical or financial capacities; problems that could be exasperated if foster-parents and children were socially or culturally mismatched.

Foster mother's motivation

The demand by the central government that those in areas considered safe should take evacuees was not always greeted with enthusiasm. Muriel Green in a Norfolk village noted in her diary for Mass Observation on 30 August 1939, 'Excitement, annoyance and worry in village owing to the expected evacuated children tomorrow. We are not having any if possible.'[5] The next day, with a touch of relief she recorded no children had arrived. The unwillingness of some householders to care for children was an issue not merely of experience but also of age. Women in their eighties found themselves asked to look after small tots, but they were rarely able to cope even with 8- or 9-year-old lads. In Great Malvern an elderly vicar wrote to the clerk to the council to suggest that his 77-year-old wife was not up to the care of evacuees, noting that due to her poor health they had not had visitors to stay for five years and that he was sometimes out carrying out parish duties. The young age of many evacuees was a problem; as a Mass Observation Investigator pointed out, '[M]ost people took it rather for granted that unaccompanied children would be about 10–14 and most of them are 5–10 and require a lot more looking after than was expected.'[6] Taking a more proactive approach to the anxieties of the local population, Hagley in Worcestershire planned to place its allocation of evacuees in a large house, employing a matron to look after them and funding the plan with a charge paid by local householders. The village was slated in the local press but defended their actions as motivated by a desire to relieve stress on the elderly and infirm. Nonetheless, they were labelled as snobs and accused of being unpatriotic and eventually bowed to social pressure and like other villages welcomed evacuees into their homes.[7]

Women were paid expenses 10s. 6d. (52.5 pence) for the first child and 8s. 6d. (42.5 pence) for each subsequent child. Frances Cooke, whose mother took in two evacuees, recalled, '[O]f course it was a bit of extra money because we were paid to have them and we weren't well off.'[8] Nevertheless, if some foster mothers clearly saw the payment of a billeting allowance as a motivating factor, others got onto the wrong side of the law by continuing to claim allowances when evacuees had left resulting in a number of prosecutions, although in some cases the authorities eventually gave up any hope of reclaiming allowances. Most women saw looking after evacuees, as their contribution to the war effort, particularly if domestic responsibilities, age or geographical location prevented them from finding an outlet for their patriotic fervour. Geoffrey Shakespeare, the MP who chaired the committee that enquired into the welfare of the evacuated and homeless, acknowledged this when he pointed out,

> The work done by hostesses in looking after unaccompanied children is worthy of the highest praise and more recognition should be given to it. Very often the hostess is unable to join one of the uniformed or more spectacular war services because she is looking after children in her home.'[9]

A number of women, mostly in large houses but also some more modest establishments, adapted their whole household to host as many as twelve children, these 'ideal good mothers' were much admired. Eric Gadd, a Hampshire headmaster and billeting officer, noted in his diary in July 1940,

> This evening visited the home of Mrs Keatley who, in a tiny cottage, billets five children aged between seven and twelve. Welcomed by a cry of greeting from bedroom window, where children in nightclothes were waiting for prayers. My teasing suggestion that they should all be sent home was greeted by a unanimous 'No Sir!' ... The secrets of success seem to be fairness, firmness and well-directed activity.[10]

Psychologists also praised such arrangements, as they 'combined the atmosphere of a family home with the appeal to the children's community spirit, and their success depended almost entirely on the women in charge'.[11] The Barnett House survey acknowledged that 'difficult children were more of a responsibility' and reported upon a child whose father had been killed at Dunkirk:

[D]erived much benefit from the care of a capable woman who had converted her house into a family hostel. His sister had been before the court on a charge of wilful damage, was retarded at school, and had few prospects of employment, but her foster-mother decided to keep her on as a domestic help. The mother was grateful for what had been done for her children.[12]

There were also those middle- and upper-class women for whom the care of evacuees was a form of social motherhood, the duty of those with privilege to care for the less fortunate, educating and improving them into bourgeois values.[13] For some, it almost appears to have been an interesting psychological experiment, an opportunity to study children close-up.

The majority of children were housed in ones or twos or occasionally threes, and their foster mothers had their own personal motivations, needs or gaps in their lives, which they hoped evacuees might fill. Sometimes caring for evacuees was seen as offering a distraction from worrying about their sons fighting in the war. Clive Dellino recalled that his foster parents 'were two of the kindest people I have ever known. They had just one son, who was older than me, and he joined the Royal Navy after a couple of years so I suppose, in a way, I filled his place and benefited from his parent's love and kindness.'[14] He spent four years with them in Yaxley, Cambridgeshire, until the bombing in London had subsided and he could safely return home. Having young evacuees could lighten the atmosphere in wartime houses and provide company for the lonely. Mrs Cartwright took in an evacuee after her husband died in an accident; her home seemed too quiet with only her and her daughter there.[15] Another recently widowed woman of 60 took in two boys and explained they gave her 'more interest in life' and took 'her mind off things by having more to do'.[16] As one foster mother noted, 'Most of the hostesses in the village seem content with their foster children, I am of course speaking only for myself when I say that my six boys are making this dreary, lonely war not only tolerable but often enjoyable.'[17]

For some women, an evacuee was the child they had always wanted; one woman from Pelsall, Staffordshire wrote to Cannock Town Clerk asking for an evacuee to look after, as the National Children's Home had no children available to adopt.[18] Pam Hobbs and her sister were billeted on a childless couple in Derby, and her foster mother explained they had gone down on their knees to thank god for sending them two ready-made daughters.[19] Bettine Saffery, her brother and two other children were billeted in Staffordshire in the home of two sisters who with their husbands ran the village post office. With no children of their own, these couples poured all their love into looking after the small charges, temporarily in their care. All four children slept in one room and on Christmas Eve were sent to bed promptly with instructions to go to sleep so that Father Christmas would come. Bettine later recalled,

> We put our stockings at the end of the bed and I remember a clock striking twelve, this must have been all put on because I remember thinking oh it's twelve o'clock and I couldn't go to sleep and then we heard bells coming up the stairs, like jingle bells sort of noise and the door opened and the other two little girls were in the other bed and my brother, he was asleep and I just pulled the covers up over my head, I was too scared to look, and the stockings were filled when I was brave enough to look so that was something else that sticks, that really sticks in my mind and that was lovely when you think about it, so they really tried to make us feel that we were special.[20]

Douglas Wood went to live with two women, a spinster in her fifties and her maiden aunt in Staffordshire for four and a half years. For these women, he was the child they never had as he recalled, '[T]hey were absolutely wonderful to me it was like erm, they were more than mothers to me actually, they just made me, it made all the difference to my life from then on ... I was shown so much kindness and love, it was wonderful really.'[21] Likewise, Dicky Blood's second and very happy foster home was a farm in Yoxall, Staffordshire where his new 'auntie and uncle' were a kindly couple who had no children of their own. After greeting him warmly and feeding him, his new auntie explained the home and care they could provide:

> There's nout posh 'bout us lad, no fancy talk or clothes, no tap watter, no electric or gas, no proper toilet, and certainly no car, no going shooting, unless we need summat for the pot. Only work and allus plenty o'that. The food inna plentiful, but it's good and ye'll not starve.[22]

What this summary did not include was the care, concern, love and support they provided, his stay on their farm left him with a lifelong love of the countryside. However evacuation was supposed to be the temporary care of other people's children during wartime, and those who grew to love their evacuees would find parting with them painful. Nora Landon, a 20-year-old volunteer at the Congregational Church in Hanley, Stoke-on-Trent recalled a friend who had taken in an evacuee,

> She was very sorry when he left 'cause she hadn't got any family of her own and, she felt as though she'd fulfilled some sort of need by taking in this little lad ...

she did look after him. She fed him well and kept him clean and took him for walks and really looked after him.[23]

Striving to provide a warm welcome

Thus many housewives responded very positively to the arrival of evacuees, by willingly opening their homes to strangers as the need arose. Hosts sometimes provided billets at the last minute to counteract the problems created by the uncertainty and disorganization of evacuation allocations. Some stepped in to help when billeting arrangements went wrong and children needed a new home. Foster mothers took in not only children but at times their relations also, so that many small cottages were filled to the brim. Michael Whitebrook remembers the scene in Newborough, Staffordshire when evacuees arrived from Ramsgate late in the evening, 'all bedraggled and tired' after 'travelling all day from early morning'. His mother was initially persuaded 'to have Olive and Clive and then a girl 'the same age and her little brother, Joan and Sydney'. Consequently, they ended up with four evacuees staying with them in a two-up-two-down cottage.[24] Peter Cotton persuaded his mum to take on an evacuee; 'later the boy's father also came to stay and she took in three children … my mam who'd got a big family, she opened her doors'.[25] These four children were not alone in being welcomed into very modest accommodation. The vast majority of evacuees entered the already crowded homes of the working class; a remarkable number of oral histories and autobiographies recount how they shared beds, slept on mattresses on the floor in corridors, halls or landings. They received care, consistency, patience from conscientious, warm-hearted foster mothers that was more important than the material circumstances in which they lived and enabled them to feel safe in unfamiliar surroundings. There are numerous examples of evacuees remembering the kindness of their foster parents. Maisie Hamilton recalls, 'Oh I loved them both, they were both really good to me, they bought me clothes from head to foot as soon as I got there … and everywhere they went I went with them.'[26] Marjorie Clowes remembered her foster mother always in the house reassuringly bustling around in the kitchen.[27]

Foster mothers' 'good mothering' of their evacuees was often exhibited via food: on their arrival they were greeted with biscuits and milk or a home-cooked meal shared with their new family. Arthur Garner recalled,

We were made very welcome and a lovely meal had been prepared for us. We all sat round a large table, and Mrs Potts put the meal in front of us. My brother David did not start to eat his meal, and Mrs Potts asked him why he wasn't eating it. And he said 'Is this all for me lady?'[28]

Likewise, Pam Hobbs' foster mother had arranged for cakes and lemonade to be ready for her new evacuees and although usually in a wheelchair stood in the doorway to greet them. Pam remembered that she hugged her and her sister and said 'we were her "poor we looves" ... and how blessed she was that her clever Freddy had managed to get two such lovely girls, she beamed from one of us to the other with obvious pleasure.'[29] Mrs Clowes, who had recently lost the youngest of her three children, was equally excited about the arrival of her small evacuee, unable to wait at home she went down the lane to meet her. Years later, that evacuee, Eileen Faires could still recall how Mrs Clowes had held out her arms to give her a cuddle, her warmth towards this little child, barely 4 years old, continued, over the next seven years. Consequently, Eileen described Mrs Clowes as 'a wonderful, wonderful lady, she had the biggest heart going I think, a most loving person'[30] whose kindness extended to other members of her evacuee's family, two aunts, and three cousins also came to stay. She was an example of a foster mother who became the first port of call for anyone in the family fleeing the Blitz. Some foster mothers also looked after evacuees' younger siblings when bombing was severe or if a child's mother was ill or injured.

For those with little experience of children caring for evacuees could be challenging. Mrs Redmund's little 5-year-old evacuee was less than enamoured about being evacuated and told her, in no uncertain terms, that he did not like her and wanted to be taken home. She recalled calming him down by taking him to the playground to go on the swings and having to lie on the bed until he fell asleep at night.[31] Most, like Tony Longdon fostered by a childless widow in Stoke-on-Trent, remembered being well-cared for[32] and Sydney Cox described the father and daughter who looked after him as 'very kind', his foster mum had never been married 'but she had been used to children'.[33] The challenges for foster mothers could be exasperated when children who had left their home clean and healthy, after a long train journey with little access to loos, and an unfortunate combination of food and no washing facilities, arrived in a very different condition. The journey also involved repeatedly crowding children together hastening the spread of nits and infectious childhood diseases.

Nella Last recalled in her diary that there had been 'a run on Keating's [insect powder] and disinfectant and soap' in a local village.[34] Foster mothers with little experience of children were ill-prepared to handle the situation, and one interviewee recalled that a neighbour came to see her mother imploring her to come and assist as

> there were things jumping about on this girls head, she was absolutely alive with fleas and of course it was quite a common thing really, and me mother told her not to be so silly and gave her some shampoo…this poor woman she just couldn't cope … they didn't understand children … she couldn't cope.[35]

The most frequently referred-to problem was bed-wetting, no doubt precipitated by a mixture of stress and anxiety in unfamiliar surroundings. Children traumatized by the separation from their parents unintentionally created work for foster mothers; Expectations and tolerance were very different in an era before washing machines although there are indications some hosts accused evacuees of bedwetting to get rid of them, in time rubber under-sheets were provided as was compensation for damage to property caused by evacuees. One homeowner was incandescent with rage about a 3-year-old who had been 'wetting the bed continually for a fortnight'.[36] Others were more sympathetic,[37] Dorothy Chadwick's mother stripped beds of wet sheets, dressed her small charges in clean clothes and undertook much extra washing regularly without a word of rebuke. Children, inevitably got into all sorts of scrapes and mishaps, causing worry and stress; Ken Marple's foster mother had to take him on the back of her bike, cycling two miles to the doctors in Abbots Bromley, Staffordshire when he nearly cut his thumb off chopping wood. Hence he remembered 'she cared for me, she really cared'.[38]

The majority of warm-hearted foster parents tried hard to make children feel welcome and many evacuees responded, in time, with genuine affection, but foster mothers' efforts were not always welcomed. Pam Hobbs recalled that she and her friend resisted an attempt to kiss them goodnight and be motherly.[39] Francis May Guy and her husband struggled to look after four siblings billeted on them from London in January 1940. She recalled, 'No amount of coaxing would make them settle … All they wanted was mum and dad … Even the nice clothes we scrounged for them got no reaction.'[40] Foster mothers could not necessarily compensate for the pain of homesickness, which prevented some children from settling down. This was not just a short-term problem and may have made foster mothers feel a failure. Katy Tuff recalled how her foster parents 'took me to their lovely home and I was given my own bedroom. They also gave me a Scotch terrier and I had never had a pet before. My foster parents were very kind. They gave me the first holiday I ever had. We went to

Blackpool.'[41] Despite their efforts she only stayed nine months as she missed her family so much.

Although visits from evacuees' appreciative, biological mothers were usually welcome, foster mothers sometimes felt that they were being scrutinized by their young guests, the billeting officers, teachers, welfare workers, sometimes psychologists and of course the children's biological mothers. They often found parental visits a trial in all senses of the word. Not only were they often expected to feed and provide accommodation for their foster children's families they were also often subjected to implied or overt criticism. Foster parents may have felt that they had all the responsibility and unpaid domestic labour that bringing up children involved but no control and sometimes no thanks for their efforts. A Mass Observation Investigator considered, 'Visiting parents frequently upset the children, and relations between foster parents and evacuees: Boy two doors away settled down well until his mother came to see him, made a scene, weeping etc., at the school gate. The boy told his landlady that he was going home to look after his mother.'[42]

Parents could and did swoop down and remove the children to another billet or return children to areas threatened by bombing. Mrs Toone, an Air Raid Precautions (ARP) warden in Billesdon, Leicestershire, whose husband was in the forces, was summoned for refusing to take in evacuees. She stated in evidence, '[S]he has had two other evacuees and while they were staying with her she had bought extra food and clothing and had arranged to take them on holiday, but their parents took them away.' She complained to the billeting officer that 'there appears to be one law for the parents and one for the householder.'[43] The problems and the foster mother's perspective are illuminated by one account in Mrs St Loe Strachey' *Borrowed Children*:

> Richard and Oliver, aged 9 and 8 respectively. Very spoiled. Two sisters aged 19 and 21 sole members of the family. Foster-parents gave up bedroom, and foster-mother her work, to have more time to devote to them. Mother arrived and spoke disparagingly of accommodation, but conceded that the people were doing their best. Mother is approaching climacteric. The younger became unwell, sore-throat and pimple – wrote to mother begging return. She removed without husband's knowledge or consent.[44]

For this poor foster mother who had given her all to care for her evacuees, their removal would have been heartbreaking and may have left her feeling she had failed, not least because so many of the commentators, working perhaps with an idealized and unrealistic notion of motherhood seemed to see many children's problems as a consequence of the shortcomings of their foster mothers, who apparently should see the value in 'adopting a positive attitude to their task immediately, and to turn duty into pleasure'.[45] For example, Mrs St Loe Strachey describes one little 5-year-old, initially evacuated with her mother and two smaller siblings who began to kick up when her mother was moved to another village. According to Strachey, once a social worker was involved, '[T]he child began to improve almost at once when the hostess felt that she was not entirely responsible and had someone to talk to about her difficulties.' She went on to state that this 'looks like an interesting case of the anxiety and insecurity of the hostess being passed on to the child'.[46]

Tensions in the domestic experience of evacuation

For all housewives the arrival of evacuees was a significant imposition into their daily lives, which some found very difficult to deal with. The Staffordshire Federation Women's Institute report to headquarters in 1939 expressed this rather strongly when they suggested, 'No longer is the countrywoman's home her own; she is trying to grapple with difficulties of housing, feeding and clothing that would have been very great in any case, but which seems almost insurmountable with the addition of strange evacuees in her home'.[47] Rumours of put-upon and struggling hosts, coping with ill-mannered guests with a strong sense of entitlement circulated in reception areas. Evacuee children and their mothers were accused of bringing disease and infestations of head lice to the countryside in the 1939 evacuation. Stories spread of evacuees' delinquent behaviour, and in Cheadle rumours of evacuees stealing garden produce were 'extremely prevalent within the district' where the billeting officer undertook to talk to the police.[48] Arguably many of these narratives were a way of expressing the anxiety, alienation and resentment at evacuation by those who felt powerless in the face of the government's policies, which adversely affected their domestic lives.

Resentment was felt particularly towards those mothers who were evacuated with their children; everybody seemed to know somebody who knew somebody whose hospitality had been abused. Constance Miles noted in her diary on 20 March 1941 the experience of her husband's elderly cousin:

> She lives in a house in Haslemere, all alone because no modern servant will stay with that kind of old person with four prize Pekes. She had pushed on her, in spite of her remonstrations, one grandmother, one mother, one big girl, one tiny

boy of two from Portsmouth. The boy behaves like an untrained animal all over her beautiful Turkish carpets.[49]

Apparently, the family responded to her requests not to push the pram into her walls by telling her she need not worry as she would get compensation from the government and did not come 'near her' or provide any care when she had bronchitis. The division of her house had resulted in this 84-year-old lady cooking on a gas ring in her bedroom.[50] Other hosts received more consideration; indeed, when Mrs Bentley in Rugeley, Staffordshire, became ill and had to go into hospital, the mother of the evacuees she had looked after at the beginning of the war moved in and looked after her and her home.[51]

Many hosts and evacuees rubbed along together, making the best of less than ideal circumstances. Max Reynolds who spent much of the war with his mother in a relatively peaceful suburbs of Wolverhampton remembered that his house had a transient population during the conflict, as his mother firstly took in a mother and two daughters from the dockland area of London, which was heavily bombed in the Blitz. Next, she had a 'tranche of people' linked to Royal Air Force Cosford and in 1944 a mother and daughter who were escaping the flying bombs. His memory is that 'it seemed to work out alright, I mean I think that, you know people took a share in the kitchen which was not large.'[52]

The Ministry of Health's investigation into evacuated and homeless people in reception areas toured the country, visiting four regions in seventeen days, after which it acknowledged the problems of housewives experienced when mothers and their children were billeted on them. Recalling one visit, Geoffrey Shakespeare MP noted that:

> It was not to be expected that the invasion of the countrywoman's home by the London mother would be achieved without friction. I can see in my mind's eye now, during our visit to Cornwall, fourteen perambulators parked outside the public house in which the London mothers were drinking their morning stout.[53]

If many of the rural hosts were appalled by their evacuee-mothers penchant for a mid-morning tipple, just as many were mightily relieved to have their house to themselves for a little while. Although Fabian Margaret Cole suggested in 1940 that 'the housewife, the member of that huge unorganised occupation which has no trade union, would not endure the violent interruption of the state into her working life',[54] most foster mothers coped. Some did so with a sense of rye humour as depicted in E. M. Delafield's fictionalized autobiography *Diary of a Provincial Lady* (1947) which portrayed foster mothers determined to see the care of evacuees as a task of national importance, while also claiming that urban children were thriving under their superior care. This included the stoical vicar's wife, who though childless prior to the outbreak of war had been most generous with her advice on child rearing. In wartime she had large numbers of children billeted on her, who ran riot in the vicarage. Her six evacuees blocked the drains, experimenting to see if a fir cone floated in the toilet. She clung firmly to the idea that nothing matters but the total destruction of Hitler. Others found it difficult to absorb ideology so uncritically.[55]

Perhaps unsurprisingly, in some households, evacuees were tolerated rather than welcomed, women did not appreciate the extra unpaid domestic labour[56] that evacuees brought or the inevitable changes to their home life. Those who had the funds to do so sought assistance from domestic servants, but they were not easy to find as they relished potentially more lucrative, alternative forms of employment. As the conflict ground on, some foster mothers found their situation stressful, difficult and very hard work and grew to resent evacuees and their families. Others regarded it as nothing but a relief when evacuees left or were removed – even if they were returning to face the bombs in danger areas. Families and their private domestic lives are constructed through: practices, connections, relationships and traditions which are both socially and individually determined – class, region, age, religion and upbringing shape the 'everyday' of domestic life and in time construct individuals sometimes tenuous sense of identity, language, phrases, manners, the timetables of eating, sleeping, washing and the distribution of responsibility for tasks, defined a sense of who people are, as families and communities. Evacuation both undermined this and brought these practices into relief.

Within families, priorities in the allocation of scarce resources often support emotional connections and hierarchies. Hence the redistribution and access to sweets, money and food to evacuees were frequently remarked upon in oral histories; Gordon Ellis remembers meeting the evacuee who stayed with his family: 'I were standing at the gate and he was brought up the path and he'd got a large bar of fruit and nut chocolate in his hand and that was what really caught my attention.'[57] This host child responded to the evacuee's possession of chocolate with classic sibling rivalry. Food was an area of tension, resentment and criticism. Choices of food and practices of food consumption are core markers of cultural identity, belonging, family, mothering, caring and housewives' skills in domestic management.[58] Foster mothers were dismayed when their use of home-grown and economical foodstuff was rejected by evacuees as unfamiliar.

Foster mothers faced a complex and often hopeless balancing act between the welfare of her evacuees and her own children, who sometimes resented evacuees. One child remembered 'they seemed to take over and all the little bits and pieces that you'd got, you had to share them as well and we didn't have much to start with'.[59] While many evacuee children remember with equal resentment harassed foster mothers making them share many of the precious items that arrived in parcels from their mothers. Readjustments in relationships created machinations and fallouts. Mrs Miles in Surrey recorded in her diary the explanation her charwoman gave of why her evacuees were going back to London:

> Pat, aged fourteen, had trouble at school and came back saying that the teacher had slapped her face and that she was going home. The billeting officer after consultation said, 'Don't stop her.' Her little brother Bernard aged ten and beginning to enjoy feeding the chickens etc was to go home too. The other lodger in the cottage, a big nice lad aged seventeen who works on the land, had got upset and jealous with the presence at close quarters of two evacuated children, he had turned quarrelsome and has gone back to Wales.[60]

Many oral history narratives convey the emotional tensions that decisions about choices of food and the minutiae of everyday domestic life led to, with personal clashes and a not entirely unjustified sense of criticism felt by all concerned. One evacuee remembers watching her foster mother doing the grates and remarking, 'My mom don't do it like that' and being smacked for her comment.[61] For others it was the enforced domestic intimacy and artificial creation of 'family life' that created anxiety for all concerned. Dorothy Jarvis recalls finding it disturbing when her foster mother went through her suitcase of clothes as, 'I didn't want people looking at my underwear at that stage, you know, you didn't show your knickers to anybody you see!'[62] She was appalled by her foster mother's imposition into her intimate and private objects of clothing and as likely as not expressed this through resentful behaviour. Foster mothers trying to protect their own intimate family lives sometimes imposed clear physical or material indicators of separation between their families and evacuees, who were expected to eat separately from their hosts, not go in certain areas or even keep out of the house during the day. These de-markers of difference, along with an absence of cuddling and physical contact from some foster mothers caused emotional trauma and humiliation on top of the inevitable homesickness to many children but also suggest foster mother's sense that their homes were not their own, that their domestic spaces were under attack.

One way of reducing the problems of enforced domestic intimacy was to have relations to stay. It was assumed that family members or friends would share some of the values, practices and assumptions about daily life which would ease the challenges of living in close proximity. Some foster mothers seem to have had little choice, Nadine Sinyard recalled her aunt turning up on the doorstep of their home in Staffordshire with her cousin and saying to her mother, 'I've brought Dorrie up for you to look after because London will be bombed.'[63] Nadine's mother looked after the little girl for the next two years. But even within families, evacuees, and their mothers who accompanied younger children were predominately from urban areas, many of their hosts were rural; cultural differences were exaggerated by the overcrowding, a housewife in Walton, Staffordshire had her cousin and three young girls from Eastbourne and their mum to stay in 1940.[64] Thanks to the government changes this host mother did at least get paid the billeting allowance, while a Staffordshire grandmother who looked after her grandchildren was dismayed not to receive an allowance because they were from Slough, which was not considered to be in a danger area.[65] For many financial constraints and difficulties were yet another issue which increased the pressure and in time resentment of foster mothers.

Practical problems and financial pressures

Whether they shared their homes with evacuees willingly or reticently, whether hosts or foster mothers were warm-hearted or pushed beyond their capabilities, there were numerous practical and financial issues raised by looking after evacuees.

The billeting allowance was not considered generous; meeting the material needs of evacuees in a time of scarcity was challenging for many foster mothers. Even for those who were better off, the costs of caring for evacuees were not inconsequential and rarely covered by the billeting allowance. Costs involved not just food but heating and water, as Mrs Loe Strachey recorded, '[Q]uite recently the hostess of a private house, which houses quite ten children, was asked by the water company whether her water meter had better not be inspected. Her consumption (and therefore her bill) had so enormously increased that the company suspected a faulty registration.'[66] Working-class housewives, for whom money, space and time were scarce, experienced difficulties most acutely. The initial assessment of available rooms for evacuees did not consider the size of the rooms only the number. The inequality of this became more obvious in 1940–1 when the need to accommodate people in reception areas was greatest and the availability of suitable billets shortest. Some cases of indiscriminate billeting led to excessive overcrowding and even greater enforced domestic intimacy, tension and difficulties for all concerned. In Stoke-on-Trent, a report produced in the late 1940s was full of examples of this including a woman and her husband with only a two bedroom terraced house who had a family consisting of a mother, her son of 16 and her three daughters between the ages of 10 and 14 billeted on them.[67]

The extra work and expense of looking after children with physical or emotional problems was in time an issue for those coping with long-term evacuees. The notes of an interview by Liverpool University investigators with one hostess who had grown up children but felt defeated by looking after a 7-year-old give an indication of the problems women were expected to grapple with:

> I am willing to go on trying, but I am tired of his dirty ways. Soils his pants nearly every day. Didn't do it for the first fortnight, stopped recently then started again. Says he has no time to go to the lavatory, must get out to play. I don't see any need to take him to the doctor, its just carelessness. He doesn't want to leave and gets upset if I say he will have to go. It has upset everything. I'm tied to the house all the time … It means a lot of work and there is all this washing.[68]

More than half the rural homes had no inside water, so washing on this scale was hard physical work involving carrying and then heating the water that used expensive and scarce fuel. Focusing attention on the work involved in the care of evacuees brought discussion about the financial costs of bringing up children into the public sphere and may have added legitimacy to the interwar campaigns for the payment of family allowances.[69] Debate about the care of evacuees suffering from non-notifiable infectious diseases also edged towards consideration of the possibility of payment for domestic labour. The Worcestershire County Medical Officer wrote to the Clerk of the Council pointing out that if more money was paid to foster mothers then evacuees would be able to remain in their billet or they would be able to find enough suitable billets and avoid the alternative of removing children to 'an isolation hospital where the maintenance rate would be higher and more important still'.[70] In time billeting allowances were temporarily increased when evacuee-children were off school ill, requiring extra care. Thus the evacuation scheme came to affirm women's domestic caring roles as work, sometimes needing to be paid for.

The tightness of some rural housewives' budgets, as they sought to look after evacuees on the billeting allowance made some very tetchy about the arrival of children's parents on visits. They did not have the wherewithal to provide cups of tea, using their precious sugar ration, or meals for visitors; in addition, they had not necessarily got the space for them to come and stay. Many were already coping with shortages of mattresses and bedding or unexpected damage to household items and soft furnishing which had taken years to make. The purchase of capital items was particularly difficult for those with limited finances and household budgets. Wear and tear on foster homes could lead to hardship and one householder from Hednesford wrote to Cannock District Council to complain about broken crockery, a torn pillowcase and spoiled bedding and asked, '[W]ho pays for this damage?'[71] This householder was not alone in their exasperation, as Staffordshire Federation of Women's Institutes noted,

> The country householder has been magnificent in the ways in way she has buckled to her problems – but she will need the strength and cheerfulness of ten if she is to come through. There is undoubtedly a growing feeling 'that the healthy, thrifty and good countryside is being sacrificed to the slums'.[72]

Government schemes, supported by voluntary agencies were set up to provide extra camp beds, pillows, blankets and clothes, but the compensation scheme to pay for damages did not always operate quickly or efficiently and favoured those housewives who were more articulate and had time to spend writing letters and pursuing officials. There were also often delays in ration books being sent to new billets or in the payment of billeting allowance when children were moved.

One of the biggest financial pressures foster mothers faced was to ensure growing children were appropriately clothed. This was supposed to be their parents' responsibility. Foster mothers had been 'promised that every child would come with a complete change of clothing [but often found they] had to spend their savings in re-clothing and re-shoeing.'[73] Biological mothers did not always have the means to clothe their children or understand clothing needed for the country, on a farm, or with a long walk along a wet rural track or road to get to school. Many foster mothers held the view that they were not getting the money and support from children's biological mothers that they were due; sometimes, children's mothers were hard to trace. Marjorie Clowes who joined a family with four sons in Talke Pits recalled that her foster mother, Mrs Sumnall, struggled to get the money that she should have had for her clothing from her biological mother.[74] Foster mothers begged, borrowed, bought and made clothes for their evacuees and were then exasperated if the youngsters returned home and neither clothes nor child were seen again.

There was also confusion and messiness about who was responsible for what in relation to evacuees, who could make decisions about health care, dentistry, schools which should ideally have been sorted out between the foster mother and their child's parents but in an era when the majority of working-class households did not have phones, communication was not straightforward. For children evacuated abroad, the British Ambassador in the United States or Governor General in Commonwealth countries was deemed to be their 'sole guardian' following the passing of the Temporary Migration (Guardianship) Act in June 1941. Nevertheless, the responsibility that many foster mothers found they had on their shoulders was immense – parents were hard to contact and, with the disruption of war and the distress of separation, were often not as communicative as some foster mothers would have liked. Marie Williamson looking after Margaret Sharp's three boys in Canada wrote repeatedly to ask if their mother approved her eldest son's having his tooth straightened, tonsils and adenoids removed, following advice from the dentist and doctor. Eventually, a telegram arrived confirming that this was acceptable.[75] With no visits home to give the foster mothers a temporary break and concern as the conflict was showing no signs of ending many American sponsors found it 'financially very hard to carry on'.[76] Some foster-mothers were able to shift their responsibilities on to others, within their family or even to boarding schools. But for others the cost of looking after evacuees became burdensome; although 6s. (30 pence) a week arrived regularly from the Children's Overseas Reception Board (CORB), currency restrictions meant that they could not appeal to children's parents for any extra assistance.

Going home and adoption

Despite the challenges, many foster mothers became emotionally attached to their evacuees; they were the children they had never had, replaced a child they had lost or were a delightful addition to their families. They cared for their evacuees, for weeks, months or even years and, consequently, it could be a sad or traumatic experience when the children they had grown to love were returned to their biological families. If this occurred before the end of the war, it was also tinged with the fear that children were still at risk of being killed by bombing. As 1945 began, it was clear the end of the conflict was near. The Home Guard had stood down, the beaches were being cleared of barbed wire, many parts of the county were no longer in danger and large numbers of evacuees had returned home. Nevertheless, when in January 1945 Bettine Saffery's foster parents were telephoned and asked if they could get her and her sister ready to return home, they did not respond well. The couple, who had no children of their own, were very distressed and wrote to Bettine's mother and explained that after five years they could not quickly prepare the children for return.[77] The two girls eventually went home in March, when victory in Europe seemed imminent, leaving their distraught foster mother standing by her gate in flood of tears. Bettine and her sister kept in touch with them and heard that 'apparently they missed us so much that they considered fostering some children from Holland or Denmark' as Bettine later considered, '[T]hey must have been devastated when we came home, it must have been awful, like giving your children away.'[78]

Ken Marple remembers seeing his foster mother, who he called mum, crying as a car drove him away after five years in Blithbury, Staffordshire.[79] Likewise, as Gwenda Brady was driven away from her billet, after three years in the Lake District, her mother remarked that her foster mother's face was as white as a sheet. Gwenda later contemplated, 'I had become the daughter Aunty and Uncle did not have and I know that they missed me very much. However I did go to Aunty and Uncle's during my next school holiday and it remained my second home for the rest of my childhood.'[80] Finding the situation awkward some children seem to have carelessly caused terrible hurt to the women who had done so much for them. When Maureen Haslam was moved from Norfolk to Staffordshire, she recalled, 'I just, I think I just went blank I couldn't say goodbye. I wouldn't look at Mr and Mrs Haylett when I said goodbye I just got on the bus and stared straight ahead.'[81] Likewise, Lily Nye was aware that although she exchanged a few letters and photographs with her foster mother and despite her mother chivvying her to write, communication stopped and everyone 'got on with their busy lives.'[82]

Some foster-mothers sought to control the situation and continue their relationship with their wartime children. Although the government organized trains and escorts to return evacuees home, a foster-mother from Standon Bridge, Staffordshire informed the billeting officers that she would escort her evacuee back home to Kent herself. She had arranged this with the permission of her evacuee's mother although the journey involved considerable time, effort and expense.[83] By physically handing the responsibility for a returning evacuee back to their parents many foster-mothers reassured themselves the evacuees they had cared for would be alright in the future. It was also an attempt to maintain a relationship between the foster and biological mothers who sometimes had become friends during brief or prolonged visits during the conflict. Oral histories and autobiographies recount numerous stories of long-term relationships between evacuees and their foster parents, when evacuees were seen as part of their foster parent's extended family, albeit an elective family that they had to some extent chosen. For years after the conflict ended, evacuees visited their foster parents in the holidays, exchanging cards and gifts or attended weddings and other family events.

Not all children returned home; parents were sometimes ill or difficult to trace, so some foster mothers continued to care for evacuees after the end of the war. Eileen Faires' father was ill and then died in 1947, so she remained with her foster mother on a farm near Leek, Staffordshire until January 1948. For her foster mother the wrench when Eileen was finally taken home was terrible, as Eileen's recollections suggest: 'I couldn't understand why they were all crying and er, I always called Mrs Clowes Aunty and Mr Clowes Uncle, and Mrs Clowes was saying to my mother she was a wicked woman for taking me away'.[84] After seven years it must have seemed to Mrs Clowes that Eileen was more her child than her biological mother's. Some stayed even longer, Peter Allen remained in Staffordshire for nine years, as his father was ill with a brain tumour and things were 'pretty dire' for his mother. His foster parents agreed to keep him until he left school at 15 and his mother found a job for him in London.[85]

Foster parents may have contemplated what would happen if an evacuee's parents were killed from bombing or fighting in the services. Some children had already lost one or both their parents, and there was concern about whether the other parent would be able to look after their children. Bernard Donnell, whose father had died some years before the war, was from a family of eight children. He was evacuated to Staffordshire in 1940; five years later Mr and Mrs Allen, who he describes as 'incredibly kind. just so wonderful … wanted desperately' for him to stay. They had two daughters and had clearly enjoyed having a boy.[86] Bernard was keen to go home and did; however, oral histories indicate a number of children 'didn't want to go back at all'.[87] Ernest Chadwick from Manchester remembers that within a week of arriving in Brown Edge he had decided he was not going back; he hid when his father came to visit him and was eventually formally adopted at the age of 18.[88] Likewise Albert Cross from Manchester remembered, 'I fell in love with Leek the moment I got off the train really, walking up Broad Street. I thought it very nice and the more I saw of it the more I liked it, I still do'.[89] Marjorie Clowes was also so well integrated into her host families that they adopted her.[90] Adoptions were unusual but not at all exceptional, a tribute to the caring and love that many foster mothers showered upon the strangers who came into their homes in wartime.

Conclusion

At the end of the war, foster mothers received a letter from the King and Queen thanking them for caring for 'children who were in danger',[91] recognizing their domestic and emotional work caring for evacuees as part of the war effort. For some it had been an unbelievable trial, a horrendous imposition by the government into the domestic, intimate space of their home, they lost control of their personal family lives in the service of the national war effort. The work of foster-mothers placed domesticity and motherhood under public scrutiny, it legitimated campaigns for family allowances and even acted as a forerunner for debates about wages for housework.

The vast majority of foster mothers invested time, money, effort and emotion into caring for the evacuees who temporarily or permanently extended their families. Regrettably, in the popular iconography and myth that now surrounds evacuation, their efforts are all too frequently forgotten. The task of caring for evacuees did not rest entirely upon their shoulders; there were many other women who volunteered or were paid to care for evacuees, who were surrogate or social mothers to evacuees, including teachers, who will be discussed in the next chapter.

6

Women paid to care: Teachers and welfare workers

The removal of thousands of children from their own mothers necessitated the employment by national and local governments of a predominantly female labour force replacing the roles and responsibilities previously undertaken within families. Many teachers employed in elementary, secondary, private schools or camps were also expected to undertake maternal tasks to ensure children's welfare beyond the classroom, accompanying them to medical appointments, keeping them occupied in the holidays and ensuring children were adequately clothed. A number of women who worked in hostels, sickbays and boarding houses, assisted children in their transit to reception areas, coordinated those responsible for children's welfare and helped to support evacuee children and their families.

Women had carved out professional careers in education and welfare since the latter part of the nineteenth century, re-enforcing, rather than challenging the idea of women as 'natural' carers of children.[1] They were often motivated by a sense of social or spiritual motherhood, a religious and maternal duty to care for the vulnerable and less fortunate.[2] The status of teaching had risen in the twentieth century as teacher-training colleges replaced on the job training,[3] to be considered an acceptable profession for middle-class young women in the inter-war years and 71 per cent of the workforce in elementary schools were women by 1938.[4] Secondary school teaching remained the fate of the majority of women graduates in the 1930s although as Carol Dyhouse points out their search for teaching posts was often 'a dispiriting task', and that they 'had had to make seemingly endless applications before securing a job.'[5] The shortage of jobs led to the stricter operation of the marriage bar in this era.[6] It was assumed that women who married would want to focus their energies on their homes and have children.[7] In the Second World War as young men were called up, the teaching profession became increasingly feminized and older. Retired male teachers or women previously forced to leave the profession upon marriage were generally welcomed back into the classroom, although some local authorities continued to try and resist married teachers.[8] Maureen Haslam later recalled,

> You'd got the odd one or two who were elderly who had been teachers who used to teach you all right, but a lot of them tried to teach you but they hadn't got a clue. The only thing that we were taught well was reading, writing and arithmetic but apart from that nothing else.[9]

Well-meaning, but not necessarily very competent, volunteers and classroom assistants were a cheap supplement to qualified teachers. Betty Duddell became an uncertified teacher at Prince's Street Junior School in Wellington, in Shropshire in November 1939, working for over three years. She remembers her monthly salary was £7–7s. –3d. (£7:37 pence) while certified teachers 'earned over £11 per month'.[10]

The Second World War evacuation scheme also produced a multitude of new working opportunities and responsibilities to support evacuees' welfare. Jean Redman was a 15-year-old girl when initially employed to help with the administration of the evacuees in Bedford town hall in 1939. After combining part-time work for the local council with half-time schoolwork for a while, she was given the opportunity to be employed full-time on evacuee issues. She worked alongside the welfare officer dealing with problems raised by evacuees and foster-parents, a messenger between people, typing letters and dealing with cases when evacuees were moved.[11] She was one of numerous women paid to care, the vast majority of whom made their contribution to the war effort with good spirit, even in the face of inconvenience and even danger, often going well beyond the call of duty.

Transporting children to safety

The government's realization that war was almost inevitable led to an order given over the radio at 9 o'clock on a Thursday, 24 August 1939 for London teachers to return to their schools. It disturbed many of the profession enjoying the end of their summer holidays 'in crowded seaside lodgings, peaceful villages, scattered houses of friends'.[12] In the next few days as evacuation plans were enacted the worlds of teachers whose schools were to be evacuated and those in reception areas awaiting the arrival of evacuees were turned upside down. In 'danger' areas, teachers found their schools were closed and they and their pupils were moved to another part of the country. Teachers had no more knowledge or control over where this would go than evacuees and their parents. Although somehow the Headmistress of Morrison Junior School, Mossley Hill, Liverpool managed to get her school re-allocated from Teifi Valley to Flintshire.[13] The upheaval and uncertainty of the disruption to teachers' working and personal lives led to a sense of doom, for some. One pupil-teacher at a girls' school noted on 1 September, '[W]e gave a pathetic little leaving party to Miss F. who had joined the staff of an evacuating school.'[14] After a presentation of a book voucher and a sponge bag, there was tea and cake, but nobody seemed very happy.

Between them, the Ministry of Health and Local Education Officers expected evacuation in England and Wales to be organized so that 'school identity should be preserved' with 'maximum possible opportunities for contact between evacuee children and their teachers'[15] who were thrust into the role of surrogate mothers. Children taking part in the government evacuation scheme initially gathered at their local schools where medical examinations and paperwork were supposed to be organized. Some schools had been undertaking regular practice runs for evacuation since the Munich crisis of 1938. A number of London schools had perfected procedures for walking in crocodiles and crossing the street en-masse to ensure their journey to the station was as orderly and as safe as possible. A teacher evacuated from Walthamstow noted in her diary for Mass Observation, '[W]e teachers became absolutely tired of the very mention of the word 'evacuation'. There was nothing that had been overlooked with regard to the organization and administration in order that this big undertaking should be carried out smoothly and efficiently.'[16]

The responsibility of getting the pupils from their school to the reception area in good spirits rested upon the teachers, assisted by couriers, volunteers, some mothers who had chosen to be evacuated with their children as paid helpers and the Women's Voluntary Service (WVS). A young woman who took on the role of courier in Stratford East London recalled how they 'lined the children up to check they had everything they had been told to bring and with many tearful farewells marched to Stratford Main Station to wait for the train to take us to some unknown place.'[17] However, as evacuees recall, railways stations were packed with soldiers, sailors, prospective evacuees and often parents all milling about. Teachers, as a Mass Observation investigator at Victoria Station noted, were: 'mostly smiling' talking confidently to parents reassuring them: 'they'll be alright'.[18] Some teachers regarded parents as a 'nuisance upsetting children with their crying' when children were looking forward to going away on a holiday; or were also exasperated by those parents who had registered their children for evacuation but had not turned up.[19] School parties were broken down into small groups as George Emptage travelling on a train for the first time, recalled 'when we got on the train we was allocated to certain compartments with a grown up'.[20] A teacher accompanying some thirty little ones of between 5 and 7 years of age from a school in Walthamstow to Hertfordshire had given some forethought to the journey and recorded in her diary, 'The children were very excited on the railway journey and the barley sugars which we teachers had found room for in our ruck-sacs were a great boom.'[21] Unfortunately the authorities had not put the same degree of forward planning into arranging accommodation for teachers, which had been overlooked, leaving her to rely upon local helpers to find her a bed that night.

All went very smoothly for some schools, the head teacher of Albany Road School in Camberwell, South London, recorded how 204 children were assembled by 11 am, transported by four trams to near Waterloo station where they boarded the 12.30 pm train, arriving at Wareham station in Dorset three hours later. Then 'the children left the train, passed through the medical tent (no casualties to report), received cups of tea and biscuits, boarded buses and were brought to Central School, Weymouth, where they were billeted in private houses.'[22] By 11 pm, all children were settled into their foster homes. For other schools, things did not go quite so smoothly. As the numbers who turned up for evacuation were lower than expected, transport was reallocated. Military mobilization, as the country readied for war, meant the rail network was awash with troops with the result that evacuee trains were frequently placed into sidings to let troop trains pass; journeys were long, access to loos minimal and children became tired, bedraggled and fractious. Teachers with their weary charges often arrived in numbers or places that they were not entirely expected. Juliet Gardiner has pointed out that Pwllheli, North Wales, received approximately four hundred evacuees that they had not anticipated and Dorothy King, the teacher of Mary Datchelor School, Camberwell whose pupils were consequently billeted across a number of villages, recalled, 'I have had few worse hours in my life than those I spent watching the school being taken off in drizzling rain and gathering gloom to those unknown villages, knowing I was powerless to do anything about it.'[23] Some schools evacuated to West Sussex similarly found themselves spread across eight villages and exasperated head teachers had to stand by as their advice was ignored by billeting officers at the stations.[24]

Teachers felt a strong sense of responsibility for the evacuees they accompanied, even if they were themselves relatively inexperienced. Nora Landon, helping in a reception area, noted that the teachers were thoughtful and kind and, 'the anchor person for the children. They were somebody they'd got with them they knew. All the rest of us of course were people that, well they didn't know who we were.'[25]

Irene Watts with only a year's teaching experience was evacuated with her pupils from Dagenham on a Thames Pleasure Boat to Lowestoft. There, she and another young teacher found themselves in charge of twenty 5–7-year-olds. After a night spent sleeping on straw on the floor of a school with rations of 'bread, margarine, crumbly red cheese and bruised apples' for children with tea and meat paste sandwiches provided as supplements for staff, accommodation was eventually found. It lacked the utilities that urban teachers were used to 'there was no electricity, no sewerage, a pump in the yard, and an earth closet round the back. But we were made very welcome.' Irene happily remained in this billet until summer 1940 when the school was re-evacuated away from the coast.[26] Barnett House Evacuation Survey commended the commitment of teachers to the welfare of evacuees. Thus the headmistress of a Girl's School from London 'tried to provide and maintain a sound balance between billet and school and supervised nearly all the children herself'.[27] Similarly, a Sister of a religious order, who had known many of her pupils at the London Catholic Elementary School since their birth, took 'an active interest in billeting and re-billeting … she tried to place them in billets which were real homes and within reasonable distance of church and school' when they arrived in Oxfordshire.[28]

For women who accompanied children evacuated abroad, there was both a greater responsibility and a greater danger. It is perhaps unfair to describe those working with CORB in 1940 as paid. They did receive £5 for voyages to Canada, £12 for South Africa and £20 for Australia but as trips took months, this was a rather small recompense for their time and costs. Interestingly the escorts did not have to be able to swim or to have extensive experience of working with children but they did have to undergo a lengthy interview; something Vera Brittain undertook after her own two children were evacuated to the United States. She summarized some of the guidance they were given on the nature of their role:

> Take charge of fifteen children, probably all ages and both sexes, and look after them on the boat from start to finish. You'll have to assume the responsibility as if you were their mother, wherever you go and whatever the conditions. It will mean getting them up and putting them to bed, seeing that they go to their meals and eat the proper food, as well as keeping them amused all through the voyage … And if it's the Atlantic it's certain to be rough, and you may find yourself in charge of fifteen seasick children all the way across.[29]

Approximately fifteen thousand people were interviewed and five hundred escorts, often described as couriers, selected. As Vera Brittain pointed out, they had the responsibility for ensuring children cleaned their teeth, took their tablets and got to sleep. More importantly, perhaps, they had to deal with a mixture of emotions from panic and homesickness to tensions within the friendship groups on board. P. L. Travers in *I Go by Sea, I Go by Land* (1941), an extraordinarily fictional portrayal of her journey with her adopted son and two friends' children to the United States in 1940, described the couriers providing a source of emotional support and care, and reassuring the children on arrival: 'This is a safe place. This is America.'[30]

Couriers worked under a lead escort, such as Nancy Tresawna, who was described as 'a lady of thirty-five and dressed in a twinset, tweeds, little stockings and sensible shoes. She was extremely nice and very efficient'. She was also dedicated to the welfare of the children under her care although she called them 'horrid little brats'. She was observed 'going from one end of the ship to the other to fetch a blanket for a child who looked a little cold.'[31] Some boats carried women and children only, to make them less of a target; nevertheless, Emlyn Davies and Sister Phyllis Matthews were among a number of escorts on the SS *Rangitane* when it was sunk on its return journey from New Zealand in November 1940. They were picked up by a German warship and eventually repatriated, by which time Sister Matthews, injured during the attack, had wounds on her face and left hand while her right arm had to be amputated. She received no compensation from the Government, even when she was recovering from her injuries and unable to work. Emlyn Davies died during the attack; her husband, who seems to have regarded his wife as on loan to the government, wrote to the CORB director asking for recompense as:

> Put brutally Mrs Davies' death had meant my finding another person to attend to the household duties of house ... Having been deprived of my wife while she was executing her duty on behalf of your board. I naturally look [to you] to make compensation as shall be adequate for the deprivation involved.[32]

His claim was turned down, but does suggest the complex blurring of volunteering and working, housewifely, maternal and national roles, which surrounded both the work of escorts, couriers, teachers and housewives at this point in time. Emlyn Davies was not the only woman to die as a result of her role helping to transport evacuees to safety. In November 1940 the SS Port of Wellington was also attacked on its way home from Australia. Edith McLean, a 50-year-old spinster and 27-year-old Joan Fieldgate were two of the escorts who were picked up and transferred first to a German prisoner ship and then to a prisoner-of-war (POW) camp in Liebenau. Joan never returned home as she died from dysentery, contracted in the camp.[33]

Teachers in the reception areas

For teachers, the journey and billeting soon appeared simple compared to the challenges of providing an education for thousands of extra children now in reception areas. The government guidelines that schools should retain their own identity did not match the facilities available. For the first two weeks of the academic year in 1939, schools were closed while teachers tried to organize existing accommodation for extra classes. Nearby buildings were appropriated, storerooms and offices cleared and halls divided, but even if there was adequate space there was rarely adequate equipment. The head teacher of Walhouse Girls School, Penkridge Road, Cannock pointed out that '[w]e have no available seats in this school at present. Every table in the hall is occupied and in the middle room last week there were forty seven girls in forty six seats ... I filled in a form to that effect last week ... at the moment every yard of floor space is being used'[34]. Ken Durston, evacuated to Somerset, recalled, 'We were all crammed up. You didn't have a single desk; it was all doubles – we'd sit two to a desk'[35] Later during the conflict, existing schools were sometimes expected to just absorb another school. Dicky Blood recalled the challenges teachers faced when his Birmingham School was evacuated to a small village school in Yoxall, Staffordshire with 80–90 children, which received an extra 100 evacuees. On the first day, 'there were kids everywhere. The evacuees seemed to outnumber the locals and were much noisier and cheekier'. Teachers tried to complete forms and registers 'while Miss Baker the school headmistress was organizing supplies of school materials, seating and hot Horlicks twice daily in the cold weather.'[36] Alternatively, Maureen Haslam recalled, '[W]e were taught in the Queen's Head, the pub and in the Working Men's club for lessons 'cause the school wasn't big enough to take all the influx of evacuees.'[37]

A number of strategies were adopted to accommodate the evacuees in reception areas, including the use of a 'double shift' whereby one school attended in the morning and the other in the afternoon thereby sharing school premises. In 1939 the Log Book for Norton Green School recorded such a system enabling them to accommodate ninety-nine Manchester evacuees; the schools swopped shifts from week to week. Such arrangements were expected to be accompanied by outdoor activities for those children not in the classrooms, as one evacuee recalled, 'We didn't go to school very much and that pleased me terrifically. We'd go to the school, all right but then the teacher would take us for a walk. We never seemed to have any formal lessons.'[38] Jan Pollard remembered that when she was evacuated to Ross-on-Wye, the teachers took them to historical sites such as Goodrich Castle, to abbeys and to farms.[39] Such arrangements significantly increased the working day of the poor teachers as the diary of May Smith in Swadlincote in Derbyshire suggests. In the first week after her school opened there was rain, outdoor activities were impractical and so after having taught in the morning she was delighted to have finished her work and be home early in the afternoon. But on 21 September 1939 she records,

> Oh dear! This shift system likes me not. Too much toil and stress involved. Feel as though I've finished my day's work at 12, instead of not having started. This morn we misguidedly took 4 classes for a ramble over Stoney's Nob and up Brindle Lane. We had an unending noisy crocodile of some 200 little dears and staggered up Springfield Road with them while faces poked out of every window and doorway and dogs leapt yapping at their gates. Grimly we plodded on, trying to look unconcerned until we got to the fields, where we relaxed a little. Halfway through we halted and Miss Smith conducted them in song, then off we set again. Trailed exhaustedly home at 11:30.[40]

May Smith then had to teach her class as usual in the afternoon. For many such teachers in reception areas, the challenges of dealing with unusual working patterns were exasperated by the roles they had 'volunteered' for as billeting officers. When in October 1940 May Smith rushed, at the end of the day of teaching, to a meeting of billeting officers she saw 'the rest of the local teaching profession assembled there' who were then instructed to find billets for numerous children due to arrive the following day.[41]

The teachers struggled on, if the weather was good overcrowding was eased by extra time spent on sports, nature walks, gardening clubs and anything else that teachers could think of to get children outdoors. Planning and managing evacuation both required a huge input of resources and time. School logbooks indicate head teachers dashing to meetings with the local education authorities (LEAs) throughout the whole period of the war; one from a senior girls' school in Hednesford, Staffordshire pointed out that a further difficulty was being given only a day's notice to be a member of an evacuation tribunal and indicated she needed more warning for such a task. Furthermore, school logbooks provide ample evidence that the numbers on school roles were never stable, constantly fluctuating, unofficial evacuees further exacerbated overcrowding. No sooner did the poor teachers think they had got a working system than external factors caused an influx of new evacuees.

In 1940 the Ministry of Information (MOI) produced a short eleven-minute film, *Village School*,[42] designed to reassure the mothers of evacuees about the wonderful education their children were receiving in the reception areas. It was shown both in cinemas and in village halls and factories or to community groups. *Village School* was filmed on location in Ashley Green in Berkshire, where two matronly teachers were looking after a multitude of local and evacuee children in a sunny rural school. Mrs James, the head teacher, has been described as the star of the film, managing three classes single-handedly, some doing arithmetic, others geography and a third group spending time on their own outside. In another building, the infants were again divided into three classes, under the care of one teacher. The viewer was reassured that through their lessons and by undertaking tasks, such as collecting milk from a local farm and gathering wood chips for winter firewood, children are 'learning more and more what they can get on with themselves'. The portrayal of the children knitting socks, helmets, mittens and scarfs for soldiers, collecting scrap iron, paper and growing vegetables assimilated the youngsters into the war effort, they too were making a contribution to the people's war. The many advantages of this rural idyll created by these two hardworking teachers in what would otherwise be a cramped school are all however weather dependent. The children eat their lunch outside, they play on the village green for an hour and half a day and the sun shines throughout. The rather more unpredictable British weather made most teachers' everyday working lives in overcrowded, rural schools rather more stressful.

Village School also explained that with thirty evacuees in the village, foster mothers looked to the teachers to sort out a range of problems, evacuees and their carers encountered. Children's emotional welfare had by 1940 sometimes suffered from a nomadic life between reception and danger areas, sporadic school attendance, experiences of bombing, family bereavement and other factors making them more challenging to teach. Then in 1940 the Board of Education wrote to Local Authorities as the summer holiday approached and suggested, '[C]hildren should during the school holiday be taken off the hands of the householders as much as possible'.[43] Buildings and playgrounds were to be kept open, teachers released from holidays in rotation and 'steps … taken to secure the services of helpers from voluntary organisations to assist in arranging and supervising out-of-school activities for the children during part of the day'.[44]

This transferred the stress of looking after evacuees in school holidays from foster mothers onto teachers and voluntary and paid helpers.

Some teachers undertook a multitude of extracurricular activities with enthusiasm; others found fulfilling the new expectations placed upon them a struggle and felt that the assumption of unswerving commitment to their part of the war effort, as portrayed in MOI films like *Village School*, added to their strain. In August 1940 May Smith was less than enamoured when yet another task added to her daily workload:

> A blow awaited at school – all windows to be covered with net – by us!
>
> Trissie offered to come after school, and Miss H but I didn't intend to. When I leave school at 4, I leave for the day, when the bally Education Committee is mean enough to pinch our holidays. So we made a start in school time, and the children stayed in the yard while we got on with the job. Glory! What a Job! Began by conscientiously doing every pane myself, but after a while let the children help – and of course they were all too willing to have a finger in the pie. Derek D cut net so vigorously that he raised huge blisters on his fingers.[45]

The determination of some teachers like May Smith to leave school promptly at the end of the day was undermined when they were expected to undertake fire watching duties in the evening, and her diary records teachers' union meetings that indicate many teachers increasingly felt exploited or deskilled.[46] Both the dedicated teachers and those for whom teaching was a meantime job, a precursor to marriage, were disgruntled or preoccupied at times. May Smith's diaries often seem predominantly concerned about her world outside work, the challenges of purchasing clothes and her two seemingly lacklustre boyfriends.

Evacuated teachers

For some teachers evacuation was the start of a new life and in Thornbury, Gloucestershire, Brigit McKearney, who accompanied sixty pupils from The Esplanade School in Harwich in July 1940, settled into town life so well that she remained, working in the local school after the war.[47] Many others did not appreciate being evacuated to an unknown area, away from their family and friends. In May Smith's Derbyshire school the gossip suggested that the Birmingham teachers were moaning about the cold in Autumn and that it was thought perhaps best they did not know what it would be like in winter.[48] Weather was only one of many unfamiliar aspects of reception areas. Some teachers found rural villages too quiet and one complained to a Mass Observation investigator that, '[W]hile I was away, there was no intellectual or social advantage proffered by anyone. The blackout made visiting friends and colleagues in the country very difficult.'[49] For others the countryside was not quiet enough. Miss Sparkes, evacuated to Cannock, Staffordshire, noted, 'The Germans followed the children it seems, at least by air as they started to raid the towns and cities in the Midlands ... Brownhills was set alight by incendiaries and the smell of charred cloth wafted across Chasetown.'[50]

The distribution of teachers rarely matched that of the shifting populations of children, some teachers were run off their feet others were struggling to find work. Specialist secondary school teachers – such as science teachers – had difficulties identifying appropriate facilities. Those who taught domestic science tended to be underemployed throughout the war, as food and other materials needed for their lessons were in short supply so this area of the curriculum was cut; alternatively they were reallocated to managing the canteen or feeding children. Thus when Susie Fisher was offered a job of teaching Domestic Science for Portsmouth High School, which was evacuated to near Petersfield, Hampshire, it was on the understanding that she would spend half her time looking after the school's domestic arrangements and organizing the catering.[51]

In many areas merging host and evacuee schools together became the most viable alternative to match teachers and pupil numbers as evacuees drifted home. Norton Green, in Staffordshire, which had initially used the shift system in September 1939, incorporated their remaining thirty evacuees with local children in April 1940. Some evacuated teachers spent much of the war in the complex position of being employed by one council and working in many respects for another; they were, however, reticent to accept the lower pay of many rural schools. Some commentators were excited about the potential merging schools provided for teacher's professional development. Teachers, it was suggested, would learn new methods from one another and introduce innovative and imaginative approaches to education, including the greater use of radio in the classroom.[52] The distinctive cultures of many schools undermined this, particularly when schools had a strong religious identity that teachers, parents and church leaders felt it was their moral duty to protect. Religion often signifies separation and difference; Jewish children were sent out of the classroom during assembly in many state schools in this era.[53] In Staffordshire, the Catholic schools, evacuated from Kent in 1940, were placed in a range of other schools in the area and removed from lessons for two hours a day to receive Catholic Instruction. This policy was not considered acceptable when Catholic children arrived in the Cannock area from Liverpool in 1941; the subsequent aggravation involved local and national government departments. The majority of the Liverpool children were not billeted with Catholic families but on the instructions of Fathers Healey and Hickson of Mount Lourdes, Hednesford, were squeezed into the local Catholic school, St Josephs. The school roll rose from 192 to 259 and with severe overcrowding many children did not have a desk.[54] Father Healey had identified potential premises for another Catholic school to be set up; but the director of education for Cannock, mindful no doubt of the transience of some evacuees, was unwilling take such an action which would be costly.

Father Healey and Liverpool teachers, backed up by letters from Liverpool parents and eventually the Archbishop of Liverpool, demanded what they saw as the inalienable right of Catholic children to have a Catholic education and saw the actions of the Cannock LEA as an attack on the principle of separate religious education. Teachers from Catholic schools in Liverpool refused to enter non-Catholic schools in Staffordshire. There were rumours of pressure and harassment of evacuees by Catholic teachers and by Father Healey who saw himself as both responsible for and having authority over the spiritual welfare of all Catholic children in the area. One Liverpool evacuee claimed to have been beaten by a Catholic teacher for attending a Methodist Sunday school with her foster parents.[55] The sentiments expressed, in what became an increasingly acrimonious row, undermined any notion of the Second World War as a 'people's war'. Many Catholic teachers, supported by religious leaders and parents appeared to consider the threat of children being educated with non-Catholics as more severe than bombing, Father Healey went so far as to describe the authorities 'as completing the work begun by Hitler'.[56]

Financial pressures and the inadequacy of government funding lay behind many problems evacuated teachers had to contend with. This began with the inadequate or inappropriate buildings in which teaching took place that must have come as something of a shock. Roy Cartwright's teacher had to content with a classroom, which was a shed behind the pub:

> It had a corrugated iron roof, which meant that in heavy rain the teacher couldn't be heard. One side was open and chickens ran in and out. A few yards away was a pigsty whose inhabitants had a habit of starting to grunt just as the class had been brought to silence.[57]

Children were quick to take advantage of teachers' uncertainty as they sought to educate their pupils in unfamiliar surroundings. The inevitable nature ramble was particularly tricky for urban teachers, apt to find themselves challenged by requests from their pupils to identify various rural fawn and flora, egged on by rural children. One described how, as much as she frantically sought to mug up, children likewise scrambled into ditches and other discrete places to find some obscure plant for her to identify. Another savvier teacher responded with exclamations of surprise at the urban child's ignorance and pointed out that the country children would definitely know and suggested asking them to illuminate.[58]

For larger schools, particularly secondary schools, there was frequently impromptu use of buildings of varying suitability. One strategy to provide space for evacuated schools in classrooms spread across a number of different schools, with the evacuated head teacher dashing between various school sites. Thus St Saviour's Church of England School from Westgate-on-Sea was based in Colton, Staffordshire, but its classes were also located in the neighbouring villages of Mavesyn Ridware and Hamstall Ridware. There were tensions between the Board of Education and the Treasury about the potential costs of hiring extra buildings,[59] and as the war progressed, requisitioning buildings and getting them appropriately fitted out became increasingly difficult as space was needed for other wartime activities. In 1940 attempts to accommodate the Junior House of Chatham House County School for Boys from Ramsgate in Uttoxeter, Staffordshire, proved to be a struggle. Alleyne's Grammar School provided some rooms as did the Wesleyan Sunday School but these lacked appropriate urinals, which a severe shortage of cement prevented from being constructed. As the school waited for the cement someone else identified the Sunday Schools rooms as suitable for a British Restaurant. As Peter Gosden points out, the wrangling between different central and local government departments about the costs incurred by evacuation made teachers working lives wearing.[60] Head teachers struggled with red tape and endless paperwork and a multitude of government circulars. Numerous weekly forms had to be filled and sent to evacuees' home authorities, including milk records, attendance records, school medical officer records and so on.[61]

For those teachers who had their own home, being billeted in someone else's house, living in one room or sharing a kitchen, with nowhere to call their own was less than ideal. Initially some teachers struggled with the expense of paying for their original accommodation and lodgings in reception areas. Returning home to see family and friends was a further unexpected cost. Married male teachers expected their wives to move with them, and if they owned a house, in time this would often have to be sold as paying their mortgage and their rent in the reception area was unsustainable. The government introduced extra financial support for evacuated teachers to address their complaints and grumbling, which were outlined in a leaflet entitled *Allowances and Travelling Facilities for Teachers and Other Transferred Staff,* early in 1940. This explained that teachers would receive two paid, return, third class rail trips home per year and be allowed another three return trips at their own expense. Weekly allowances of 5s. (25 pence) a week were also introduced for those who were not provided with billets and found accommodation with families or friends. Those who were householders were also compensated for the difficulties they faced. The scale of payments was organized to give greater support to those with lower salaries and the examples provided in the leaflet give an indication of financial strain evacuation placed on teachers. For example, 'a woman assistant teacher, Salary Scale I, salary £180 a year who contributed 15s. (75 pence) a week to the rent of her mother's house where she normally lives', or a female assistant teacher, who shared a flat with a friend and paid half rent would receive an allowance of 11s. (55 pence).

Teachers also organized extracurricular activities for those under their care: cycle rides, walks, even hiking holidays in North Wales. Jan Pollard recalled her domestic science teacher took her and her younger sister to see the Walt Disney film *Pinocchio*.[62] The extracurricular activities gave teachers an opportunity to monitor evacuees' welfare and are indicative of shifting relationships between pupils and teachers that Phillip Gardner and Peter Cunningham have identified.[63] Pam Hobbs recalled the Saturday excursions her favourite young teacher took her charges on provided an opportunity to discuss anxieties:

> She actually encouraged us to talk about our families and problems we had or concerns about war news from home. Although she was barely older than some of my sisters, she knew how to assuage young Peter's fears and made us all feel good about our small achievements at school. She also assured us that this war would not last forever.[64]

Thus evacuated teachers went beyond providing education to undertake maternal care of their charges. The *Cambridge Evacuation Survey* concluded that 'there is very clear evidence that an undue burden of duties which should properly belong to Social Workers has been laid upon the teachers'.[65] One teacher, recorded for Mass Observation the range of 'tasks [that] have been the teacher's lot' which included 'taking children (and sitting for two hours) to the clinic, being very tactful and tolerant with foster-parents, washing children who come to school a little worse for wear and attending to their education'.[66]

Schoolteachers, LEAs, parents and foster parents all had some level of responsibility for evacuees, but there was some uncertainty and complexity about where the final responsibility lay that teachers had to navigate. Teachers and social workers or field workers, as they were sometimes called, tried to ease issues between foster home and parents, carried messages and kept in contact with both sets of parents. Obtaining consent for medical and dental treatment became an administrative nightmare. In one case a final decision on who could give permission for a child with a toothache to have an extraction went between LEAs and teachers, as the parents could not be traced at their original address in Kent. In the meantime, a child languished in pain while school head teachers worried about how to fund medical visits. The headmaster of St Gregory's RC School inquired how to get money refunded for the transport costs of two children and the accompanying staff to attend both Wolverhampton and Stafford Hospitals.[67] He was it seems caught in an endless administrative maze trying to ensure his staff and school were not out of pocket. Clothing was a further area of ambiguous and contested issues of responsibility that created extra work for teachers. London County Council compiled an extensive memorandum on *Boots and Clothing for Evacuated children not accompanied by their parents*, suggesting that perhaps teachers should undertake a weekly review of clothing, before completing a 'Form C' which was sent to parents. Teachers found themselves in the unenviable position of negotiating between foster parents and children's families, and many were very relieved when the Women's Voluntary Service stepped in to alleviate the problem.

Boarding and camp schools

The government evacuation scheme predominantly billeted children in private homes, but this was not suitable for all, and there was a consequent mushrooming of professional services and establishments set up to cater for children who were ill, unmanageable or repeated bed-wetters. Children were accommodated in purpose-built camp schools, boarding houses and hostels, while those teachers who already taught at rural boarding schools found that their classes significantly increased as parents with the money to do so chose to send their children to safety in an environment they had some control over.

Teachers at independent schools had a mixed fate in wartime. Miss Bailey, the headmistress of St David's School in Purley, was enjoying two weeks' break in a remote part of the Scottish Highlands in August 1939, avoiding the stress of a daily newspaper. Organizing the majority of her school to be evacuated to Upton Wold Farm in the Cotswolds quickly followed her return to London. A number of the parents chose not to shift their children from a day school in the London suburbs to a boarding school in the countryside, and for the next four years the school operated over two schools 100 miles apart with teachers alternating between the two venues.[68] Mrs Gough, the headmistress of Adcote School in Shrewsbury, 'brought forward the start of the autumn term to the 9 September 1939, but even so many pupils, some of them complete strangers started arriving ten days earlier'.[69]

The difficulty of finding accommodation, relocations, operating across several sites and falling numbers as children were privately evacuated abroad, led to the demise of some schools. In addition, the government requisitioned some independent schools. Miss Davey ran a small Physical Training College with thirty pupils in Kensington at the outbreak of war; her premises were commandeered while she was on holiday in Cornwall. After an attempt to decamp into unsatisfactory premises in Cornwall, she secured premises in Bournemouth. By 1942 parents' anxiety at their girls being educated on the South Coast meant she finally closed her school.[70] Thus even teachers in the privileged atmosphere of private schools found their working lives disrupted, uncertain and precarious. Berkhamsted School for girls hosted 24 staff and 110 girls from Hampstead High School. Furthermore, whatever their personal views or skills, teachers had to include contributions to the war effort into the curriculum. Teachers assisted their pupils in growing vegetables, knitting comforts for troops or at Bruton School for Girls in Somerset providing women and children from bombed areas of Bristol with two weeks of rest and recuperation.[71]

A number of teachers in grammar, high schools or specialist schools in danger areas became boarding schools teachers when they were evacuated and their working days expanded as they and their pupils were located in country houses or even holiday camps on the South Coast at Selsey, West Sussex. When Pamela Hobbs passed her 11+ she left her domestic billet and went to join Westcliff High School for Girls evacuated in Chapel-en-le-Frith, Derbyshire. She was picked up at the station by a teacher who took her to a temporary boarding house which 'had dormitories, a dining hall and library and at 8:30 each morning the girls assembled and walked together in a long crocodile to their school in another house in the village'.[72]

Head teachers were dogged by problems around accommodation. King Edward's Girls Grammar School from Birmingham was lucky enough to be based in the Hall of the Bishops Palace in Lichfield from 1940 until 1943. The

Headmistress must have considered this a suitable site for her school of 160 girls, particularly when she was allocated number nineteen for her accommodation. However the buildings were extremely cold in winter, there was a constant threat that the military would requisition the buildings they used and two houses she had identified for boarding houses were commandeered for nurses in the event of an invasion.[73] The teachers from Clarendon House Girls School of Ramsgate in Kent considered their billet in Baswich House in Stafford a particularly unsuitable building. It was rather too isolated for women to occupy alone at night apparently and the headmistress wrote a number of letters about the potential danger of 'any unbalanced man who might either get into the building for reasons of his own, or who might happen to know there were only women on duty at night'.[74]

The challenges of unsuitable accommodation were a particular blight on the working lives of teachers of physically or mentally disabled children, as Sue Wheatcroft's research demonstrates.[75] The government evacuation scheme that relied upon untrained and unpaid housewives to look after evacuees was not considered feasible for disabled children. Thus many specialist schools undertook a transition from day schools to boarding schools, providing round the clock residential care. This presented particular challenges for teachers, once again extending their responsibilities and working hours. In August 1940, more than two hundred girls and fifty staff were moved from London to Peckforton Castle in Cheshire, under the stewardship of Jessie Thomas. Despite the challenges of running the school in a building, constructed for a very different purpose, Jessie Thomas received glowing reports from His Majesty's Inspectorate (HMI), but not all teachers fared so well. Unfortunately, when inspectors visited the holiday camp in East Sussex, which housed 243 children, 26 teachers and 23 attendants, they noted the head 'appeared nervous and overworked'.[76] In Somerset the inspectors also found all was not running smoothly in a school set up in a holiday camp where teaching assistants refused to work weekends, leaving the teachers and head to try and cope.[77]

The stresses of undertaking twenty-four-hour care of children in unsuitable premises took its toll on many teachers, as the report written by the inspectors who visited the Bristol school for deaf children in 1942 makes clear. The school had evacuated to Ledbury Park in Herefordshire, whose owners seem to have been motivated by the rental income rather than social responsibility and making a contribution to the war effort; they continued to live in the house and were free with their criticism. The school lacked appropriate ventilation, outdoor space, kitchen equipment, urinals or a sick bay. Miss Virgo, the headmistress returned to the school six weeks before the inspection, following a nervous breakdown and extensive sick leave. 'Two assistant teachers had also been ill, and a third admitted to hospital; all illnesses had been attributed to the stress.'[78] Poor Miss Virgo, who had prior to this unsatisfactory evacuation been very well regarded, walked out of the school carrying her suitcase and gave in her resignation to the Bristol LEA.

Residential schools, hostels and infirmaries to look after sick evacuees were also accommodated in large houses, built for other purposes with some adaptions to allow for the children. These establishments were generally intended for youngsters who needed care beyond the scope of most foster mothers. The children's stay was supposed to be temporary, a few weeks or months, until they were ready to return to domestic billets. When children had a contagious disease this was a clear-cut process; thus nurses at Barrow Hall in Staffordshire took care of approximately thirty children with impetigo or scabies for a period of three months, first in isolation beds and later running around the generous grounds. But by 1943 there were also three thousand children across the country in 215 hostels in England and Wales for 'unmanageable children' and smaller cottage homes, which dealt with those who responded to the stress of evacuation by continuing to wet their beds. There was a wide divergence in the attitudes, warmth, skills and training of the women who predominantly worked in these establishments. As Wheatcroft argues, '[M]ost of the staff did hold practical qualifications of some kind, such as catering or household management, some were qualified nurses, teachers or social workers.'[79] Eighteen of the forty-eight looked at, in the *Survey of Hostels for Difficult Children* by the Ministry of Health in 1944, had men in charge, although many women were employed to undertake domestic or household tasks which the youngsters could not do themselves.[80] Indeed the Ministry was of the opinion that in the larger hostels there should be a clear distinction between the caring or teaching staff and the domestic staff to maintain teacher's professional status. In smaller more informal establishments, the assumption that women would do both caring and domestic work, as the 'natural' carers of children, was maintained.

Smaller cottage homes, which looked after evacuees, presided over by women, attempted to recreate a homely atmosphere. Janie Hampton's research has revealed how the Balendoch hostel was set up in Perthshire in 1940 for forty children aged between 5 and 15. Some stayed there for the duration of the war, others while their foster parents had a break. The three women who ran Balendoch did not have formal qualifications, although they had previously organized a summer camp for brownies and girl guides in

Broadstairs in Kent.[81] They were surrogate mothers who took the children to church on Sundays and camping in summer; they introduced the children to the countryside and bought and wrapped presents for them at Christmas. The hostel had a strict timetable, all children were allocated jobs such as table laying and washing up; there was also clear discipline but expediences more akin to domestic rather than institutional care. One of three motherless Ritchie sisters who spend a number of years at Balendoch mused, 'Those exceptional ladies should have received medals for what they did. They were the parents I never had. They were the saints who gave stability and love to over forty children.'[82]

Children at Balendoch and cottage homes usually attended local schools and there are accounts of the wardens taking their young charges into the school on the first day and introducing them to the teachers who they chatted to, just as many mothers would have done. Hostels and cottage homes differed from the residential nurseries, where women, some trained nurses, psychologists or psychoanalysts, looked after younger children who were orphans, motherless or whose mothers were working.[83] Constance Miles, a billeting officer in Surrey, noted in 1942 that she had been to see 'about a dozen three-year-olds at a local war home. Where the mothers are, I don't know. I believe they are making munitions.'[84] All these facilities were responses to failures in a primarily domestic approach to evacuation. In contrast, camp schools were built as a more utopian and professional alternative approach to caring for evacuees.

The National Camps Act, passed in April 1939, allowed for the building of camps for urban children to enjoy a holiday while being introduced to the benefits of rural life. In Staffordshire two camp schools, Pipewood for girls and Shooting Butts for boys were constructed, each intended to provide all year boarding school education for 240 pupils between the ages of 10 and 15 from Birmingham. Pipewood school was constructed out of low wooden huts in 35 acres of grounds, the four (later five) huts which were used for dormitories, each had twenty-four double-decker beds for pupils and two beds for teachers who woke the pupils up each morning and read to them each evening. The teachers in many of these schools were dedicated, idealistic and some perceived themselves as developing a model for post-war reconstruction.[85] An ex-teacher from Pipewood later described how the school offered 'its pupils a really comprehensive education and one which recognised the equal importance of each individual'.[86] Lily Wilson was a recently married young woman with a husband in the forces when she joined the Pipewood in 1940, remaining there for three years when her husband was posted abroad. She may have slept in a dormitory with the girls but also recalled, 'I only taught half the day, I don't know how many classes, I took the English, and I took the dancing and the sports.' In the rest of the day she undertook her marking, wrote to her husband and started up a guide company. Her reflection of her relationship to her pupils was 'not only a kind of surrogate mother to them' but also a friend as she was so close to their age.[87] The school maintained teachers professional status by adhering to the division between domestic staff under the school manager and teachers who looked after the girls both in and out of school hours.[88]

Teachers at Camp Schools were expected to teach practical skills to equip evacuees for domestic or rural life; girls practised answering the telephone as if in an office at Pipewood.[89] One of the teachers, a farmer's daughter, taught them about the care of rabbits, bees, pigs, hens, vegetable-growing and even how to catch kill, pluck and cook a duck. Teachers seemed to have utilized the camp school environment in innovative ways, keeping charts of the productivity of the school hens to teach arithmetic. Lessons were outside in the fine weather, while in winter daylight was used to maximum effect by undertaking activities outside in the afternoon and formal lessons when it was dark after tea. At Christmas, teachers filled Xmas stockings for each girl who remained in the safety of the Staffordshire countryside, although the holiday season was preceded by a carol concert on the monthly visit day when special buses from Birmingham brought parents, who were offered lunch for 6*d*. The visit days did not provide time off for the teachers; the young teacher Lily Wilson recalled how upset the girls who did not have visitors were and that teachers spent 'with them because it was awful when they didn't get a visitor of their own'.[90]

The ethos of always keeping the girls busy so that they could not dwell upon anxieties and misery created by the war relied upon immense dedication from the teachers. Their only respite seems to have been a short break in the afternoon on Christmas day, a lie-in on Boxing Day and the regular one hour of rest that pupils were expected to take each day after lunch, on their beds in their dormitories, often reading. Activities were arranged within and beyond the school grounds, concerts at the nearby Royal Air Force base in Hednesford, attending church 2 miles away on a Sunday, shopping and cinema trips in nearby Rugeley where arrangements were made to ensure that older girls, who wished to, could attend a commercial college to gain vocational skills on Saturdays. All served to expand these teachers' role into a maternal one; providing intimate care and education included guidance on menstruation. As Barbara Hewit later recalled, they were like mothers to us really, er, looked after us and, er, seeing that we were, erm, fed well and, er, if we had any knocks and bruises you know (laughs) er, looked after us especially, er, at, erm, our monthly time, you know, when we were, er, needed protection and, er, the teacher that, er, the one in the dormitory, kept a little box and she had all the, erm, er, sanitary protection there.[91]

Similarly, Ethel Ridley recalled the support that was provided when she first menstruated:

I got up one morning and discovered my pyjamas were full of blood I run down to one of the dormitory teachers in her room and she sort of sorted me out and then we went across to the hospital and saw the nurse and she used to sit making the sanitary towels… With erm, cotton wool and gauze and I think they were a ha'penny each to buy, and the nurse there always used to have a chat with you if you were worried about them.[92]

Many evacuees in camp and other schools appreciated their teachers' dedication, Olga Harvey recollected, '[W]e were all grateful for these teachers, I mean they gave up their lives for us, you know.'[93]

Conclusion

Teachers were, as David Limond argues, often seen as 'keepers of national morale in times of war … and as advocates of reorganization and change that came in the immediate post-war years'.[94] Reflecting on her involvement in the first phase of evacuation from Walthamstow to St Albans one teacher longed to 'build up an A1 nation, not to be fodder for the battlefield but to be representatives at the discussion table of the modern Utopian Europe'.[95] Many teachers had been dedicated and committed and some were idealistic, echoing the ideological centrality of children in wartime. Nevertheless, many wartime innovations were not permanent, at the end of the war day nurseries closed and to the dismay of the teachers so did the camp schools. Some teachers saw this as a missed opportunity for what should have become a new approach to education.

The glimpses of teachers' lives, in their own histories and many memories of evacuees, suggest that the profession became feminized not just in terms of the workforce but in the shifting relationship between what were public and private responsibilities in the looking after of children. Teachers increasingly undertook the maternal and emotional care of evacuees, but in the post-war era emphasis was placed on professionalization. As Phillip Gardner and Peter Cunningham argue there was a growing understanding of the degree to which the future of the nation rested upon the work of teachers;[96] consequently a number of new teacher training colleges were set up and the minister of education, Ellen Wilkinson, made the decision to move towards only employing Qualified Teachers in maintained schools. However, as Laura Tisdall argues the growth of a new range of experts in child psychology undermined 'traditional claims to authority made by both parents and teachers' and made new demands on teachers in the years that followed evacuation.[97]

7

Social motherhood: An army of volunteers

Both the organization of evacuation and the day-to-day care of evacuees made enormous demands on teachers and foster mothers. From the very beginning of the conflict, their burden was reduced by the support of volunteers who undertook a multitude of practical tasks. Women, through women's organizations such as the Women's Voluntary Service (WVS) and the Women's Institute (WI), provided care and 'mothering' for evacuees and their mothers outside homes and schools.[1] Volunteers gave out much-needed cups of tea, arranged children's parties and holiday clubs, mended evacuees' clothes, offered leaflets and advice on bed-wetting, organized clothes exchanges and set up social centres for evacuee mothers. Little wonder that the Ministry of Information (MOI) film *Britannia Is a Woman* (1940) in praising women's wartime work described evacuation as 'The biggest feat so far of women's voluntary work' while Ernest Brown in a forward to a pamphlet on the Government Evacuation scheme pointed out,

> The general public hardly realises how arduous and how important a service is being rendered by this great army of volunteers ... It is to the billeting officer and local voluntary workers that all these difficulties are brought and it is he, or more often, she who is called upon to act as a guide, counsellor and friend in matters ranging from the unruly high spirits of small boys to the tracing of lost relatives.[2]

Volunteering was by no means a new phenomenon for women and as Eileen Yeo has pointed out, in discussing the charitable activities of Victorian and Edwardian middle-class women, an area women used to extend their spheres of influence.[3] Although women's philanthropic activities can be interpreted as Yeo suggests as 'important in nation-state building and middle-class formation,'[4] in the early twentieth century many women with strong links to the Labour Party, such as Professor Millicent MacKenzie in Cardiff or Edith Rigby in Preston saw charitable activities as integral to their own radical political agendas that included women's suffrage campaigns.[5] Thousands of women undertook a plethora of activities for the eighteen thousand charities set up in the First World War,[6] many of which were focused on infant and material welfare.[7] These voluntary activities, like evacuation itself, blurred boundaries between private family and public responsibilities for children's welfare. They raised questions about when and under what circumstances were the feeding, clothing and safety of children purely private, domestic issues, or instead could or should they rely on input from external groups. Such questions were more pronounced when voluntary organizations became the mouthpiece of put-upon foster mothers, voicing their dissatisfaction and critiques of government priorities and assumptions about evacuation.

Yeo's analysis draws attention to the tensions that, often well intentioned, women created in dealing with working-class women, whose lives were framed by very different economic circumstances and cultural values.[8] James Hinton's study of the WVS suggests that in wartime, middle-class do-gooders created tensions and hierarchies of class were remarkably tenacious.[9] However, women volunteers' interactions and motivations were complex, varied and contradictory. While some were full of public spiritedness and patriotic fervour, others needed to feel useful, to find an activity that would divert their thoughts from worrying about their own loved ones in danger. Not all wartime volunteers were wealthy or elite women; they were from the industrious classes, who become included in the broadening perception of 'the people' that the idea of the people's war encompassed.[10] Many volunteers came from the lower middle or better-off working class who valued their respectability and had their own front doors, insurance, frugally balanced budgets and husbands in regular work. There was something inherently democratic and potentially radical in some of the activities provided by one group of women for others or for the children of others. It removed the taint of charity of the Victorian and Edwardian era, replacing it instead with the ethos of community, social welfare what Sue Bruley has described as 'neighbourliness' in her analysis of Welsh Mining Villages.[11] Arguably the voluntary activities also carried a sense of the universalism that was embedded in both the Beveridge Report (1942) and the post-war welfare state.

Voluntary work in support of the evacuation scheme required women to support not just the neighbours they knew but also many women they did not know or necessarily share cultural values with. Nevertheless, for a number of women – like the Barrow-in-Furnace Mass Observation diarist Nella Last, volunteering gave access to a female cultural space, one in which they could develop skills, confidence and a sense of identity.[12] The seeds of the sisterhood of second-wave feminism in the 1960s and 1970s can be found in volunteering and wartime women's organizations. Nevertheless, women's voluntary contribution to the evacuation scheme was not universally well received; wartime provided opportunities for many different groups to demand that their skills and expertise should be both utilized and recognized as war-work for the national good. Volunteers were perceived to be interfering amateurs by some teachers and psychologists such as John Bowlby who argued caring and social work should be undertaken by professionals only.[13] However, in a struggling and cash-strapped wartime economy, the evacuation scheme continued to rely on volunteers. Nevertheless, the growing popularity of the ideas of psychologists like Bowlby would in the post-war era gain traction and women volunteers were sometimes sidelined by a new army of experts who came to the fore in the emerging welfare state.

Transporting and welcoming evacuees

From the moment evacuation began in 1939 until it officially ended in March 1946, women volunteers help to transport evacuees between their homes and their billets. The arrangement to care for and welcome evacuees at disembarking stations as they got off trains were organized by both volunteers and statutory bodies. Ideally on arrival children had medical inspections undertaken by professionals and light refreshments provided by volunteers. George Emptage recalled, '[W]e got examined by a nurse and got a label tied round our neck or pinned to our jacket to say who we was. And after a while we had a drink and after a while buses drew into the school playground and we were counted onto the buses.'[14] The sometimes ad hoc and small-scale domestic, maternal care that volunteers provided – in this case providing children with a drink – sought to ease the trauma of evacuees on their arrival in towns such as Burton or Hednesford, Staffordshire[15] They were occasionally accompanied by huge banners hung in halls announcing the community's welcome to the new arrivals. These were speedily put together and often financed by enthusiastic volunteers from local WIs, WVS, church and other women's groups. The process of transporting children and their mothers to their new homes, on foot, bus or by car, also relied on volunteers. Mrs St Loe Strachey recalled how for 'a confused hour, those of us who had volunteered as drivers drove to remote farms and distant villages.'[16]

The well-meaning arrangements of these volunteering women were almost invariably thrown into disarray by misinformation about when and who would arrive. Volunteers valiantly attempted to cope with uncertainty and chaos and for some the culture shock of interacting with children with very different regional accents, cultural and class backgrounds. Nora Landon, a young volunteer at the Congregational Church in Hanley, Stoke-on-Trent recalled how those arriving in 1939, were first fed and then went onto an overnight a reception centre in their church hall where her mother stayed overnight to look after them. But she explained on one occasion rather than children, mothers and babies turned up and 'it was pandemonium, and bedlam and whatever you might call it! Oh dear, the mothers were crying and so were the babies. Oh dear. But it was a very worthwhile thing to do yes.'[17]

In a world where phones were not common and email and mobiles non-existent, the goodwill and efforts of volunteers were sometimes in vain. The town of Stone in Staffordshire carefully prepared for evacuees, remaining in a state of readiness for two weeks, welcoming hall, drinks and food at the ready each day. Then they were informed that no evacuees would be coming to their area. Mindful of the problems that had occurred in the first wave of evacuation in 1939 and the outpouring of analysis and criticism which followed, communication and organization were generally improved between statutory and voluntary bodies in 1940. Nevertheless, Brownhills in Staffordshire had prepared for over a thousand evacuees only to find no one arrived. Alternatively, Ken Maple remembers the efficiency of the WI sorting out the billeting when he arrived in Blithbury, Staffordshire in 1940. He was informed who his foster-parents would be while he was on the bus, in advance of his arrival in the village.[18] In Kendal, Cumbria the billeting officer turned to the WVS for help[19] and in Tamworth, Staffordshire the Town Clerk admitted he did not know how the billeting could have been managed without the WVS.[20] Likewise in Hampshire, schoolteacher Eric Gadd, who struggled with the challenges to billeting the 'unbilletable', praised 'the Women's Voluntary Services Volunteers, who scrubbed and cooked for them'[21] but in Rugeley, Staffordshire there was friction between some voluntary and statutory groups.

Hinton's analysis of the WVS has indicated both its regional diversity and the frictions that occurred when middle-class women, who considered that social leadership and deference was their right, clashed with professional workers from local authorities and schools. In April 1940, Rugeley WVS stood ready to help when three hundred teachers and children were due in the area if and when air raids began. They were anxious about the situation, as they noted, 'Rugeley is already overflowing with troops who have taken up all available billets and many more are expected.'[22] Maybe their negativity was not appreciated, perhaps members sympathized too strongly with the foster mothers who did not want to shoehorn anyone else into their homes. Their local organizer might have been considered to be an amateur do-gooding, upper-class busybody whose opinions were not appreciated in a mining town like Rugeley. Either way, there was tension between the WVS and the billeting officers who considered any attempt to contact them as interference, which left the WVS reliant on hearsay to know what was going on. It seems to have been assumed that WVS volunteers would be standing around ready to be called upon at a moment's notice rather than consulted. And a certain amount of irritation creeps into the narrative report Rugeley WVS put into headquarters around the arrival of 250 children from Kent in June 1940 where the organizer recorded,

> As the WVS were not officially asked by anyone in authority in Rugely to help in any way with the evacuees we could do nothing on our own in regard to billets etc. Only after many visits and meetings with the Town Council and the Teachers was I able to get them to make some preparation for the reception of the children and it was only the day before it was announced that 250 children from Margate would arrive that I and my workers were asked to stand by and help the Teachers. On arrival of the children the Teachers took full charge and would not allow us to help.
>
> So great was the chaos and confusion that some sisters and brothers got separated and it was 4 ½ hours after the arrival of the train which had left Margate about 9 am that the last child was found a billet.[23]

She was even more irritated that thirty of the WVS had offered to take evacuees home, and had been refused only to discover that some of 'superior type of child' had been billeted in miners' cottages. Oral testimony suggests that some middle-class children were surprised but not unhappy when billeted with miners' families. What is also perhaps indicated by this interchange is that the role of the WVS in providing care to make the evacuees feel welcome and their intimate knowledge of the local community that could match up billets and children were perhaps not valued. Only small-scale evacuation was left to the WVS; in July 1940 WVS members met ten children from Margate at the station and escorted them to their billets.[24] However, as the conflict went on and teachers and other professionals felt more stretched the WVS were increasingly incorporated into a number of areas of evacuation organization. In Bingley in Yorkshire in 1943 the WVS were asked to assist in the reallocation of crowded families from Leeds while others from Hull and London found themselves advising on adoption in relation to under-fives.[25]

Volunteers were also needed to facilitate the endless to-and-froing of evacuees that went on; both the WVS and WI helpers with cars delivered children to billets and moved them between billets and transported them to sickbays. However in Rugely, four WVS members volunteers who were on-call drivers to take children to the sick bay the other side of Lichfield became unhappy with the petrol allowance allocated for the task.[26] The WI and WVS also assisted children returning home for holidays or permanently at various point during the conflict and facilitated the safe travel of unaccompanied children, sometimes by meeting them at stations where they had to change trains, or travelling with them until they were safely placed on a train that their parents would be able to meet. Other transport roles were more traumatic; Anne Lee Mitchell undertook to drive a mother to her evacuee child's funeral.[27]

When in the summer of 1944 the doodlebugs began to hit in London and the South, a large-scale evacuation of women and children from London and the South Coast had to be undertaken at speed. As it was summer time and many urban teachers were on holiday, volunteers were required. Over the next few weeks over a thousand WVS volunteers from across the country travelled to London to escort evacuees on trains to the safety of the Midlands and the North. The volunteers were also responsible for ensuring that the trains had urns of tea on them.[28] In Derbyshire, councillor Mrs C. D. Locchrane reported that the 'the WVS Street representatives had given wonderful help in dealing with the unofficial evacuees who are still arriving in the town'.[29]

Housewives mobilized: The WVS

Transportation of children and their mothers to billets was only one of the challenges of evacuation; ensuring that evacuees felt welcome and would stay in the relative safety of the reception areas proved more of a struggle. Women mobilized for special occasions such as Christmas parties and to give mundane or even emergency care. Volunteers filled the gaps in local and national government provision, giving emotional and material support for evacuee children, their hosts and visiting parents. Numerous organizations and individuals were involved in this work, but propaganda posters implored women to offer their services at their local council or at any branch of the WVS.[30]

The Women's Voluntary Service was set up when the threat of war seemed imminent in the summer of 1938, led by the Dowager Lady Reading. It operated in conjunction with the Home Office, who provided its funding which included first-class travel for full-time volunteers going to meetings;[31] an indication of the social status of the women involved in the higher echelons of the organization. They were organized, locally, regionally and nationally with an advisory committee of representatives of the chief women's organizations in the county at the time. Its initial aims were focused on air-raid precautions, but its remit quickly expanded to include support for evacuation, emergency feeding, first aid, the collection of salvage, the knitting of socks and gloves for merchant seamen and other activities that Patricia and Robert Malcolmson have charted in their history of the organization in wartime.[32] The monthly narrative reports local centres completed each month listed possible areas of work to be reported on as: Evacuation, Air Raid Precautions (ARP), Transport, Hospital Services, Canteens, Hospital Supply depots and work parties, Meetings, Salvage, with a space for other activities.

In many ways the WVS harnessed women's domestic skills and extended their sphere of activity beyond their own domestic spaces into a more public arena, this could involve giving advice on bed-wetting and helping at sick bays.[33] As the first wave of evacuees was due in Worcester in 1939, WVS 'members were asked to assist the local education authority by making 900 paillasse covers to be filled with straw to supplement the mattresses already available' something they did with relays of working parties at the Guildhall.[34] In some areas they cleaned houses in preparation for evacuees arriving while in Bath, Somerset they furnished houses the town clerk made available for evacuee families. Thus the MOI film *Willing Hands* (1944) described the WVS as 'quiet unspectacular women' doing unspectacular jobs, maids of all work in green uniform'. The amount of propaganda produced about the WVS suggests a certain sensitivity about the status of this public enacting of domestic tasks for strangers evoked. Lady Stella Reading seems defensive when she asserted, '[T]oo many people think of volunteers as a means to an end, as cheap labour. True voluntary service is nothing of the kind. It is, in fact, the gift of a thoughtful person of their skill, their energy and their time.'[35] Undeniably women in the WVS and other organizations provided not cheap but unwaged domestic labour for the national war effort, the *Leek Post and Times* noted, 'It is common knowledge that many millions of pounds are being spent daily to pursue the war but it is not everyone who realises that it is a speedier victory when that money is supplemented with voluntary war work'[36] and goes on to praise the organization. James Hinton sees in the organization an example of how the social relations of voluntary work contributed to the continuities of upper- and middle-class power.[37] Class divisions were remarkably tenacious, in the WVS and the people's war more generally[38] but there were spaces and places in this organization, which had over one million volunteers by 1943, where they were challenged, became a little less clearly defined. Over twenty-seven thousand members of the WVS joined their 'Housewives' Service', 'a grass roots service ... based in the intimacies of the street where women, particularly those with young children spent most of their time'.[39] The service involved ordinary women undertaking both civil defence and a range of practical activities that would assist their neighbourhood in wartime especially if there was an air raid. The Housewives Service were encouraged to look after children under school age for evacuee mothers who could then shop and run errands, without leaving a young child on the hands of the family's host. In working-class and lower-middle-class districts the women who were recruited were extending women's caring role as mothers beyond their home; a wartime reworking of 'social motherhood'.[40] The geographical and class proximity between helper and those they were helping suggests neighbourliness and sisterhood, not hierarchy and social control.

As an organization with its roots in ARP it was perhaps logical that the WVS would be asked to play a major role in providing rest and reception centres for those who, as part of the people's evacuation, fled the cities in response to the Blitz of 1940 and 1941 or the doodlebugs in 1944. When Vera Brittain visited in Oxford the Majestic Cinema shelter for London' evacuees in Autumn 1940, she found that Public Assistance and the Medical Officer played a role but the care and support of hundreds of evacuees required assistance from an army of volunteers. 'The doughty ladies of the WVS busily worked to provide tea and sandwiches',[41] but as their ten-year report acknowledged in 1948 that 'the task of caring for people shaken in mind and body called for the highest degree of understanding, patience and sympathy'.[42] Oral histories and Mass Observation investigators suggest that the compassion of the volunteers who staffed such centres was, perhaps inevitably, varied. Their own attitudes and values coloured their approach to people with very different social experiences from their own. However volunteers also exhibited acts of practical kindness and thoughtfulness; the WVS volunteers at the Chadderton Rest Centre, which received ninety-six evacuees on 14 July 1944, gathered up all the nappies, washed them and put them through a wringer they borrowed for the occasion.[43] In the Mere and Tilbury Rural District of Wiltshire, aware of the problems caused for 258 mothers not having been allowed to bring their prams when they left London, the WVS spent two days collecting prams locally and delivering them to the mothers, even those who had moved into billets in outlying villages.[44]

There was a slight ad hoc and responsive, rather than planned, approach to the organization of shelters and rest centres. In Middlesex the Red Cross Society took over houses, equipped them and staffed them with volunteers to provide a safe space for homeless people suffering from shock or illness after intense bombing in London.[45] In Leek, Staffordshire four centres were prepared in conjunction with the Local Authority and sixteen others were organized and run by the WVS alone.[46] In Cheadle, Staffordshire, the WVS ran a shelter for the homeless in conjunction with the Mothers' Union, between them equipping the house with beds for nursing mothers.[47] Inevitably, in some areas shelters stood ready for action and were not needed, in York the WVS staffed and equipped 11 hostels, but only needed to use 1 for evacuees. Newspaper reports of the centres focused on the domestic and very feminine tasks needing to be undertaken by women, in so doing they downplayed the organization and management skills utilized to prepare the emergency hostels and rest centres.[48]

Rugeley WVS carefully made arrangements for expected evacuees escaping from bombing in nearby Birmingham. Their records note plans for 120 to be accommodated at the Town Hall, 50 in the Comrades Club and 25 in the Methodist Schoolroom. They organized rotas intended to have 6 members on duty at the Town Hall doing three-hour shifts and 'a case of Bovril, Tea, Coffee, Milk was got ready as well as a number of feeding bottles and blankets.'[49] They made arrangements with the Co-op society to cook food, principally bread and jam with the addition of porridge at breakfast and stew and potatoes at lunch, as the manager of the Co-op had identified a large stock of tins for use.[50] Despite all their organizational efforts, not all accommodation was needed, and some were mothballed until 1944 when the WVS in the Midlands and North set up rest centres to accommodate those fleeing the doodlebugs in London and the South.

The mismatch between the provision of clothes by urban mothers and the expectations of rural foster mothers was another problem alleviated by the work of volunteers. The MOI film *Britannia Is a Woman* (1940) explained, '[W]inter is more rigorous in country districts and we all know what the winter of 1939–40 was. For the issue of warmer clothes, supply depots are set up in every district.' Financial considerations encouraged foster mothers to look for assistance with the burden of caring for evacuees from agencies outside their home. Many housewives operated on very tight budgets, and unexpected costs such as the provision of winter coats and shoes caused consternation and complaint. Local government departments found themselves increasingly involved in the minutiae of domestic life as what should and could be paid for by foster mothers or families was disputed, often with a plethora of letter writing. Ministry of

Heath memorandums made it clear that the primary responsibility for clothing evacuees rested with their biological parents, but this was easier in theory than practice, contact could be slow and very time-consuming for teachers who acted as go-betweens. A teacher in charge of Liverpool evacuees recalled that dealing with clothing and boot repairs was a real headache 'until the WVS came to our aid'.[51]

Two thousand WVS clothing depots were set up across the country relying upon donations of clothes from Britain, the Lord Mayor's fund in London, the Commonwealth and America. The WVS also appealed for clothes though local newspapers. On the 19 October 1940 the *Bath Weekly Chronicle and Herald* 'featured a large photograph of a young child being newly clothed by a WVS member, along with a message to readers appealing for clothes for evacuees'.[52] WVS volunteers, sorted, checked and catalogued clothes which were delivered, in special WVS vans to wherever they were required, to be distributed to evacuees, refugees, those who had lost all their belongings in bombing raids and even those in the forces who found themselves in need. When 250 children arrived in Rugeley, Staffordshire from Margate, the WVS Narrative Report noted, they had provided several families with clothes and shoes for their charges.[53] Newcastle-under-Lyme, Staffordshire, reported in March 1941 that the work supplying clothing to evacuated families had gone steadily forward, regularly recording that they had clothed seven or eight large families of evacuees.[54] While Bingley WVS in Yorkshire administrated a wellington boot scheme, proudly recording that in one year they had given out thirty pairs on presentation of a form signed by both a child's doctor and their head teacher.[55]

Many of the donated clothes were a little worse for wear and so a veritable army of women undertook make-do and mending, up and down the country. Cheadle WVS, Staffordshire noted they paid for repairs to shoes,[56] Malvern, Worcestershire, in one month had mended 74 socks, 64 pairs of pants and 3 vests and 1 glove. Rugeley WVS took over the mending of all the clothes belonging to children at the nearby boys camp school, Shooting Butts, noting that 'the camp is entirely run by men and the mending was in a dreadful state when we took over … the WVS members take quantities of the mending home'.[57]

The introduction of clothes rationing in Britain on 1 June 1941 made running clothes depots a trickier process, the WVS volunteers momentarily closed for training and then opened again, with a stronger emphasis on exchanging clothes to ensure the circulation of items across a wide variety of individuals. Outgrown clothes and shoes could be swopped for vouchers or better fitting items,[58] clothes brought in were assessed and given a points value that could be saved if there was nothing suitable in stock. Some items, which were limited or rare, could only be exchanged for similar items – for example, football boots could only be exchanged for football boots.[59] To get an evacuee initially started with a set of clothes was often reliant upon a work party making an outfit or donations. A number of evacuees in Staffordshire remembered going to the Rugeley WVS clothing depot to get new boots, and Iris Jones Simantel recalled, '[A]ll my clothes came from the Women's Voluntary Service (WVS). It ran a clothing distributions and exchange service. Some clothes came all the way from America and I remember how proud I was of a red plaid dress they gave me. It had a "Made in America" label.'[60] The work of clothing depots not only helped to meet evacuee's clothing needs and relieved the pressures on foster mothers but involved an external, public body, taking a role in what was once a private and family responsibility.

Parties, protests and the Women's Institute movement

The WVS was not the only women's organization to help clothe and care for evacuees nor did they work alone, but while the WVS was formed as a wartime service for civil defence their main ally, the WI movement was a very different and more independent organization. Formed in 1915, the WI had strong links with the feminist movement[61] and became known as the rural housewives' trade union.[62] It had aligned itself with other inter-war women's groups' commitment to peace, supporting the League of Nations Union and inviting the Women's International League for Peace and Freedom to gather signatures at its National Conference in 1933. The National Federation of Women's Institute's (NFWI's) constitution was non-sectarian and the organization sought to be open to all women of whatever faith and with a number of Quaker members, the NFWI did not condone activities which supported war, although many of its members joined organizations which did, including the WVS. Thus, although James Hinton has suggested the WVS 'colonised other women's organisations'[63] the relationship between the different organizations was more complex and regionally varied.

Volunteers in the WI prepared to care for evacuees, as early as the 1938 Munich Crisis, when one institute had made arrangements for a crèche, with blankets, cots and lodging for ninety-one children.[64] During the conflict, individual institutes supported victims of war in a number of different ways. They co-operated in knitting the clothes for evacuees, but Mucklestone village in Staffordshire was disconcerted when, in Autumn 1939, they entirely re-clothed a contingent of evacuees, only to have the children return home within weeks. WI members in Winslow, Buckinghamshire arranged regular meetings to make clothing for children, who had lost their possessions during the London Blitz prior to evacuation.[65] Members of the WI, the WVS and other women's organizations often worked together to arrange welcoming parties and Christmas parties for evacuee children.[66]

As the WI member Mrs Rural explained in the MOI film *Countrywomen* (1941) a member who was an artist 'started a voluntary painting class for evacuee and village children on a Saturday mornings' and then organized an exhibition in the village hall:

> We arranged for all the children to come to the village hall as soon as they arrived. Poor things they were in a state. We gave them a tea party in the hall before we took them to their new homes. I'm afraid their appetites were bigger than expected. So nice to see village children and evacuee children together.

The parties were so common that the plot of children's book *Just William and the Evacuees* published, in 1940, is predicated on the village children's jealousy at the number of parties organized for evacuees.[67]

The minute books of numerous local WIs and local newspapers describe how volunteers struggled to maintain the significance of Christmas for children despite the privations of wartime.[68] Winslow WI in Buckinghamshire entertained evacuees and small children with singing, dancing and a competition.[69] After rationing was introduced in January 1940, volunteers were able to obtain an allocation of extra tea, milk, sugar, margarine and preserves for Christmas parties, which sometimes became mammoth operations organized by multiple statutory and voluntary bodies. The WVS in Bingley, Yorkshire, recorded in their narrative reports that they held a Christmas party attended by eighty children on 2 January 1943 and had given Junior America Red Cross gifts to them all.[70] A modest affair compared to the party in Rugeley, Staffordshire, the previous year, when 528 children and some mothers had tea, games and a film show, each child receiving a bar of chocolate on leaving and a cracker from the Christmas tree presented by Father Christmas. Evacuees' local education authorities (LEAs) usually contributed to the cost of the parties but according to their own priorities, procedures and funding arrangements. Records demonstrate the struggles of local authorities to coordinate the funding for the Christmas parties; Cannock, Staffordshire, had to collect financial contributions from educational authorities in London, Manchester and Liverpool, among others. It was, however, volunteer women who made the sandwiches and cakes, sourced and wrapped presents and put on entertainment for children including films, plays and community singing. In Uttoxeter, Staffordshire, the WVS not only organized a Christmas party in 1941 for evacuees but also, more unusually, a party for the foster mothers in the New Year.[71]

The WI was, however, the only women's organization which provided both practical assistance to evacuees and also used the experiences of the put-upon foster mothers to challenge some of the cultural assumptions about domesticity, drawing attention to the unpaid, domestic labour of women. Many rural housewives who were members of the WI bore the brunt of the government's decision to evacuate children in private homes. Consequently, NFWI surveyed their members following the 1939 evacuation and published a report in 1940 entitled *Town Children through Country Eyes.*[72] To a modern-day reader this makes for very uncomfortable reading, as it articulates the resentment of the put-upon and frustrated housewives who were battling with the lived experience of a government scheme which, despite numerous readjustments and government circulars, relied upon housewives' unpaid and undervalued domestic labour. Staffordshire Federation of the Women's Institute's contribution to the NFWI's survey of evacuation accused evacuee children and their mothers of being, slovenly and dirty, bringing disease and infestations of head lice to the countryside. Stories spread among WI members of evacuees' delinquent behaviour and urban women's poor maternal and housekeeping skills[73] and articulated what can only be described as Towneyism.[74] It was NFWI which took an active role in political campaigning during and after the war in relation to this; the organization, which was already campaigning for equal pay during the Second World War used an overtly feminist discourse to argue that domestic rural women were the 'Nation's Cinderella.' in the Women's Institute magazine *Home and Country.* An article pointed out,

> The planners of the evacuation could – and calmly did – assume that the housewife need not be paid anything for the time, energy, labour and skill spent in cooking, washing, ironing, mending and 'minding' doing housework for three or four extra children. They did not ask the school buses to run free services with unpaid drivers; or the farmers to charge nothing for milk and vegetables, or cobblers not to send in accounts for mending evacuating children's shoes.[75]

The article brought discussion about the financial costs of bringing up children into the public sphere and highlighted women's unpaid domestic labour. Attention was drawn to the discrepancy in the earnings of those who worked in war work outside the home, for example in munitions, and the unpaid domestic labour involved in looking after evacuees. The article's arguments would be echoed by the Wages for Housework campaign of 1970s feminism and may have added legitimacy to campaigns for the payment of family allowances.[76]

The significant government responsibility for children's lives which evacuation involved made mothering the focus of discussion and debate in the public sphere also unleashed a range of criticisms upon mothers of evacuees. John Welshman has documented how in 1943, the *Our Towns Report*, which was published by the Women's Group on Public Welfare in response to the 1939 evacuation, drew attention to poor clothing, disease, nutrition, personal hygiene and habits of inner-city working-class evacuees. Although some of the responsibility for these perceived failures was placed upon inner-city housing, a significant degree of blame was also levelled at urban women's mothering and domestic skills.[77] Yet in the MOI film *The Countrywoman* (1942), Mrs Urban, whose initial response to the countryside is to exclaim, 'What am I going to do here?', is soon introduced to village life including communal allotments, jam making and of course the local Women's Institute which was busy discussing post-war planning. Mrs Urban decides to visit the institute and see what the organization does for herself. She is reassured that there are quite a few evacuee members. For as Mrs St Loe Strachey noted the WI acted 'as a nucleus around which the foster-mothers could discuss their problems and gain a social outlook and spirit of friendship, which helped them over many of their troubles.'[78] In joining a WI, evacuee mothers joined an already existing organization; many other social centres were set up in wartime particularly to meet their needs.

Social centres and canteens

Many individual volunteers and women's groups or organizations responded to the realization that looking after evacuees was a responsibility which could not be managed by foster mothers or schools alone. They provided a variety of further support, organizing canteens, social centres, mother and baby clubs and nurseries. Women, by undertaking domestic labour in public spaces, alleviated the domestic labour of foster mothers; hence, politicians and Ministry of Health circulars encouraged the setting up of centres for communal feeding, particularly in rural areas where evacuees were billeted too far away from school to return home for lunch.[79] Shere in Surrey was one of the earliest villages to organize a canteen giving lunch to evacuees in September 1939. Mrs Miles, a local housewife who helped out, recorded in her diary, 'It's the second day of the canteen in our village, cold beef and hot suet pudding for the children – so many tiny ones, who all in the most distressing manner, carry gas masks that seem almost as big as they are.'[80] Despite teething problems, the volunteers running the canteen were determined to get things on an organized footing and on 15 November 1939 Mrs Miles noted, 'Diana and I went to visit the communal kitchen and saw a pleasant scene, three happy ladies peeling potatoes (with the new patent knife) and another carrying buckets. Smart black and white lino, good stove and so on.'[81] Canteens and social centres also provided social space, support and scope to learn and develop new skills for women evacuated with young children. In many respects they are proto-types of many of the women's groups that emerged during 1970s feminism.

Across the country, women worked to turn public places into spaces that offered domestic comforts to evacuees and alleviated the stress evacuation placed upon their hosts. Some churches provided premises; the Cathedral restrooms in Exeter were used as a social centre for evacuees from Autumn 1939. The Bishop of Crediton was chairman of the management committee, assisted by a volunteer who accompanied evacuees from London and the centre, staffed entirely by volunteers provided clothing for children and lunches for a moderate charge each day.[82] A Christmas party was held at the Deanery for evacuee children with presents supplied by the choristers and local WIs.[83] St Martin's Church rooms in Dorking, Surrey was also used as a centre, run by the WVS – it enabled evacuee mothers and their children to spend time together and mothers to leave their children to have a break or go shopping. The organizers explained that the centre would be a benefit to the '[h]ousewives whose homes now accommodate these temporary guests. With the centre providing somewhere else to go, the mothers and children will not be compelled to spend so much time in their billets'.[84] The government and London County Council sponsored some centres, for example, one in Market Harborough, Leicestershire which was used by 100 mothers and 180 children.[85] Centres relied upon local volunteers, often from women's groups; in the LLC centre in Ayscoughfee Hall, Spalding, Lincolnshire women from Baptist and Methodists churches, the Mothers' Union and Toc Hall worked with women who accompanied evacuees from London.[86]

In 1940 as the bombing and threat of invasion intensified, the need to ensure women, children and the infirm stayed safely in reception areas became a concern to both local and national governments, who both looked towards women of a certain age to volunteer with or through women's organizations to provide facilities for evacuees. Many volunteers were already working hard, setting up a Saturday clubs for evacuees; in Worcester and in Staffordshire the WVS had nineteen centres for communal feeding operating.[87] As the first summer holiday of evacuation approached, the Board of Education wrote to Local Authorities suggesting that 'children should during the school holiday be taken off the hands of the householders as much as possible'.[88] There was a growing awareness that neither teachers nor put-upon foster mothers could cope with the huge demands that evacuation placed upon them, it was decided buildings and playgrounds should be open during the holidays and 'steps taken to secure the services of helpers from voluntary organizations to assist in arranging and supervising out-of-school activities for the children during part of the day'.[89] Establishing more communal feeding centres was seen as one way of relaxing: 'the tension caused by the existence of two families in one house'.[90]

As 1940 drew to a close and bombing and informal evacuation intensified, a number of WVS centres organized Christmas clubs and activities for children who could not be encouraged to play outside during the shorter, colder days of winter. In Uttoxeter, Staffordshire this was located in the Town Hall two afternoons a week during the school holidays. In summer, Uttoxeter WVS organized indoor games in a local hall for girls and small children, cricket in the recreation ground for older boys and rounders for smaller ones. Volunteers managed a programme of activities aimed at alleviating foster mothers' workload. The attendance averaged two hundred children who were entertained by a percussion band, a conjurer, film showing and sports.[91] Despite the efforts of the WVS, in January 1941 a conference on evacuation attended by Staffordshire Urban District Councils noted there was still a need for new services as a result of evacuation, including mothers' clubs, nursery centres, communal meal facilities and occupational, recreational and instructional centres.[92]

As the war ground on, local authorities encouraged by the central government, appear to have increasingly sought to slide the responsibility for services to support evacuees over to women's organizations, many of who responded favourably. All manner of groups including the WVS, church groups, the Women's Section of the Royal British Legion in Felpham and even in Taunton the British Women's Temperance Association, co-operating with the Mothers' Union set up centres, clubs, communal feeding facilities, restrooms or canteens for evacuees or their mothers.[93] The centres often also developed evacuee-mothers' domestic skills; across Oxford centres encouraged them to make their own and their children's clothes.[94] In April 1941, Rugeley WVS reported their Mothers and Babies Social Club was operating three afternoons a week. It had lectures on thrift, country dancing, cookery, drama and obtained a piano. As they were committed to ensuring that no one would be prevented from joining by a shortage of funds, there was no charge for attendance. A box left out for donations collected sufficient money to make the group almost self-supporting. The WVS attributed the low number of evacuees returning home to the club's activities.[95] Seeping through the pages of the Rugeley WVS narrative reports was a sense of the increasing role taken by evacuee-mothers in running the club; they made decisions about activities and entertainments including organizing a cinema afternoon, Christmas party, pantomime and play-centre for the Christmas holidays. In this area and many others, volunteers, usually housewives, many whom were not in the first flush of youth, organized, lobbied and acquired items necessary to run clubs and centres.

MOI films and local newspapers encouraged and endorsed the importance of volunteers, describing their work such as providing Sunday clubs for parents visiting evacuees as important in helping alleviate some of the practical problems of evacuation. The *Coventry Evening Telegraph* pointed out in August 1941 that evacuated mothers needed 'something to do in those idle hours when time hangs and longing for home increases, in saying this one is not unmindful of what has already been done by way of rest centres, play centres for games and outings'.[96] An article in the *Warwick and Warwickshire Advertiser and Leamington Gazette* in 1941 praised 'the loyal and enthusiastic army of voluntary workers' who were running 'clubs, communal feeding centres and advice bureaux for the benefit of adult evacuees and nurseries and playrooms for their children'.[97] The article went on to explain how across the country War Visitors Clubs enabled evacuee mothers to make friends, attend classes, chat, knit and mend clothes while young children were kept occupied. Halls, homes and even a pavilion were adopted to provide spaces of social interaction; in Torquay the club was apparently called the Evacuated Mothers' Union.

Volunteers' work in centres was valued; a Christmas card received by the junior organizer of the WVS community-feeding centre in Kettering expressed this appreciation:

FROM HOUSEHOLDERS TO ALL HELPERS

You have cleared your hurdles, won your way

Lessoned our work in the middle of the day

Saved our hair from turning grey.

WE THANK YOU

FROM THE 'KIDS' TO THE LADIES

We have enjoyed your meat, fish and Irish stew.

We have loved the 'taters' and 'afters' too,

But 'Go Blimey' the 'suckers' whew.

WE THANK YOU[98]

Nevertheless, the trials and tribulation of keeping centres and canteens going seep into the pages of personal diaries; in mid-July 1940, Mrs Miles recorded her alarm at the sudden arrival of fifty more evacuees who needed feeding at the canteen next day. In August 1941 she described the children as little, shabby and very resistant to eating their cabbage, no doubt the produce of some volunteer 'digging for victory' in their garden.[99] Mrs Miles was not the only volunteer who observed the small size of many working-class urban children. While many better-off women may have managed to avoid having evacuees billeted upon them, voluntary work brought them into contact with the poverty and deprivation of some urban working-class children for the first time. Ruth Inglis has suggested that in many reception areas 'the volunteers who greeted the children were shocked at their undernourished appearance. The incidence of tubercular disease was alarmingly high.'[100] The degree to which this re-enforced or challenged views that they had about the causes and solutions of poverty, deprivation, or the need for welfare and maternal care remains hard to gauge.

As evacuees' stay in reception areas became more permanent, the social centres and canteens developed. In Uttoxeter, Staffordshire the WVS reported that by April 1941 the club for evacuated mothers and babies met on Wednesdays for sewing, knitting and mending and on Fridays for social activities. The club had a membership of thirty-six and in January 1942 moved into a semi-furnished house in which they set up a 'Home from Home Club' and a full-time community centre with facilities for bathing and household washing.[101] The social and creative opportunities offered by evacuee centres were shaped by the facilities available, and negotiation and compromise between volunteers and attendees. In reading the Rugeley WVS narrative reports there is an increasing sense of 'neighbourliness', evacuee-mothers rehearsed and performing a play in the Town Hall and obtained a full-time centre by the beginning of 1942. The Ministry of Health helped with the acquisition of necessary items including a gas boiler and other equipment to wash clothes, and it was the Ministry that leased the building, which enabled evacuee mothers to get out of their billets for at least part of every day. The Centre became communal space to meet friends and undertake tasks such as washing and sewing that they would have been done in their own homes prior to the war.[102] Daily opening led to an explosion of classes and activities including dressmaking, keep fit, toy making, leather working, tailoring, shoe and boot repair and doll making. The organizers were pleased with the standard of work produced in the club, some of which was successfully entered in exhibitions including one in Birmingham to which they sent gloves made from cloth and old fur.

After three years of evacuation, a 1942 Ministry of Health circular to LEAs entitled *Woman Power and the Evacuation Services* acknowledged the importance of women's contribution to the evacuation scheme, and again encouraged local authorities to utilize women exempt from conscription due to their age or domestic responsibilities. In Surrey, Mrs Miles's commitment to the local canteen had not wavered and she noted in her diary that on one day she had washed up sixty plates at the children's kitchen.[103] For a comfortably off, middle class and no longer young women accustomed to domestic servants, such tasks represented genuine work for the war effort. The village also introduced an adult communal kitchen relying on unpaid women's labour as the WVS mobile canteens delivering school dinners to rural schools portrayed in the MOI film *Willing Hands* (1944) did throughout the country. The operation of these centres and canteens stretched ideas of domestic labour and mothering. They must have encouraged women to wonder which tasks should be undertaken by individuals in their private homes and which might become collective responsibilities in the post-war world.

As the needs of the war economy become more intense, with encouragement from local authorities and the Ministry of Labour some evacuee centres morphed into day nurseries to enable evacuee -mothers to work. The WVS nursery in Hurstpierpoint, Sussex, was set up in 1941 relying upon two WVS volunteers collecting children in the morning and initially returning them to their foster-homes at lunchtime.[104] Nursery hours were extended so their mothers could find employment. A conglomeration of organizations worked together to support the opening of a residential nursery in Uttoxeter. The paid staff were funded and appointed by Waifs and Strays while voluntary help came from the Red Cross, St John's Ambulance and WVS members. The local biscuit manufacturer, Mr Elkes, provided the premises and furniture at a nominal rent.[105] In Rugeley it was the WVS who organized the nursery that opened in March 1942 and reached full capacity by October 1943. However, a number of these nurseries and centres were set up rather late in the conflict, in 1943 many evacuees and their mothers had returned home. Numbers rose again during the doodlebug bombing in 1944 when a new evacuee-centre was set up in Leek, Staffordshire for London mothers which laid on tea, light refreshments, table tennis and other pastimes in a room at The British Legion[106] and communal feeding was quickly organized at the Senior School in Cheadle, Staffordshire.[107] As the war came to an end in the summer of 1945 many nurseries and clubs closed. In Rugeley only the make-and-mend class continued, accompanied by a few social activities and a local women's committee took over the evacuee-centre rooms, how long it continued is unknown.[108]

Conclusion

Securing the safety of women and children from aerial bombing through the evacuation scheme relied upon the labour of armies of volunteers, unsung heroes, who supported schoolteachers, foster parents and evacuee mothers struggling on a day-to-day basis with the practical and emotional challenges evacuation created. Volunteers undertook a multitude of tasks; they drove youngsters to medical appointments, held Christmas parties, darned socks, set up canteens and social centres. In doing so, what were once private domestic activities, carried out by mothers and families, shifted into the public realm. The feeding, clothing and transporting of evacuees and a multitude of the practical tasks to care for children began to be undertaken communally, publically, often by relative strangers. The boundaries between the private domestic sphere of motherhood and the public activities of voluntary bodies were blurred; they began to seem less fixed or natural. They have been areas of debate and contestation ever since. The practices, organization and commentaries that surrounded, evacuation extended what were once assumed to be private domestic and maternal roles into the public sphere for the war effort. Debates about nursery provision, communal washing facilities, social spaces for mothers and young children and whether they are the responsibility of local or central government, voluntary organizations, charities, private enterprise or individuals started in the war and continue eighty years later. Likewise, discourses and practices of motherhood continue to be questioned, challenged and scrutinized, but myths and narratives of wartime evacuation frame contemporary debates. They also, therefore, need to be thought about critically, and this will now be done in the last chapter.

8

Myths, memories and memorials
of evacuation

This book has sought to explore some of the multiple, contradictory and messy histories of evacuation for mothers and women but although myths of wartime evacuation remain a touchstone in Britain's national narratives of its past, they are always selective. Thus when the *Doctor Who* 2011 Christmas special featured the story of a widow who with her two children who fled from the London Blitz to Dorset, it was unusual in portraying both a mother and her children's experiences of evacuation.[1] Most narratives of evacuation in popular culture and heritage sites find little place for the experiences and emotions of millions of women whose family and working lives were disrupted by this government scheme. History is shaped by the concerns, pre-occupations and anxieties of the present; consequently, the myths of evacuation have shifted and moved; as children have increasingly taken up a more central place in British culture women and mothers have tended to slip out of focus in histories of evacuation.

Evacuation myths in wartime

The process of mythologizing, constructing and reconstructing evacuation's place in histories of the Second World War, the 'people's war' began in 1939, when as Calder argues the myth of the Blitz was also being constructed.[2] The media played a role in mythologizing evacuation, beginning with the radio broadcasts, newsreels and newspaper reports that appeared in September 1939 and the Ministry of Information (MOI) films that were shown the following year. Olive Shapley who worked for the BBC in wartime acknowledged that programming on evacuation sought to reassure children's parents about government policy and producers also felt the 'receiving families needed encouragement in their wartime role, coping with unfamiliar changes'.[3] Perhaps because these reports were produced for an audience of parents, they focused on the experiences of children. Shapley's radio documentary entitled *We Are Evacuated*, which was made up of recordings from a small Lancashire mill town that was a reception area for evacuees, was aired in the first days of the war. She later recalled that she introduced these recordings to the audience by explaining,

> When we arrived, the streets were given over to children: the high school girls sauntering arm in arm up the main street in their tidy brown uniforms, children playing football in the steep cobbled side streets, children going shopping for their new mothers, children making friends with policemen and ARP (Air Raid Precautions) wardens.[4]

These reassuring images were echoed the following year in the MOI film *Westward Ho* (1940) which depicted children with their friends leaving London on a train bound for the holiday resort of Torquay, as the voice of God narrator explained, 'Nobody is supposed to know where the party is going but these kids have a pretty good idea they will be beside the seaside before very long ... These children are setting out what to them is a great adventure.' Over images of children playing on the beach, looking at jelly-fish or gardening the narrator explains, 'Here you can see children from the evacuation of last September who have settled down to their new lives.' Propaganda films, posters and women's magazines emphasized the evacuee experience, portraying it in terms of an adventure in the healthy outdoors. In the years after, extracts of these films, images and headlines from newspaper have been reproduced in other media texts. Their representations of the events, experiences and emotions of evacuation have been incorporated into documentaries, museum displays and educational material, again and again. Yet MOI films were propaganda, government-backed investments of time, money and scarce resources led to their production. Their aim was to explain how the government wanted people to behave, not necessarily how they did behave. Indeed a post-structuralist reading could interpret the plethora of posters, newsreel coverage, radio broadcasts and public information films produced, conveying all was well with evacuation, as an indication of the government's anxiety that all was far from well, even as *Women's Own* reassured mothers that 'None of us can deny that space and fresh air and country food are best for growing girls and boys' in January 1941.[5]

As Louise Sherman has pointed out, evacuation novels 'appeared almost immediately' and quickly became 'a substantial sub-group of children's fiction' of the Second World War.[6] The first novels, like *Westward Ho*, portrayed evacuation as an adventure. Being away from home, family and parental supervision was a literary device that gave children a license to take control of their lives; evacuation provided perhaps a more democratic and accessible alternative to the boarding school novels which have played a central role in children's fiction[7] from Thomas Hughes's *Tom Brown's School Days* (1857)[8] to the J. K. Rowling's Harry Potter novels (1999).[9] The two subgenres were combined in *The Chalet School Goes to War* (1941)[10] when having fled Austria after it is annexed by Germany, the school is then forced to evacuate from Guernsey when an invasion becomes imminent. Finally established in Wales, the girls in the school have a communal and protected evacuation experience, enjoying rural life and enthusiastically taking to gardening and digging for victory. In the Chalet School books, teachers play a role as idealized mothers, and seeming to emphasize this, one of them, Joe, becomes the mother of young triplets; in other texts, mothers are much more marginal characters.

Enid Blyton's *Children of Kidillin* (1940)[11] involves two London children and their dog who were evacuated to the Scottish Highlands to stay with their cousins. Violet Methley's *Vaccies* (1940)[12] narrative features siblings Kevin, Moon and Oke who stay with their mother's retired governess at the seaside, while in C. S Lewis's *The Lion, the Witch and the Wardrobe* (1950)[13] four children are evacuated to a large house where a wardrobe gives them access to the magical kingdom of Narnia. Importantly in these landscapes, children are distanced physically and emotionally from adult supervision, free of maternal discipline, censure or care. In *The Lion, the Witch and the Wardrobe* Peter reflects, 'I tell you this is the sort of house where no one's going to mind what we do. Anyway, they won't hear us.'[14] Foster-mothers' roles are limited to physical welfare, housing, food, warmth, clothing, leaving children free to roam. But when the children go through the wardrobe into Narnia, the white queen is a possessive and all-devouring mother figure, who enchants Edmund by giving him Turkish delight. Lucy explains, '[S]he's a horrible witch, the White Witch … She made an enchantment over the whole country so that it is always winter here and never Christmas'[15] hinting there are dangers for children denied the warmth of a 'good mother'. Nevertheless, foster and biological mothers in these early evacuation novels are often shadowy characters, absent or marginalized, their lives eclipsed by those of the children. In *Vaccies*, the children's biological mother is mentioned only fleetingly, on the last page, her return at the end signals the narrative's closure, as a new equilibrium has been restored. 'There won't *be* any bothers Moon declared "Not now we're all vaccies together." '[16] In *Children of*

Kidillin, the evacuee's mother is never mentioned and their aunt, their foster mother, is only glimpsed, she appears on three out of ninety-three pages and her role is ultimately to ensure order and discipline as she inhabits a separate reality, seemingly in the dark about of the children's world as suggested by the narration of one scene, '[S]o when mother came into the room she saw four children all working hard, and did not know that two of them were ashamed and frightened, and one was angry and hurt and one was very miserable and homesick.'[17]

In the world created in these fictional texts, mothers provide physical necessities and therefore can easily be replaced by domestic servants who are rather marginal characters. In *The Lion, the Witch and the Wardrobe*, the children have been sent to stay with an old professor who, it is explained, 'had no wife and he lived in a very large house with a housekeeper named Mrs Macready and three servants (Their names were Ivy, Margaret and Betty, but they do not come into the story much)'.[18] Indeed they did not, although in *Vaccies* and *Children of Kidillin* governesses and maids of all work set the parameters of behaviour and lunch times leaving children to roam free. In *Vaccies*, 6-year-old Oke wanders in a remarkably self-sufficient fashion around the seaside town to which he has been evacuated, initially accompanied by his tortoise, kept in his gas mask case, and later by a dog. He takes buses and climbs hills, confronts and captures a leopard and stays the night at the house of a stranger when too late to return home.

The iconographic images of the evacuees from the media were grounded in the government evacuation scheme for working and lower middle children, yet much of this early children's literature focused on private evacuation, and middle- and upper-class children's actions propel the narrative forward. *Vaccies* features working-class evacuees but slips into a discourse of evacuees as dirty. A small baby is dragged around in his pram by his sister, as he sucks on a toffee apple, a practice which adds to the little mite's grubbiness and offers a silent but nevertheless clear critique of urban working class evacuees' mothers. They, it is suggested, are inadequate, not because they sent their children away but because their mothering had not ensured that their children were resourceful, disciplined and independent like the middle-class 6-year-old Oke. Evacuees in these books may have escaped the bombing but not the anxiety and fears and threats of wartime, even in the rural or coastal backwaters to which children have been sent, Britain was under threat. Boys, as Owen Dudley Edwards points out, were in 'training for war'[19] longing to be heroes, and catch German spies. As the uncle, Captain MacLaren, points out in *Children of Kidillin*, 'When countries are at war everything is different.'[20] But unusually in *Vaccies*, girls too could be heroic; 14-year-old Moon rescued a baby accidentally swept out to sea in a pram; although only 14, she too was a good mother figure.

Most of these early fictional narratives were set in the homes of the wealthy and privileged, sheltered from the privations of war, but in *Vaccies*, fears of financial shortages, rising prices and the problems faced by working-class foster mothers were articulated by a busybody neighbour, while Mrs Noakes, who looked after Geranium (Gerry), a working-class child, and her baby brother, is a self-sacrificing angel in the house. She quickly dismisses any mention of economic hardship, explaining, 'Now, I'm sure I have never complained– nor had any cause to. I own I'm proud of being a good manager and I've made the allowance the Government gives do me very well. And, what's more, it gives me great pleasure to see children enjoy their food, bless them!'²¹ Mrs Noakes was a 'feeder' whose competence as a domestic manager and her frugal home cooking ensured that Gerry was better looked after than she had been previously by her biological mother. This portrayal of evacuation, at least, suggested that working-class evacuees could thrive under the care of a skilled foster mother, in the midst of wartime evacuation.

Post-war reconstruction

Children were a familiar trope used in wartime documentary films as symbols of British resilience and the future that Britain was fighting to protect. In *Christmas under Fire* (1941) children were portrayed happily settling down to sleep in an underground shelter, playing at being soldiers or nurses or preparing for Christmas, while children played games in rural playgrounds, and thrived on subsidized milk in the MOI film *Village School* (1940). However, as the post-war peace came into sight, a baby became a signifier of the future that Britain was fighting for in the MOI film *Diary for Timothy* (1945). The narrator directly addressed a small baby boy, born in an Oxfordshire nursing home on the fifth anniversary of the outbreak of war. The baby is reminded that the miner, train-engine driver, farmer and a wounded pilot, all shown in the film, were fighting for him and his future. The film ends as the war ends and Timothy is invited to think what he is going to do in the future. The narrator asks, 'Are you going to make the world a better place, you and the other babies?' Little Timothy lives in a well-appointed vicarage, in the clean air of Oxfordshire with all mod cons and was shown enjoying a bath. More than half of all rural homes did not have an inside tap, even in the 1950s, yet as Wendy Webster points out the film articulated 'a unity of aspiration across class boundaries for the reconstruction of British Society'.[22] As plans developed to rebuild society in the aftermath of the Second World War, the small child with a label on, carrying a gas mask and a cardboard suitcase waiting at an urban railway station, parting from their mother, signified the disruption of war. The mother and child in their comfortable domestic home, portrayed in *Diary for Timothy*, became one of the iconic images of the longed for peace. If mothers had been encouraged to accept separation from their children who were evacuated during the conflict, as Angela Davis argues, '[T]he belief that women should contribute to society through marriage and motherhood was entrenched within post-war thinking.'[23]

In this post-war thinking, an inaccurate but widely held popular perception also developed that children from inner-city slums had spent their wartime in the country houses of the wealthy to the mutual benefit of both. Apparently, children enjoyed a healthy outdoor life and were educated and cultured, while the upper classes learnt how the other half lived and consequently supported the formation of the welfare state when the first majority Labour government was elected in 1945 and the National Health introduced in 1948. Arguably the encounters with the 'other', the working class urban children, which evacuation facilitated did nudge problems of urban poverty and deprivation away from being understood as symptoms of biological and inherited degeneracy to be seen more often in terms of mother's lack of education, poverty, skills or appropriate housing. These it was thought could be addressed by government and expert intervention via the welfare state. But this narrative of evacuation as a catalyst for social change, first articulated by Richard Titmuss,[24] reiterated by Arthur Marwick[25] and most recently by John Welshman,[26] was only one of the multitude of stories of evacuation, *a* story but very definitely not *the* story although it has a strong purchase in British popular culture.

This version of evacuation is a backdrop what is perhaps the most famous emblem of evacuation, Paddington Bear, which reached the bookshops in 1958.[27] Michael Bond's popular hero who appeared in numerous children's stories was a small bear. He evoked memories of the Second World War evacuees, as he was found on Paddington Station, lost but with a suitcase and the label on his coat saying 'please look after this bear, thank-you'. Michael Bond himself admits the story was inspired by own memories of, '[C]hildren being evacuated from London with a label around their necks and all their possessions in a suitcase, and this became part of Paddington as well.'[28] At Mrs Brown's instigation, Paddington was brought into the family home as company for the children. Like working-class urban evacuees, until they received the benefit of re-education,

Paddington's table manners and habits left much to be desired. He was almost immediately instructed to have a bath so he could 'come down nice and clean.'[29] The next day, Paddington was taken shopping by Mrs Brown and his trademark duffle coat was purchased. Like so many evacuees he was re-clothed, equipped for his new life but he still constantly threatened to bring chaos to the household and his disorderly presence was often signified by dirt, paint, sticky marmalade and butter on his fur, resonating with the sticky toffee apple sucked by the baby in *Vaccies*. Paddington like the Gerry and her baby brother was assimilated into a loving household where he thrived thanks to the care of not one but two loving foster mothers, Mrs Brown and Mrs Bird the housekeeper. This positive portrayal of foster mothers would in time be challenged, but it fitted with the 1950s and 1960s narrative of Britain's good war.

Mythically the Second World War was apparently a conflict in which little isolated, idiosyncratic and quirky Britain heroically struggled against huge odds to support democracy and defeat a wicked enemy. The narrative of children who had to be separated from their parents so they could be protected from enemy gunfire has an important place in this selective narrative of the Second World War and the construction of the enemy as evil. Likewise, the Luftwaffe's bombing raid on Coventry in November 1940 that led not only to the loss of innocent civilians but also to the partial destruction of a Cathedral. The iconic images of the damaged building, maintained in the rebuilding, affirm the idea of a heartless and cruel enemy. Forgotten in this narrative are the young, scared German crews of the bombers who were trying to hit the numerous factories of Coventry that played a crucial role in Britain's military war effort churning out army vehicles and munitions. The emblematic image of the bombed Coventry Cathedral in popular imagination is a justification of the aggression of Britain and her allies, including the saturation bombing of Dresden in February 1945 that killed upwards of twenty-five thousand people. Unexpected bombing of the civilian population is also an important backdrop for the emblematic evacuee, the innocent children whose life was disrupted and destroyed by war. Both contribute to what Angus Calder refers to as Britain's 'good war'.[30] The evilness of the foe was affirmed once the horror of the Holocaust, the bombing of Coventry and the disruption of children's lives. But myths are selective, if not deeply inaccurate; nevertheless, the appeal of the people's war, Britain's good war lies deep in the psyche of British nationhood and has been remarkably tenacious.

Middle and upper classes media professionals, writers and academics created many of the early narratives and stories of evacuation. They used visual images of the government evacuation scheme but the voices of those involved at the sharp end of evacuation – be they mothers or children – rarely came through. The growth of social history in the 1960s and 1970s changed this. The publication of Edward Thompson's *The Making of the English Working Class*[31] in 1963 which explored the role the working class played in shaping their own history and destiny during the industrial revolution was a key text in questioning whose histories were being told. His often quoted statement that he was 'seeking to rescue the poor stockinger, the Luddite cropper, the "obsolete" hand-loom weaver, the "utopian" artisan, and even the deluded follower of Joanna Southcott from the enormous condescension of posterity' articulated what became known as the *history from below* or *people's history*.[32] This new social history focused on the experiences, perspectives and lives of ordinary people and owed much to left-wing politics. In its wake came the formation of the Oral History Society and the *History Workshop Journal* in 1976, and a mushrooming of local and community history groups, movements Raphael Samuel once optimistically described as 'history made by a thousand hands, which can democratize the past'.[33]

A plethora of evacuation narratives began to surface, many produced by local, school and community groups, the publication of autobiographies of evacuees, oral history projects undertaken at a local level while at the national level the Imperial War Museum recorded a number of oral histories of evacuees in the 1980s.[34] This democratization of the past challenged some of the narratives of evacuation constructed in film and children's literature in wartime and the immediate post-war era. Instead it drew upon rumour and gossip, the mainstay of so many of ordinary people's social interactions in wartime and ordinary people's memories of the conflict. The narratives that emerged, like evacuation itself, were infinitely varied and frequently contradictory, complex and like the emotions that they evoked unstable, conflicting and ambiguous.

New and different myths and memories of evacuation

The new personal histories and narratives of children's wartime evacuation experiences that surfaced in the 1970s, 1980s and 1990s were interwoven with and shaped by shifting and changing cultural attitudes towards motherhood and childhood. In the post-war world, a mother and her young children were expected to be inseparable as never before. The social construction of childhood shifted to produce what Juliet Mitchell once described as 'His Majesty King Baby'.[35] Laura Tisdall argues, the focus on the child-centred caregivers led to a situation in which 'in the early years, a mother was expected not only to subjugate all her own needs to her child but to enjoy her own self-sacrifice and to take pleasure from this self-sacrifice.'[36] Parents were encouraged to put children first, to produce the future citizens; against such high expectations, mothers were liable to be found wanting.

The growing availability of divorce and the visibility of single-parent families following both the 1969 divorce act[37] and the feminist movement in the 1970s alongside an increasingly high profile given to fathers and alternative caregivers were perhaps the impetus for a new spate children's fiction focusing on evacuation. In an era of child-centred parenting, these narratives judged mothers prepared to let their children be evacuated harshly. There was an assumption that all children were troubled and traumatized by the separation from parents during evacuation. Nina Bawden's *Carrie's War* (1973)[38] and Michelle Magorian's *Goodnight Mister Tom* (1981)[39] both depicted the government evacuation scheme and children billeted in more modest homes than those that featured in early evacuee literature. Furthermore, the children in these novels do not stride around their new environments with confidence, as 6-year-old Oke did in *Vaccies,* they are timid, troubled and uncertain.

In *Carrie's War,* the heroine is evacuated to Wales with her younger brother, their mother is a shadowy figure, out of touch with her daughter's welfare and even growth. Her lack of appropriate maternal understanding of her daughter is signified when she sends a dress that is too small to Carrie for her birthday. Carrie spends much of the novel feeling guilty, concerned her actions have brought death and destruction to others, anxious and uncertain about the adults' responses to things she cannot control. Her thoughts are like 'bits of jigsaw whirling around in her head'.[40] Near the end of the novel as the two children prepare to be reunited with their mother, their foster mother, Auntie Lou, runs off to marry a GI, leaving the brother for whom she had kept house for many years. Carrie and her brother muse, 'What would he do, what would he say? The thought of it scared them so much they turn all the lights off and go straight upstairs.'[41] Carrie's mother can be compared favourably to young Will's mother in *Goodnight Mister Tom.* She is a hypocritical and mentally unstable woman who physically and mentally abuses Will and leaves him tied up in a cellar where he is unable to care for his baby sister who dies in his arms. By comparison, his rural foster father, although initially uncertain and aware that he does not understand this 'mothering lark' – turns out to be a 1980s 'superdad'.[42] He is heroic because he is able to do the mundane, nurturing and caring that so many women undertake every day, unnoticed. Will recovers from his mother's abuse and under Tom's care thrives in a rural community, as he affirms on the last page of the book – he is able to grow.

In both these novels written in a child-centred culture, hosting evacuees is transformative for foster parents. Auntie Lou pronounces in *Carrie's War*, 'Oh there's happy I've been with you two, there's been life in this house, first time I've known it,'[43] while Tom's fostering and later adoption of Will not only helps him get over the grief of losing his own wife and child but are also catalysts to integrate him into his community. He even takes on the role of choirmaster at church. *Goodnight Mister Tom* was adapted for television in 1998, starring the well-known actor John Thaw as Tom. It was judged the Best Drama the following year at the National Television Awards winning the Lew Grade Award for Most Popular Television at the BAFTA Film Awards. *Carrie's War* has frequently been read in schools and was also adapted for television in 2004.

Despite the disapproval of the separation of children and parents that many of the texts involve, they, like the television drama of Michelle Magorian *Back Home* (2001), have as their point of closure the re-establishment of new wartime, rather than pre-war, families. In some of these fictional portrayals, there was an element of nostalgia perhaps, ideals of community and social responsibility in a mythical past which offer a way to rejecting the social and political turmoil of the present.[44] Nostalgia is also identifiable in some of the oral histories and autobiographical narratives of evacuation that have emerged since the 1970s and 1980s, but it is tempered or challenged by discourses of the confessional culture of reality television that also emerged in the 1980s.[45]

Two identifiable, competing popular strands of children's experience of evacuation were recognizable in the latter part of the twentieth century. The first positive portrayal of evacuation suggests urban children were given access to a new, healthy, rural life where fresh air, locally grown fresh food and warm-hearted and decent 'rural folks' enabled the previously unhealthy and untrained urban children to thrive. Alternatively, a more negative portrayal is of the urban evacuee as alienated, teased in school as a 'townie', 'vacee/vackie' or 'refugee' who experienced ostracism and even physical and/or mental abuse in the homes in which they were billeted. Two Staffordshire autobiographies of evacuation epitomize this. *Dicky Blood's War* (2003) recounts a young Birmingham evacuee's three-year stay in Yoxall,[46] after an initial mediocre billet he went to live with a childless couple Mr and Mrs Roe on their farm which as he later recalled led to a 'couple of happy weeks of discovery' as he 'roamed at will around the farm' and the immediately adjoining area.[47] His autobiography contains many stories of home-cooked food, going ferreting and taking cows to be covered by the local bull, all of which instilled in the young evacuee a lifelong love of the countryside. Alternatively, *Family Values* (1998) tells a much more harassing account of Mary Rose Benton's evacuation from Kent to Stafford in 1940 – an experience that led to two years of physical and mental abuse, which emotionally scarred her for life.[48]

In these autobiographies and many oral histories of evacuation, women are judged and by implication categorized as good or evil mothers. Melanie Klein's psychoanalytic model, which 'splits the mother into two very different breasts: a "good breast" and a "bad breast"', sheds light on the harsh judgement of many foster mothers. 'The bad breast is hated with a passion; the infant wants to bite, wound and destroy this object of unholy frustration. But the good breast is revered with an equally thorough, though more benign intensity.'[49] Positive narratives of evacuation or personal memories are full of good mothers, whether biological or not, who are nurturing, caring, loving and warm and constantly feeding the children they are keeping safe. Alternatively, the bad mothers withhold love; these cold, rejecting, uncaring women are discussed in terms of their requisitioning of children's rations, keeping evacuees hungry, denying the food and love that children need to develop. They are central to negative myths, memories and recollections of evacuation. Mary Rose Benton recalls of her foster mother in Stafford, '[A]t some point she began to starve me ... I went to bed hungry, and woke up in the night to find I was chewing the blanket, I now had to scavenge for food.'[50] I am not suggesting that such events did not occur, but rather that certain tropes are used selectivity to convey cruelty, and lack of love, certain aspects of a negative experience are told and retold and picked up which often focus on food. As with stereotypes, there is always an element of truth in myth, but they lose the complexity and contradictory nature of experiences and emotions, particularly when reproduced for a popular audience in film and fiction and television programmes. In drawing upon and reworking Klein's theories, E. Ann Kaplan writing in the 1990s suggests, 'Popular culture represents all three types of mothers in its main mother paradigms, namely the all-sacrificing "angel in the house," the over-indulgent mothers, satisfying her own needs and finally the evil, possessive, destructive and all devouring one.'[51] To these problematic discursive constructions of motherhood, the absent mother needs to be added. Not just a mother who is temporarily removed, withheld, away, even dead, but one is absent, unmentioned, replaced by domestic servants, siblings even in the 1980s by 'super-dads' as in *Goodnight Mister Tom*.

Twenty-first-century myths of evacuation

The memory boom that has occurred since the latter decades of the twentieth century[52] has gone hand in hand with the increasing attractiveness of social history as a leisure activity, the popularity of the Second World War in television history and the wider circulation of evacuees' stories in oral history collections, autobiographies or media. These memories, narratives and myths prioritized the experiences of children who were evacuated and facilitated both the establishment of the Evacuees Reunion Association (ERA) in 1995 and the collection of 14,336 stories of children and evacuation as part of the BBC's People's War website between June 2003 and January 2006.[53] As Britain entered the new millennium there were still people with memories of their own experiences of evacuation; many more were part of what Marianne Hirsch refers to as a post-memory generation, who understand evacuation through imagination. They encountered cultural memories of evacuation via children's literature, family histories, education, heritage and media industries rather than through direct experience.[54] Evacuation stories like the people's war, are now national narratives of Britishness, so embedded within culture that, using Alison Landsberg's concept of prosthetic memory, it is possible to suggest that many people 'have an intimate relationship with memories' of evacuation,[55] which may create empathy 'not simply a feeling of emotional connection but a feeling of cognitive intellectual connection, a coming together with other's circumstances'.[56] Her concept of prosthetic memories rests upon assertions that such memories are not 'authentic', rather they are 'sensuous memories ... worn on the body' and evoke an intimate relationship between audiences and memories of the past.

For any audience, there are now a multitude of different contributions to the lexicon of iconography of contemporary personal and cultural memories and understanding of evacuation to draw on.[57] Individual and collective experiences, family stories, representations in popular culture, academic and popular books, museums and heritage sites have all played a part in the narratives and tropes of evacuation and the Second World War. Nations are inevitably imagined, people do not know each other and in an increasingly mobile, diverse and divided Britain people do not necessarily share a language or values. But shared narratives, as Benedict Anderson argues, enable those in nation states to feel they are part of an 'imagined community'.[58] Shared stories of the past can provide points when nationhood is articulated, they offer connection, just as national teams competing in football matches or the Olympic games do. The transition of the multiple lived experiences of thousands of evacuees and their birth and foster families into a familiar iconic, national narrative of Britain in the Second World War was neither a simple nor a natural one and is shaped, framed, reinforced, challenged and stretched.

Myths, as Calder points out, are purifying, selective, they remember but also forget[59] as all national, personal and community histories do. There is an inevitable tendency for individuals, communities or nations to evoke those versions of the past, which affirm their sense of self. The narratives, stories and events, most frequently retold are those that are useful for identity construction, when they no longer serve such a purpose they can be forgotten, discarded, swept aside; although this is not necessarily a conscious process. Evacuation like the bombing of Coventry, Churchill's speeches, food rationing and the formation of the welfare state in 1945, supports perhaps the greatest myth of the Second World War – that it was a 'people's war'. The notion that the country united for a common cause 'all in it together', experiencing an equality of sacrifice to defeat an evil foe, is a very appealing national narrative for a country that has been deeply divided in the years since this conflict. The small child, their gas mask in hand, who apparently happily went off to the safety of the countryside, playing their part in the national war effort, fits well with the myth of nation keeping calm and carrying on, so often quoted and re-quoted in advertising rhetoric and media texts. A multitude of historians, over more than fifty years, have challenged and deconstructed this myth[60] and have persuasively argued that in many ways the Second World War was a conflict, which may have engrained rather than challenged class and gender divisions, a war in which those with money could eat or live in hotels, while the poor waited in food queues to obtain modest rations or where racism and anti-Semitism were rife.[61] The people's war myth has been stretched and gently challenged in a number of books and even in television series like *Foyle's War* (2002–7) with narratives which draw attention to the activities of profiteers, British Nazi sympathizers, hotels which operate as bolt holes for the well off to avoid the privations of the war and evacuees killed in their billets. Yet as the twenty-first century began, the iconic status of the Second World War still sold films and supports a whole nostalgia industry of posters, mugs and 1940s weekends on heritage trains such as the Gloucester and Warwickshire steam railway.[62]

When, between 2010 and 2012, the Staffordshire Museum and Archives Service undertook the first detailed oral history project of evacuation to focus on a reception area, it provided a unique insight into the complex process of reconciling personal memories and cultural values, myths and memories.[63]

Psychologists argue a process of working through the past, navigating a range of emotional experiences to create a coherent story is an essential element of recovery from trauma.[64] Personal and cultural memories of evacuation are entwined with shifting ideas and practices about children and childcare, which circulated in the late twentieth- and early twenty-first-century 'risk society'.[65] Children are increasingly a lifestyle choice, a focus of consumer spending,[66] and receive more parental time, scrutiny and protection in smaller families than would have been imaginable to those who lived through the Second World War. In constructing their life stories from disjointed, partial snippets of memory,[67] interviewees had a range of resources to draw upon: popular discourses, school and academic histories, representations of the evacuation in popular culture all contributed possible explanations for what seemed to many unexplainable in an era when the elevation of bonds between parents and children made wartime parents acquiesce in separation from their children almost incomprehensible. A number of themes, which emerged in the oral histories, highlighted their search to understand their parent's decision to have them evacuated, themes that also occur in many other autobiographies and memoirs.

Parental concern for children's safety was a common one, something that was easier to comprehend for those evacuated in 1940 who had experienced bombing, memories and experiences of bombing provided a legitimate rationale for evacuation. Thus one man evacuated as a young lad explained, 'I went home to Ramsgate once, but I remember sitting in an Anderson shelter when all the ack-ack and the bombs were dropping. I was pleased to get back to Stafford.'[68] A number of evacuees claimed to have witnessed the bombing of Coventry while evacuated in Staffordshire, an incident which could serve to justify evacuation but which would not have been visible from the billets these children were in during November 1940. However, the bombing of Coventry has mythical status in British popular culture as an apparently unexpected and devastating attack on civilians – it is a narrative of their experience that justifies evacuation and more subtly suggests that although many children evacuated to Staffordshire did have an idyllic wartime escape from the stresses and anxieties of aerial bombardment, evacuees were painfully aware that the cities in which their parents, relatives and friends still lived in were being bombed. Arguably, tropes in oral history narratives like this convey, to borrow a term from media analysis of soap opera, emotional realism.[69] They are an attempt to narrativize emotional experiences, to locate those emotional experiences in the mundane and ordinary, part of everyday life.

Another familiar trope was the suggestion that parents and children had little choice or control over evacuation. Many memories of their journey to Staffordshire involved meeting or seeing trains of soldiers[70] who perhaps operated as a signifier of wartime. The military mobilization and the conscription of all men between the ages of 18 and 41, as the country readied for war and troops, were shipped to France, meant the rail network was awash with troops in September 1939 and summer 1940. If soldiers were going into battle, evacuees were being removed from its potential front line, whether this was the South Coast and Kent countryside where invasion was expected to happen or urban areas such as London or Birmingham and Coventry where the factories were pouring out the machinery of war. Trains of evacuees were frequently placed into sidings to let troop trains pass; yet memories of soldiers are so frequent as to suggest something more, perhaps that evacuees like soldiers saw themselves as victims of the war effort. Soldiers sharing sweets, oranges and Horlicks tablets and waving at the children connoted a shared experience, between evacuees and soldiers, of the sacrifice and powerlessness of those sent where government decreed. A perspective that sees evacuation as almost compulsory displaces the responsibility from parents to the government and enables evacuees to make 'meaning ... of experiences through narrative'.[71]

In no area of evacuation, narratives whether oral histories or autobiographies is the issue of emotional realism more acute than the often-repeated narrative of evacuees arrival in reception areas. Unaccompanied children and some mothers with children tell of finding themselves standing in halls, roads, market squares even a field while host families viewed and selected them. Gordon Warren recalled arriving in the village of High Offley, near Gnosall, 'Well we all just stood around with our gas masks you know hanging from our necks, waiting for someone to say "we'll have him" or "I'll have her".'[72] Mary Rose arriving in Stafford remembers that 'there were hundreds of children, many crying and calling for their mothers'.[73] Jean Wilks, who was 5 when evacuated, recalls, '[I]t was absolutely horrendous then we had to walk around the streets ... and people were at the side of the street saying "we'll have her" or "we'll have him". And picking, picking children out just like that ... and it was really upsetting to be honest.'[74] Such scenarios would have been traumatic, but the majority of narratives, in oral histories or autobiographies, describe the narrator as the last person or group to be picked. Not all children or their mothers can have been the last or the last group to be selected but the emotions evoked by the possibility, the fear and potential humiliation of that happening remains. This is the emotional reality of their stories, for evacuees who left home went to an unknown part of the country and faced rejection, this is their dominant memory, one that feeds the negative myths of evacuation, focuses on the child and silences the narratives of mothers and women.

By contrast, the live-action animated film *Paddington* (2014), which gained critical acclaim and received two nominations at the British Academy Film Awards – Best British Film and Best Adapted Screenplay – maintains and reworks positive myths of evacuation. Near the beginning of the film, Paddington is sent to London by his aunt, who, homeless after an earthquake, enters a retirement home for bears. As she stows him away in a lifeboat on an ocean liner, she reassures him about the welcome he will receive by explaining how

> There was once a war … thousands of children were sent away left at railway stations with labels around their necks and unknown families took them in and loved them like their own.

These words comfort both Paddington and the audience as Mrs Brown supported by Mrs Bird the housekeeper are 'good mothers' to Paddington, and in a child-centred culture, Mrs Bird points out that the family needs Paddington as much as he needs them; children and indeed animals are now intrinsic to the perception of media construction of the 'happy home'. The film was so popular that a sequel, titled *Paddington 2*, was released on 10 November 2017, the same year that a new memorial dedicated to the Second World War evacuees was opened at the National Memorial Arboretum.

The ERA, which was instrumental in the inclusion of evacuees in Remembrance Day parades, regarded the memorial as the achievement of a long-term ambition of their organization. Karen Follows, manager of the British Evacuees Association, explains on the National Memorial Arboretum website, 'The memorial encapsulates the emotion of the bewildered children perfectly. The Evacuees had their childhoods taken from them and their lives were changed forever.'[75] Originally formed to enable members to share their stories or recollections of evacuation and contact former friends or families, ERA has tended to privileged negative myths of evacuation and the view that evacuees were victims of war.[76] The memorial positioned among monuments to those who died fighting in numerous military conflicts reaffirms this. Renowned sculptor Maurice Blik designed the memorial, he was a child holocaust survivor and intended to encapsulate the fear and confusion of evacuees. The bronze statue portrays figures of a number of children but their bodies are deliberately distorted, hands are reversed, some torsos twisted 180 degrees, clothes are on back the front, gloves missing. This connotes the evacuee experience as one in which maternal care is absent, where children rely on each other, metaphorically signified by their holding of hands in a line. Although the ERA website suggests that 'this memorial is not simply a memorial for the evacuated children but all those involved in the evacuation process. i.e. the train drivers, teachers, nurses, billeting offices, and of course, the foster parents'.[77] Its design silences the voices, experiences and emotions of the numerous women who cared for evacuees.

The evacuee memorial is positioned next to the children's playground; evacuation is repeatedly used as a hook through which children can be encouraged to engage with national narratives of the Second World War. Thus the educational offering that both the Bewdley Museum and the Severn Valley Railway in Worcestershire jointly provide for schools in 2017 included the *Blitz & Evacuation Workshop*. Children are equipped with a replica identity card and a label prior to their visit and at the Engine House at Highley, children 'will experience at first hand the contrast between town and country life. The evacuees will have lunch followed by a second workshop session where they will have fun playing wartime games'.[78] Events such as this and dressing up in 1940s clothes and traipsing down to the bottom of the school playing field in a long crocodile pretending to be evacuees, watching *Paddington* films and reading *Goodnight Mister Tom* introduce children to particular versions of the past which swings between negative and positive myths of evacuation. But in the multiple competing myths, memories and narratives of evacuation, some are in danger of not being heard.

Conclusion

There are overlaps and collisions between the numerous historical and fictional myths and narratives of evacuation, which intertwine and reinvent themselves as cultural attitudes are created, reinforced and changed over time. The contemporary emphasis on the child-evacuee as the innocent victim of war or as an emblem of the post-war peace unfortunately silences many other narratives of evacuation. Women, perceived in the 1930s and 1940s, by virtue of their gender and biology to be natural carers of children, are often forgotten, and as more negative myths of evacuation have emerged, it is women who are also often judged harshly.

Afterword: Shifting discourses of motherhood

This book has sought to explore the histories of numerous women whose lives and families were turned upside down by evacuation, as both the government and individuals sought to limit the death and injury aerial bombing inflicts. The focus has been on women, not because evacuation was solely about women, but because experiences and emotions of motherhood were so central to evacuation. Mothers had to wave their children goodbye as they set off to unknown destinations under the government evacuation scheme or themselves take their children to find a new home in the relative safety of the countryside. Women had to struggle with the challenges of mothering other people's children or share their homes with mothers and their children. Volunteers and teachers undertook social mothering enacting numerous maternal, caring activities to help and support evacuees, with varying degrees of success.

Discourses of motherhood were and remain complex and contradictory, during evacuation and since then have been, stretched, reworked, renegotiated, unstable and in flux. Motherhood in wartime and since had been both an unattainable ideal, shaped by material circumstances, and a lived experience entwined with emotion.

During the Second World War many young women, as Claire Langhamer suggests, fantasized about romance and placed increasing emphasis on intimacy;[1] with peace, many women attempted to translate their dreams into marriage. Although the post-war housing crisis made establishing a home problematic, as Denise Riley has argued many young women had what could be seen as a traditional view of the family and longed to give up work on marriage.[2] Many historians see the post-war era and particularly the 1950s as the heyday of domesticity, motherhood and family[3] and like Gillian Swanson argue that 'the centrality of the relationship between mother and child to emotional well-being … gained new emphasis during the war'.[4] Certainly, the Beveridge Report in

1942 stated that 'in the next thirty years housewives as mothers have vital work to do in ensuring the continuance of the British race and the British ideals to the world'.[5] This then provided the blueprint for the post-war welfare state, which emphasized women's roles as mothers and carers while also accepting that these roles required work, skill and training or at least guidance.

Many of the proponents of a welfare state drew upon their interpretation of wartime evacuation to support their arguments for the establishment of a new post-war society. Evacuation was an unprecedented attempt to organize the personal domestic life of individuals by the state, an unparalleled attempt to manage mothering. The government evacuation scheme and its reliance on domestic billeting of evacuees resulted in both voluntary and governmental agencies becoming increasingly entangled in shifting complex understandings, responsibilities and costs of caring for children. The state was forced to concern itself with the minutiae of bedroom resources as it, for example, had to address the financial consequences of bed-wetting. Evacuation loosened the bonds between biological mothers and their children; teachers, volunteers, voluntary organizations and foster mothers took over many areas of children's care that once would have been the responsibility of the family. Evacuation was very much a public issue, and consequently, it accelerated the tendency for domesticity and motherhood, and particularly working-class motherhood, to be subjected to judgement and governance. Evacuation made mothering the focus of discussion and debate by politicians, women's organizations, teachers and the newly developing army of childcare experts who unleashed implied criticism upon the mothers and foster – mothers of evacuees. Perhaps as significantly, the plethora of sometimes competing voices and writings on how mothers should behave and the impossible circumstances in which women sought to mother in wartime invited self-doubt, self-criticism and guilt.

That mothers had the expertise to know what was best for their children had been being questioned from the beginning of the twentieth century,[6] but evacuation provided new opportunities for welfare reformers, psychologist and psychoanalysts to jostle for prime position as experts on childrearing. Bowlby's maternal attachment thesis, which had its roots in the interwar era, was further developed by his response to evacuation, when he argued that separation of children from their mother could impede emotional and physical development.[7] It did not go uncontested, but it did gain influence with welfare workers and health professionals and increasingly in popular discourses and culture.[8] Donald Winnicott's radio broadcasts in the 1940s and 1950s also promulgated the idea that women's main contribution to society was motherhood and stressed the importance of a mother's natural and attentive relationship to her baby.[9] The influence of psychologists' theories and childcare experts, even when they have access to many millions of listeners through the radio or engage in populist writing, remains hard to gauge.[10] Yet the notion that children need their mothers as their primary carer gained traction in post-war Britain as Angela Davis' oral history interviews suggest.[11] Most problematically the child-centred approach to motherhood and the pattern of maternal care, which was advocated by Winnicott and many of those involved with the welfare of children, was one where the mother as an individual received little consideration. It was 'a social arrangement in which the positive liberty of some is bought at the cost of denying it to others'.[12] This approach to the gender division of labour in the household, not only restrained mother's liberty but also implied that mothers who do not conform to these perceptions of motherhood as intuitive, all-absorbing, self-sacrificing and enjoyable were immature or unnatural.[13]

Yet the messy history of wartime evacuation, the very different experiences and emotions that this policy aroused amongst mothers and foster mothers, teachers and volunteers suggests that perhaps government policies and expert opinions do not evoke such smooth transitions into the actions and practices of ordinary people's everyday life. A messy women's history of evacuation is contradictory and contains competing narratives of women surviving, doing their bit for their children as much as the war effort, and muddling through. It has attempted to understand these women on their own terms, the angst biological mothers who waved goodbye to their children, the put-upon foster mothers struggling to cope, frightened mothers fleeing from bombing with children in tow, pressurized teachers and volunteers handing out much-needed cups of tea. All their narratives, interpretations, experiences and emotions are different and incompatible, and their voices would have been lost by any attempt to weave them into seamless top-down or chronological history of evacuation.

Furthermore, the narratives of evacuation are also about women making their own histories in wartime situations over which they had limited control; these messy histories are also full of people power. Foster mothers and biological mothers made impossible decisions, as they weighed up what was 'for the best', utilizing and circumnavigating systems to decide whether or how they and their families should be involved in evacuation. Private evacuations and the people's evacuation during the heaviest periods of bombing, the to-ing and fro-ing between billets and between home and billets are all articulations of the strength of mothers' resourcefulness and their struggle to protect their children in wartime, as they chose to do, in the face of propaganda and pressure. The work of teachers, volunteers and foster mothers during evacuation provides ample evidence of women looking after each other and each other's children, of social and regional hierarchies but also of sisterhood and support. The multifarious responses and small seemingly mundane actions of kindnesses by women in response to wartime evacuation is both an example of women heroically carrying on with the daily grind of everyday life, of their resistance and independence, but also perhaps contained the seeds of 1970s feminism.

Notes

Introduction

1 See, for example, Margaret R. Higonnet, *Behind the Lines: Gender and the Two World Wars* (New Haven, CT: Yale University Press, 1987). Penny Summerfield, *Reconstructing Women's Wartime Lives: Discourse and Subjectivity in Oral Histories of the Second World War* (Manchester: Manchester University Press, 1998). Sonya O. Rose, *Which People's War?: National Identity and Citizenship in Wartime Britain 1939–1945* (Oxford: Oxford University Press, 2003). Susan R. Grayzel, *At Home and Under Fire: Air Raids and Culture in Britain from the Great War to the Blitz* (Cambridge: Cambridge University Press, 2012). Lucy Noakes and Juliette Pattinson, eds, *British Cultural Memory and the Second World War* (London: A&C Black, 2013).

2 Judith Butler, *Gender Trouble* (London: Routledge, 2002).

3 Karen Hunt, 'A Heroine at Home: The Housewife on the First World War Home Front', *The Home Front in Britain* (Basingstoke: Palgrave Macmillan, 2014), pp. 73–91. Harold L. Smith, ed., *War and Social Change: British Society in the Second World War* (Manchester: Manchester University Press, 1986).

4 See, for example, Richard Titmuss, Problems of Social Policy, History of the Second World War, United Kingdom Civil Series 410 (London: HMSO, 1950), p. 100. Travis L. Crosby, *The Impact of Civilian Evacuation in the Second World War* (Abingdon: Taylor & Francis, 1986). John Welshman, 'Evacuation and Social Policy during the Second World War: Myth and Reality', *Twentieth Century British History* 9.1 (1998), pp. 28–53.

5 For example, Martin Parsons, *War Child: Children Caught in Conflict* (Stroud: History Press, 2008). James Stuart Musgrave Rusby, *Childhood Temporary Separation: Long-Term Effects of Wartime Evacuation in World War 2* (Irvine, CA: Universal Publishers, 2008).

6 See Mass Observation Archive, then held in the University Sussex Collections, accessed June and July 2012, http://www.massobs.org.uk.

7 See Children on the Move Project, Staffordshire Archives and Museum Service Project and materials accessed through joint project carried out with them between 2010 and 2013, http://www.childrenonthemove.org.uk/ (accessed 30 September 2013).

8 Barnett House and Evacuation Survey Committee, *London Children in War-Time Oxford: A Survey of Social and Educational Results of Evacuation: By a Barnett House Study Group* (Oxford: Oxford University Press, 1947), p. 40.

9 James Hinton, *Protests and Visions: Peace Politics in Twentieth-Century Britain* (London: Hutchinson, 1989), p. 44.

1 Setting the scene

1 See for example Travis L. Crosby, *The Impact of Civilian Evacuation in the Second World War* (Abingdon: Taylor & Francis, 1986). Niko Gärtner, *Operation Pied Piper: The Wartime Evacuation of Schoolchildren from London and Berlin 1938–46* (Charlotte, NC: IAP, 2012). John Welshman, *Churchill's Children: The Evacuee Experience in Wartime Britain* (Oxford: Oxford University Press, 2010).

2 Penelope Leach, 'Anna Freud Centenary Lecture: Attachment: Facing the Professional Demands of Today's Research Findings', *Journal of Child Psychotherapy* 23.1 (1997), pp. 5–23.

3 Viviana A. Zelizer, 'The Price and Value of Children: The Case of Children's Insurance', *American Journal of Sociology* 86.5 (1981), pp. 1036–56, 1038.

4 Anna Davin, *Growing Up Poor: Home, School and Street in London, 1870 to 1914* (London: Rivers Oram Press, 1996), p 212.

5 Ellen Ross, ed., *Slum Travellers: Ladies and London Poverty, 1860–1920* (Oakland: University of California Press, 2007).

6 Julie-Marie Strange, '"She Cried a Very Little": Death, Grief and Mourning in Working-Class Culture, c. 1880–1914', *Social History* 27.2 (2002), pp. 143–61.

7 Jill Liddington, *The Life and Times of a Respectable Rebel: Selina Cooper: 1864–1946* (London: Virago, 1984), p. 391.

8 Marijke Gijswijt-Hofstra and Marland Hilary, eds, *Cultures of Child Health in Britain and the Netherlands in the Twentieth Century*, Vol. 71 (Amsterdam: Rodopi, 2003).

9 Jay Winter, *The Great War and the British People* (New York: Springer, 2003).

10 Estelle Sylvia Pankhurst, *The Home Front: A Mirror to Life in England during the World War* (London: Hutchinson, 1932).

11 Charles Webster, 'Healthy or Hungry Thirties?' *History Workshop*, Editorial Collective, History Workshop, Ruskin College, 4 (1982), pp. 110–29.

12 Davin, *Growing Up Poor*.

13 Maggie Andrews, *Domesticating the Airwaves: Broadcasting, Domesticity and Femininity* (London: A&C Black, 2012).

14 Ruth Davidson, '"Dreams of Utopia": The Infant Welfare Movement in Interwar Croydon', *Women's History Review* 23.2 (2014), pp. 239–55.

15   Eleanor F. Rathbone, *The Disinherited Family* (London: Edward Arnold, 1924).

16   Gerry Holloway, *Women and Work in Britain since 1840* (London: Routledge, 2007), Kindle 50%.

17   Judy Giles, *The Parlour and the Suburb: Domestic Identities, Class, Femininity and Modernity* (London: Berg, 2004), p. 122.

18   Elizabeth Roberts, *Women and Families: An Oral History 1940–1970* (Oxford: Wiley-Blackwell, 1995).

19   Maggie Andrews, *The Acceptable Face of Feminism the Women's Institute as a Social Movement* (London: Lawrence and Wishart, 1998).

20   See ibid., and Alun Howkins, 'The Rediscovery of Rural England', in Robert Colls and Philip Dodd, *Englishness Politics and Culture 1880–1920* (London: Routledge, Kegan and Paul, 1987), pp. 62–88.

21   Taylor, P. Women Domestic Servants 191901939, CCCS Stencilled Paper 1976, p. 1, http://epapers.bham.ac.uk/3000/2/Taylor_1976_SOP40.pdf (accessed 4 May 2018).

22   https://www.theguardian.com/lifeandstyle/2011/apr/02/britain-child-migrants-australia-commonwealth (accessed 12 April 2018).

23   Kathleen Dayus, *The Girl from Hockley* (London: Virago, 2008), p. 313.

24   Steve Humphries and Pamela Gordon, *A Labour of Love: Experience of Parenthood in Britain 1900–1950* (Basingstoke: Sidgwick & Jackson, 1993).

25   http://www.historyandpolicy.org/docs/dfe-jenny-keating.pdf (accessed 30 April 2018).

26   http://www.todayifoundout.com/index.php/2011/06/until-he-was-nine-eric-clapton-thought-his-mother-was-his-sister/ (accessed 3 February 2018).

27   Pat Thane and Tanya Evans, *Sinners? Scroungers? Saints?: Unmarried Motherhood in Twentieth-Century England* (Oxford: Oxford University Press, 2012).

28   http://www.historyandpolicy.org/docs/dfe-jenny-keating.pdf.

29   Tony Kushner, 'Local Heroes: Belgian Refugees in Britain during the First World War', *Immigrants & Minorities* 18.1 (1999), pp. 1–28.

30   http://www.bbc.co.uk/news/uk-england-tees-30004430.

31   Susan Grayzel, *At Home under Fire: Air Raids and Culture in Britain from the Great War to the Blitz* (Cambridge: Cambridge University Press, 2012).

32   Ariela Freedman, 'Zeppelin Fictions and the British Home Front', *Journal of Modern Literature* 27.2 (2004), pp. 47–62.

33   See for example http://www.dailymail.co.uk/news/article-2724769/The-original-Blitz-Amazing-photographs-damage-Britain-WW1-air-raids-look-100-years-later.html or https://www.expressandstar.com/news/2016/01/31/black-country-zeppelin-raids-100-years-on/.

34   Jerry White, *Zeppelin Nights: London in the First World War* (London: Random House, 2014).

35   Ibid., p. 218.

36 Tami Davis Biddle, *Rhetoric and Reality in Air Warfare: The Evolution of British and American Ideas about Strategic Bombing, 1914–1945* (Princeton, NJ: Princeton University Press, 2009), p. 102.

37 Brett Holman, 'The Air Panic of 1935: British Press Opinion between Disarmament and Rearmament', *Journal of Contemporary History* 46.2 (2011), pp. 288–307, 290.

38 Ibid., p. 294.

39 Neil Christopher Fleming, 'Cabinet Government, British Imperial Security, and the World Disarmament Conference, 1932–1934', *War in History* 18.1 (2011), pp. 62–84.

40 James Hayward, *Myths & Legends of the Second World War* (Stroud: History Press, 2009), p. 86.

41 Andrew Rigby, 'The Peace Pledge Union: From Peace to War, 1936–1945', in Peter Brock and T. P. Socknat, *Challenge to Mars: Pacifism from 1918 to 1945* (Toronto: University of Toronto Press, 1999), pp. 169–85.

42 Michal Shapira, 'The Psychological Study of Anxiety in the Era of the Second World War', *Twentieth Century British History* 24.1 (2012), pp. 31–57.

43 Richard Overy, *The Morbid Age: Britain and the Crisis of Civilisation, 1919–1939* (London: Penguin UK, 2009).

44 Michele Haapamäki, *The Coming of the Aerial War: Culture and the Fear of Airborne Attack in Inter-War Britain* (London: I.B. Tauris, 2014).

45 For further details see http://www.basquechildren.org/colonies/history and Peter Anderson, 'The Struggle over the Evacuation to the United Kingdom and Repatriation of Basque Refugee Children in the Spanish Civil War: Symbols and Souls', *Journal of Contemporary History* 52.2 (2017), pp. 297–318.

46 Anthony Grenville, 'The Kindertransports: An Introduction', *Yearbook of the Research Centre for German & Austrian Exile Studies* 13 (2012), p. 9.

47 Andrea Hammel and Bea Lewkowicz, eds, *The Kindertransport to Britain 1938/39: New Perspectives*, Vol. 13 (Amsterdam: Rodopi, 2012).

48 Edward Timms, 'The Ordeals of Kinder and Evacuees in Comparative Perspective', *Yearbook of the Research Centre for German & Austrian Exile Studies* 13 (2012), pp. 23–39.

49 Historical England, *Civil Defence: From the First World War to the Cold War*, p. 4, https://content.historicengland.org.uk/images-books/publications/iha-civil-defence/heag145-civil-defence-iha.pdf/ (accessed 3 March 2018).

50 J. B. Haldane, *ARP-Air Raid Precautions* (Vancouver: Read Books, 1938, reprinted 2013).

51 Ibid.

52 Ibid.

53 House of Commons Debate, 2 February 1938, vol. 331 cc305–47.

54 Richard M. Titmuss, 'Problems of Social Policy. History of the Second World War', *The Social Worker Speaks* 204 (1950), p. 23.

55 Timms, 'The Ordeals of Kinder and Evacuees', pp. 23–39.

56 Ibid.

57 Ryder Richardson, Colin (Oral History) in Imperial War Museum Collection https://www.iwm.org.uk/collections/item/object/80019493 (accessed 12 February 2018).

58 Staffordshire Archives. D 1441/1/88 Letter to Ministry of Health 1/3/1940.

59 Hayward, *Myths & Legends*, p. 88.

60 Figures are from Richard Padley and Margaret Cole, *Evacuation Survey: A Report to the Fabian Society* (London: Routledge, 1940), p. 4.

61 Staffordshire Archive and Museum Service. On the Move Project. R2010.004.0047.

62 Barnett House, *London Children in War-Time Oxford: A Survey of Social and Educational Results of Evacuation* (Oxford: OUP for Barnett House, 1947), p. 12.

63 Richard M. Titmuss, 'Problems of Social Policy. History of the Second World War', *The Social Worker Speaks* 204 (1950), p. 102

64 See for example Juliet Gardiner, *Wartime: Britain 1939–1945* (London: Headline Review, 2004). Niko Gartner, 'Administering "Operation Pied Piper" – How the London County Council Prepared for the Evacuation of Its Schoolchildren 1938–1939', *Journal of Educational Administration & History* 42.1 (2010), pp. 17–32. Richard Titmus, *Problems of Social Policy* (London: His Majesty's Stationery Office and Longmans, 1950).

65 Juliet Gardner, *Daily Mail*, 5 March 2005, https://search-proquest-com.apollo.worc.ac.uk/docview/321590263?pq-origsite=summon&accountid=15133, p. 4.

66 Richard Titmus, *Problems of Social Policy* (London: His Majesty's Stationery Office and Longmans, 1950).

67 Figures are from Padley and Cole, *Evacuation Survey*.

68 Ibid., p. 50.

69 *HC Deb 08 February 1940*, vol 357 cc415-6W415W.

70 Daniel Todman, *Britain's War: Into Battle, 1937–1941* (Oxford: Oxford University Press, 2016), p. 341.

71 Vera Brittain, *England's Hour: An Autobiography 1939–1941* (London: A&C Black, 2005), p. 28.

72 Gillian Mawson, 'Guernsey Mothers and Their Children: Forgotten Evacuees', in Maggie Andrews and Janis Lomas, eds, *The Home Front in Britain: Images, Myths and Forgotten Experiences* (Basingstoke: Palgrave Macmillan, 2014), pp. 139–51.

73 House of Commons Debate. 8 February 1940, vol. 357 cc415-6W415W.

74 Gardiner, *Wartime*, p. 204.

75 Vera Brittain, *Englands Hour: An Autobiography 1939–1941* (London: A&C Black, 2005), p. 31.

76 Paula Bartley, 'Ellen Wilkinson and Home Security 1940–1945', *The Home Front in Britain* (Basingstoke: Palgrave Macmillan, 2014), pp. 108–38.

77 Julia S. Torrie, *'For Their Own Good': Civilian Evacuations in Germany and France, 1939–1945* (Oxford: Berghahn Books, 2010).

78 Richard M. Titmuss, *Problems of Social Policy. History of the Second World War* (London: His Majesty's Stationery Office and Longmans, 1950), p. 359.

79 Sean Longden, *Blitz Kids: The Children's War against Hitler* (London: Hachette UK, 2012), p. 145.

80 Titmuss, *Problems of Social Policy*, p. 313.

81 Sean Longden, *Blitz Kids: The Children's War against Hitler* (Hachette UK, 2012), p. 81.

82 Ibid., p. 91.

83 Mass Observation Archive TCS/2/G.

84 Hayward, *Myths & Legends*, p. 92.

85 Frances Partridge, *A Pacifist's War* (London: Chatto & Windus, 1978).

86 Longden, *Blitz Kids*, p. 87.

87 Ibid., p. 87.

88 Ibid., p. 179.

89 Mass Observation Archive TC 5/2/K.

90 Titmuss, *Problems of Social Policy*, p. 273.

91 Ibid., p. 261.

92 *At Home Today* BBC Radio Broadcast, 22 July 1942.

93 Mass Observation Archive File Report 916 Evacuation October 1941.

94 Longden, *Blitz Kids*, p. 414.

95 Ibid., p. 419.

96 *Leek Post and Times*, 28 July 1944.

97 Staffordshire Archives and Archeological Service Record Office. D 1425/1/4.

98 Yuki Tanaka, Toshiyuki Tanaka, and Marilyn B. Young, eds, *Bombing Civilians: A Twentieth-Century History* (New York: New Press, 2010).

2 Nationalizing hundreds and thousands of women

1 Richard Padley and Margaret Cole, eds, *Evacuation Survey: A Report to the Fabian Society* (London: Routledge, 1940), p. 13.

2 Ibid., p. 3.

3 *Gloucestershire Echo*, 9 January 1939.

4 *Express & Echo*, 26 April 1939.

5 *Yorkshire Post*, 6 April 1939.

6   *Leeds Mercury*, 4 April 1939.

7   *Shipley Tomes and Express*, 8 April 1939.

8   *Cheshire Observer*, 1 April 1939.

9   Mass Observation Archive Topic Collections /1/A.

10 Mass Observation Archive, Diarist 5282, p. 4/5.

11 Ibid.

12 T. C. Gardener, 'Local Government and Finance', in Richard Padley and Margaret
    Cole, *Evacuation Survey: A Report to the Fabian Society* (London: Routledge,
    1940), p. 76.

13 Staffordshire Archives and Museum Service. On the Move Project. R2010.004.0040.

14 Dorothy Sheridan, *Wartime Women: An Anthology of Women's Wartime Writing for
    Mass-Observation 1937–45* (London: Vintage, 1991), p. 65.

15 Padley and Cole, *Evacuation Survey*, p. 253.

16 Ibid., p. 3.

17 For further discussion see Maggie Andrews, *The Acceptable Face of Feminism: The
    Women's Institute Movement as a Social Movement* (London: Lawrence and Wishart,
    1998 and 2015) and Sonya O. Rose, *Which People's War?: National Identity and
    Citizenship in Wartime Britain 1939–1945* (Oxford: Oxford University Press, 2003).

18 House of Commons Debate, 14 September 1939, vol 351 cc 802–86. https://api.
    parliament.uk/historic-hansard/sittings/C20.

19 Andrews, *Acceptable Face of Feminism*, 2015.

20 Mary Douglas, *Purity and Danger: An Analysis of Concepts of Pollution and Taboo*
    (London: Routledge, 2003).

21 The Womens Library NFWI Collections 5WFM/E/2.

22 Mary Douglas, *Purity and Danger: An Analysis of Concepts of Pollution and Taboo*
    (London: Routledge, 2003), p. 44.

23 Ibid., p. 50.

24 For more about the idealization of rural life see Alun Howkins, 'The Rediscovery
    of Rural England', P. Colls and R. Colls, eds, *Englishness: Politics and Culture
    1880–1920* (London: Croom Helm, 1987), pp. 78–92 and Andrews, Maggie. *The
    Acceptable Face of Feminism: The Women's Institute Movement as a Social Movement*
    (London: Lawrence and Wishart, 1997), new edition 2015.

25 Mass Observation Archives. Diarist 5282 p. 36.

26 Padley and Cole, eds, *Evacuation Survey*, p. 2.

27 *Burrows Worcester Journal*, 21 December 1940.

28 Staffordshire Archive and Museum Service D 144/1/87a.

29 Government Circular 1913, 17 November 1939, this and other circulars were
    accessed via Staffordshire Archives and Museum Service Staffs Record office D
    144/1/87a.

30   Robert Malcolmson and Patricia Malcolmson, *Women at the Ready: The Remarkable Story of the Women's Voluntary Services on the Home Front* (London: Hachette UK, 2013), p. 109.

31   Government Circular 1987, 26 March 1940.

32   Travis L. Crosby, *The Impact of Civilian Evacuation in the Second World War* (Abingdon: Taylor & Francis, 1986).

33   *Bedford Times and Independent*, 31 May 1940.

34   Joan Simeon Clarke, 'Family Life', in Richard Padley and Margaret Cole, eds, *Evacuation Survey: A Report to the Fabian Society* (1940), pp. 157–65, p. 159.

35   Le Gros Clark and Richard Toms, *Evacuation: Failure of Reform* Fabian Society Tract Series No 249 published by the Fabian Society February 1940.

36   May Smith, *These Wonderful Rumours: A Young Schoolteacher's Wartime Diaries 1939–1945* (London: Virago, 2012), p. 180.

37   John Bowlby, 'Psychological Aspects', in Richard Padley and Margaret Cole, eds, *Evacuation Survey and Report to the Fabian Society* (Routledge, 1940), pp. 186–96, 188.

38   John Stewart, *Child Guidance in Britain, 1918–1955: The Dangerous Age of Childhood* (London: Routledge, 2015).

39   Susan Isaacs, Sibyl Brown, and Robert Thouless, eds, *The Cambridge Evacuation Survey* (York: Methuen, 1940), p. 92.

40   University of Liverpool, *Our Wartime Guests: Opportunity or Menace? A Psychological Approach to Evacuation* (Liverpool: University Press of Liverpool, Hodder & Stoughton, 1940), p. 10.

41   Barnet House Study Group, *London Children in Wartime Oxford: A Survey of Social and Educational Results of Evacuation* (Oxford: Oxford University Press, 1947).

42   Paul Addison and Jeremy Crang, *Listening to Britain: Home Intelligence Reports on Britain's Finest Hour* (London: Vintage Book, 2011).

43   Worcestershire Archives and Archaeological Service, Oral history interview WW2/78.

44   Evelyn Waugh, *Put Out More Flags* (London: Penguin, 2012), first published 1942.

45   Staffordshire Archives and Museum Service, On the Move Project. R02010.004,0035.

46   Staffordshire Archives and Museum Service. Cheadle Evacuation Minute Book. D 1425/1/4.

47   University of Liverpool, *Our Wartime Guests: Opportunity or Menace? A Psychological Approach to Evacuation* (Liverpool: University Press of Liverpool, Hodder & Stoughton, 1940), p. 8.

48   House of Commons Debate, 14 September 1939, vol 351 cc802–86. https://api.parliament.uk/historic-hansard/sittings/C20.

49   Mass Observation Evacuation 1939–44 Box 1 TV 5 94 Topic Collections /1/A.

50   Smith, *These Wonderful Rumours*, p. 120.

51   Ibid., p. 16.

52   Ibid., p. 137.

53   Elizabeth Monica Delafield, *The Diary of a Provincial Lady* (London: Penguin UK, 2014).

54   Constance Miles, *Mrs Miles's Diary* (Simon & Schuster, 2013).

55   *Sunderland Daily Echo and Shipping Gazette*, 14 June 1940.

56   *Hull Daily Mail*, 18 November 1940.

57   Mass Observation Archive, Report on Evacuation 1940, p. 6.

58   The *Berrows Worcester Journal*, 9 September 1939.

59   *Leek Post and Times*, Leek Library, 11 August 1944.

60   Staffordshire Archive and Museum Service, On the Move Project. R2010.004.0063.

61   Worcestershire Archives and Archaeological Service. 9196-493-332-A-F.

62   Judith Niechcial, *Lucy Faithfull: Mother to Hundreds* (Judith Niechcial, 2010).

63   Clarke, 'Family Life', p. 164.

64   Geoffrey Field, 'Perspectives on the Working-Class Family in Wartime Britain, 1939–1945', *International Labor and Working-Class History* 38 (1990), pp. 3–28, 4.

65   John Welshman, 'In Search of the "Problem Family:" Public Health and Social Work in England and Wales 1940–70', *Social History of Medicine* 9.3 (1996), pp. 447–65.

66   Clare Debenham, *Birth Control and the Rights of Women: Post-Suffrage Feminism in the Early Twentieth Century*, Vol. 31 (IB Tauris, 2013).

67   Welshman, 'In Search of "Problem Family"'.

68   John Welshman, 'Evacuation, Hygiene, and Social Policy: The Our Towns Report of 1943', *Historical Journal* 42.3 (1999), pp. 781–807.

69   Welshman, 'In Search of the "Problem Family"'.

70   Pat Starkey, 'The Feckless Mother: Women, Poverty and Social Workers in Wartime and Post-War England', *Women's History Review* 9.3 (2000), pp. 539–57, 551.

71   Hygiene Committee of the Women's Group on Public Welfare, 'Our Towns Up Close: A Study Made in 1939–1942 with Certain Recommendations' (London: in association with the National Council of Social Service, 1943).

72   Welshman, 'Evacuation, Hygiene', p. 796.

73   See for example John Macnicol, 'The Effect of the Evacuation of Schoolchildren on Official Attitudes to State Intervention', *War and Social Change* (1986), pp. 3–31. Bob Holman, *The Evacuation: A Very British Revolution* (Lion, 1995). Anne Digby, *British Welfare Policy: Workhouse to Workfare* (London: Faber & Faber, 1989).

74   John Welshman, 'Evacuation and Social Policy during the Second World War: Myth and Reality', *Twentieth Century British History* 9.1 (1998), pp. 28–53, 28.

75 Michal Shapira, '"Speaking Kleinian:" Susan Isaacs as Ursula Wise and the Inter-War Popularisation of Psychoanalysis', *Medical History* 61.4 (2017), pp. 525–47, 527.

76 Shapira, ' "Speaking Kleinian" ', p. 525.

77 Ibid.

78 For further discussion of this see Maggie Andrews, *Domesticating the Airwaves: Broadcasting, Domesticity and Femininity* (London: Bloomsbury, 2012).

79 *Daily Herald*, 12 December 1936.

80 BBC Written Arhcives. T310.

81 Ibid.

82 Evacuation is a story of tragedies' (D. W. Winnicott): World War II and British Child Psychology *Wellcome Institute*: Thursday 19 January 2012 Speaker(s): Angela Davis, University of Warwick, See also Angela Davis, *Modern Motherhood: Women and Family in England, 1945–2000* (Oxford: Oxford University Press, 2012).

83 John Bowlby, Emanuel Miller, D. W. Winnicott, 'Evacuation of Small Children, Correspondence to the British Medical Journal 16 December 1939.

84 Ibid.

85 Government Circular 1987, 26 March 1940.

86 Dorothy Burlingham and Anna Freud, 'Infants without Families', *Reports of the Hampstead Nurseries* (1974).

87 Dorothy Burlingham and Anna Freud, *Young Children in Wartime. A Year's Work in Residential War Nursery* (George Allen and Unwin, 1942), p. 43.

88 Dorothy Burlingham and Anna Freud, *Young Children in Wartime: A Year's Work in a Residential Day Nursery* (George Allen and Urwin, 1942).

89 Jane Ussher, *Women's Madness, Misogyny or Mental Illness* (London: Harvester Wheatsheaf, 1991).

90 Burlingham and Freud, *Young Children in Wartime*.

91 Susan Isaacs, Sibyl Brown, and Robert Thouless, eds, *The Cambridge Evacuation Survey* (Slingsby Yorkshire: Methuen, 1940).

92 Jenny Willan, 'Susan Isaacs (1885–1948): Her Life, Work and Legacy', *Gender and Education* 23.2 (2011), pp. 201–10.

93 Ben Mayhew, 'Between Love and Aggression: The Politics of John Bowlby', *History of the Human Sciences* 19.4 (2006), pp. 19–35.

94 Memo from g. m to E Heath 20 July 1944 quoted in Carlton Jackson, *Who Will Take Our Children?* (Methuen, 1985), p. 50.

95 John, 'Psychological Aspects', p. 192.

96 Barnett House and Evacuation Survey Committee, *London Children in War-Time Oxford: A Survey of Social and Educational Results of Evacuation: By House Study Group* (Oxford: Oxford University Press, 1947), p. 26.

97 Ibid., p. 99.

98 See for example Judy Giles, 'A Home of One's Own: Women and Domesticity in England 1918–1950', *Women's Studies International Forum* 16.3 (1993), pp. 239–53, Pergamon. Adrian Bingham, '"An Era of Domesticity?" Histories of Women and Gender in Interwar Britain', *Cultural and Social History* 1.2 (2004), pp. 225–33. Nicola Verdon, '"The Modern Countrywoman:" Farm Women, Domesticity and Social Change in Interwar Britain', *History Workshop Journal* 70.1 (2010), pp. 86–107, Oxford University Press. Carla Cesare, *Sewing the Self: Needlework, Femininity and Domesticity in Interwar Britain* (Diss. Northumbria University, 2012).

99 House and Evacuation Survey Committee, *London Children in War-Time Oxford*, p. 23.

100 Ibid., p. 96.

101 Mrs. St. Loe Strachey, *Borrowed Children: A Popular Account of Some Evacuation Problems and Their Remedies* (London: John Murray, 1940 reprinted 2007).

102 Ibid., p. 117.

103 See, for example, Padley and Cole, *Evacuation Survey*. Denise Riley, '"The Social", "Woman", and Sociological Feminism', in *Am I That Name?* (Basingstoke: Palgrave Macmillan, 1988), pp. 44–66. Sarah Benton, 'The 1945 'Republic'', *History Workshop Journal*, no. 43 (1997), Oxford University Press. Paul Addison, *The Road to 1945: British Politics and the Second World War Revised Edition* (London: Random House, 2011).

104 Janice L. Doane and Devon L. Hodges, *From Klein to Kristeva: Psychoanalytic Feminism and the Search for the 'Good Enough' Mother* (Michigan: University of Michigan Press, 1992), p. 21.

3 Mothers who waved goodbye

1 Vera Brittain, *England's Hour: An Autobiography 1939–1941* (London: A&C Black, 2005), p. 44.

2 Olive Schreiner and Carol Barash, *An Olive Schreiner Reader: Writings on Women and South Africa* (Kitchener: Pandora Press, 1987), p. 206.

3 Jessica Mann, *Out of Harm's Way* (London: Headline, 2014), p. 42.

4 Richard Padley and Margaret Cole, eds, *Evacuation Survey: A Report to the Fabian Society* (London: Routledge, 1940), p. 5.

5 Ruth Inglis, *The Children's War: Evacuation 1939–1945* (Peterborough: Fontana Press, 1990), p. 4.

6 Staffordshire Archive and Museum Service. On the Move Project. R2010.004.0015.

7 Ben Wicks and David Rider, *The Day They Took the Children* (London: Bloomsbury, 1989), p. 164.

8 Private Papers of E.M. Ridley, Imperial War Museum Archives 5998.

9 Pam Hobbs, *Don't Forget to Write* (London: Ebury Press, 2009), p. 53.

10 *Leek Post and Times*, 12 January 1945.

11 Informal discussions at Birmingham Wives group May 2018.

12 Mass Observation Evacuation Report 1940, p. 17.

13 quoted in Jill Wallis, *A Welcome in the Hillsides: The Merseyside and North Wales Experience* (Gwespyr: Avid Publications), p. 24.

14 Juliet Gardiner, https://search-proquest-com.apollo.worc.ac.uk/docview/321590263?pq-origsite=summon&accountid=15133 (accessed 12 January 2018).

15 Mrs St. Loe Strachey, *Borrowed Children: A Popular Account of Some Evacuation Problems and Their Remedies* (London: John Murray, 1940), p. 21.

16 Terence Frisby, *Kisses on a Postcard* (London: Bloomsbury, 2010), p. 21.

17 Hobbs, *Don't Forget to Write*, p. 54.

18 Staffordshire Archives and Museum Service On the Move Project. R2010.004.0003.

19 Wallis, Jill, *A Welcome in the Hillsides*, p. 28.

20 Mass Observation Archives. Turton 1400 MO TCS/1/A.

21 Frisby, *Kisses on a Postcard*, p. 23.

22 Mass Observation Archives TCS C/1/C 1 Observer KB 31/ (accessed 12 June 2012).

23 *Leek Post and Times*, 17 May 1941.

24 *Working Women in This War by Tom Harrisson Reprinted from Industrial Welfare and Personnel Management December 1939 Vol xx1 N 253*, p. 5.

25 University of Liverpool, *Our Wartime Guests: Opportunity or Menace? A Psychological Approach to Evacuation* (London: University Press of Liverpool, Hodder & Stoughton, 1940).

26 Imperial War Museum Posters of Conflict Collection an online collection available through *vads* an online collection for the visual arts http://www.vads.ac.uk/results.php?cmd=advsearch&words=imperial+war+museum+posters+of+conflict&field=all&oper=or&words2=&field2=all&mode=boolean&submit=search&IWMPC=1 (accessed 17 January 2013).

27 *Woman's Own*, 11 January 1941. Jane Waller and Michael Vaughan-Rees, *Women in Wartime: The Role of Women's Magazines 1939–1945* (Osborne Park: Optima, 1987), p. 20.

28 Wallis, 'A Welcome in the Hillsides', p. 184.

29 Jennifer Purcell, *Domestic Soldiers: Six Women's Lives in the Second World War* (London: Constable and Robinson, 2010), pp. 70–3.

30 Geoff Blore, *Dicky Blood's War* (Bloomington, IN: Dreamstar Books, 2005), p. 21.

31 Staffordshire Archives and Museum Service. On the Move Project. R2010.004.0022.

32 Sonya Brett interviewed for the BBC People's War website. Submitted 297 December 2003. http://www.bbc.co.uk/history/ww2peopleswar/stories/00/a2157400.shtml (accessed 13 May 2014).

33 Sonya Brett interviewed for the BBC People's War website. Submitted 297 December 2003. http://www.bbc.co.uk/history/ww2peopleswar/stories/00/ a2157400.shtml (accessed 10 May 2014).

34 Walsall Archives ACC 1268/1/5/7.

35 Ibid.

36 Mass Observation File Report 520 Moral and Women, p. 8.

37 Mann, *Out of Harm's Way*, p. 34.

38 Ibid.

39 Brittain, *England's Hour*, p. 50.

40 Ibid., pp. 57–8.

41 Mann, *Out of Harm's Way*, p. 49.

42 Ibid., p. 139.

43 Sean Longden, *Blitz Kids: The Children's War against Hitler* (London: Hachette UK, 2012), p. 127.

44 Brittain, *England's Hour*, p. 184.

45 Mary F. Williamson and Tom Sharp, eds, *Just a Larger Family: Letters of Marie Williamson from the Canadian Home Front, 1940-1944* (Waterloo, Canada: Wilfrid Laurier University Press, 2011).

46 Oral Transcript in Imperial War Museum Collection https://www.iwm.org.uk/ collections/item/object/80019493 (accessed 16 May 2018).

47 Ruth Inglis, *The Children's War: Evacuation 1939-1945* (London: Fontana Press, 1990), p. 24.

48 Vera Brittain, *Wartime Chronicle: Diary 1939-1945* (London: Gollancz, 1989), p. 100.

49 Barnett House and Evacuation Survey Committee, *London Children in War-Time Oxford: A Survey of Social and Educational Results of Evacuation: By a Barnett House Study Group* (Oxford: Oxford University Press, 1947), pp. 38–9.

50 Staffordshire Archive and Museum Service. On the Move Project. R2010.004.0004.

51 Staffordshire Archive and Museum Service. On the Move Project. R2010.004.0022.

52 Staffordshire Archives and Museum Service. On the Move Project. R2010.004.0006.

53 Clive Dellino interviewed for BBC People's War website, submitted on 13 November 2003, http://www.bbc.co.uk/history/ww2peopleswar/stories/53/ a2032453.shtml (accessed 12 May 2014).

54 Hobbs, *Don't Forget to Write*, p. 102.

55 Ibid., p. 128.

56 Williamson and Sharp, *Just a Larger Family*. Kindle edition Appendix 2.

57 Letter written in 06/12/41 in the Private Papers of J. Ingham in Imperial War Museum Archives, 15368.

58 Carlton Jackson, *Who Will Take Our Children?* (Methuen, 1985), pp. 122–4.

59 Jackson, *Who Will Take*, p. 76.

60 Walsall Archives ACC 1268/1/5/7.

61 Hobbs, *Don't Forget to Write: The True Story of an Evacuee and Her Family* (London: Random House, 2009), p. 145.

62 Hobbs, *Don't Forget to Write* (Ebury Press). pp. 141–50. Ruth Inglis, *The Children's War: Evacuation 1939–1945* (Peterborough: Fontana Press, 1990), p. 25.

63 Staffordshire Archive and Museum Service, On the Move Project. R2010.004.00.

64 Staffordshire Archive and Museum Service, On the Move Project. R2010.004.0090.

65 Barbara Fox, *When the War Is Over* (London: Sphere, 2016), p. 216.

66 Staffs CED/1/7/2.

67 Fox, *When the War Is Over*.

68 Staffordshire Record Office CEQ /15/3.

69 BBC Radio. January 1940, Records in the BBC Written Archives.

70 Mann, *Out of Harm's Way*, p. 220.

71 BBC Written Archives 24 /6 1942 R 11/12.

72 A more extensive discussion of this phenomenon can be found in broadcasting and evacuation in Maggie Andrews, *Domesticating the Airwaves: Broadcasting, Domesticity and Femininity* (London: Bloomsbury, 2012).

73 Vera Brittain, *One Voice: Pacifist Writings from the Second World War* (London: Bloomsbury, 2006), p. 60.

74 George Lock interviewed for BBC Peoples War Website Submitted 3 July 2005, http://www.bbc.co.uk/history/ww2peopleswar/stories/50/a3692450.shtml (accessed 10 May 2014).

75 *Staffordshire Advertiser,* 13 December 1941.

76 Cutting from a Thanet newspaper, reproduced in Peter Hyawood, *To a Safer Place: Memories of Kent Evacuees* (Dover: Buckland Publications, 2000).

77 Peter Askins BBC People's War website, submitted 21 August 2005, http://www.bbc.co.uk/history/ww2peopleswar/stories/88/a5234988.shtml.

78 *The Evacuee*: The magazine of the Evacuee Reunion Association November 2011, p. 10.

79 John Bowlby, 'Psychological Aspects', in Richard Padley and Margaret Cole, eds, *Evacuation Survey and Report to the Fabian Society* (London: Routledge, 1940), pp. 186–96, p. 191.

80 Staffordshire Archive and Museum Service. On the Move Project. R2010.004.0040.

81 Staffordshire Archive and Museum Service. On the Move Project. R2010.004.0003.

82 Staffordshire Archive and Museum Service. On the Move Porject R2010.004.0005.

83 Ibid.

84 Blore, *Dicky Blood's War*, p. 170.

85 Staffs R2010.004.00 Interview with Sydney Cox.

86 House and Evacuation Survey Committee, *London Children in War-Time Oxford*, p. 41.

87 *Daily Record*, 21 January 1943.

88 Ibid.

89 Mrs Lydia Coxhead interviewed for BBC People's War website, submitted 20 February 2005, http://www.bbc.co.uk/history/ww2peopleswar/stories/50/a3692450.shtml (accessed 12 May 2014).

90 Eric Brady, *Class War* (St Albans: Piper's Ash Books, 2007).

91 Jan Pollard, *Evacuee a Real Life WW2 Story* (London: London Scholastic Children's Books, 2015), p. 103.

92 Dorothy Sheridan, *Wartime Women: An Anthology of Women's Wartime Writing for Mass-Observation 1937–45* (London: Vintage, 1991), p. 207.

93 Dorothy Burlingham and Anna Freud, *Young Children in Wartime. A Year's Work in Residential War Nursery* (London: George Allen and Unwin, 1942), p. 43.

94 Staffordshire Archive and Museum Service. On the Move Project. R2010.004.0063.

95 Ruth Inglis, *The Children's War: Evacuation 1939–1945* (London: Fontana Press, 1990), p. 25.

96 Ibid., p. 144.

97 James Stuart Musgrave Rusby, *Childhood Temporary Separation: Long-Term Effects of Wartime Evacuation in World War 2* (Irvine, CA: Universal Publishers, 2008), p. 251.

98 Brittain, *England's Hour*.

99 Mann, *Out of Harm's Way*, p. 295.

100 Ibid., p. 297.

101 Staffordshire Archive and Museum Service. On the Move Project. R2010.004.0021.

102 Staffordshire Archive and Museum Service. On the Move Project. R2010.004.0022.

4 Mothers who were evacuated with their children

1 Mass Observation Archive, Second Evacuation, Box F 35 SXMoA1/2/S/2/A TCS/2/A.

2 Mass Observation Archives, TCS/2/G Investigator on Paddington Station 9 September 1940.

3 A Survey of Evacuation, 'Town Children through Country Eyes' (1940), p. 19.

4 Maggie Andrews, *The Acceptable Face of Feminism the Women's Institute as a Social Movement* (London: Lawrence and Wishart, 1998; reprinted 2015).

5 Dorothy Sheridan, *Wartime Women: An Anthology of Women's Wartime Writing for Mass-Observation 1937–45* (Vintage, 1991), p. 64.

6 *The Worcester Evening News and Times*, 2 September 1939.

7 Dennis Thorn informal interview in Abbots Bromley 2012.

8   Ben Wicks and David Rider, *The Day They Took the Children* (London: Bloomsbury, 1989), p. 104.

9   Richard Morris Titmuss, *Problems of Social Policy* (HM Stationery Off., 1950), p. 168.

10 Sheridan, *Wartime Women*, p. 58.

11 Ibid.

12 Mass Observation Evacuation Report 1940, File 11, p. 19. Mass Observation Online, http://www.massobservation.amdigital.co.uk/Documents/Preview-FileReports (accessed 30 July 2017).

13 George Seward, BBC People's War website, submitted 24 January 2006, http://www.bbc.co.uk/history/ww2peopleswar/stories/16/a8799916.shtml (accessed 15 July 2015).

14 Evelyn Margaret Fee, IWM Collection, https://www.iwm.org.uk/collections/item/object/80006057 (accessed 28 February 2018).

15 Ibid.

16 Mass Observation File Report 1940, File 11, p. 12. Mass Observation Online, http://www.massobservation.amdigital.co.uk/Documents/Preview-FileReports (accessed 30 July 2017).

17 Wicks and Rider, *The Day They Took the Children*, pp. 95–6.

18 Mass Observation Evacuation Report 1940, File 11, p. 20. Mass Observation Online, http://www.massobservation.amdigital.co.uk/Documents/Preview-FileReports (accessed 30 July 2017).

19 Report of Evacuation – From Staffordshire Federation of Women's Institutes November 1939, Women's Library, 5 FWI /H/56 (accessed 12 June 2012).

20 *Home and Country Magazine*, November 1939.

21 Worcestershire Archives and Archeology Service Oral Histories – Not part of a catalogue when accessed in 2015, Diana Morrison WW2/15 – Evacuated to Brighton from Croydon.

22 Private Papers of R W Coomber, IWM Collections, 3101, https://www.iwm.org.uk/collections/item/object/1030003151 (accessed 30 October 2015).

23 Ibid.

24 Ibid.

25 Jean Gibbins, BBC People's War website, submitted 2 September 2005, http://www.bbc.co.uk/history/ww2peopleswar/stories/34/a5496834.shtml (accessed 3 July 2016).

26 Staffordshire Archive and Museum Service, On the Move Project. R2010.004.0035.

27 Titmuss, *Problems*, p. 167.

28 Staffordshire Archive and Museum Service, On the Move Project, R2010.004.0089.

29 Staffordshire Archive and Museum Service, On the Move Project, R2010.004.0057.

30 Brenda Bryant, BBC People's War website, submitted 9 June 2003, https://www.bbc.co.uk/history/ww2peopleswar/stories/22/a1073422.shtml (accessed 3 July 2016).

31 Mr Messer, *HC Deb 08 February 1940, vol 357, cc415-6W415W*.

32 Jean Gibbins, BBC People's War website, submitted 2 September 2005, http://www.bbc.co.uk/history/ww2peopleswar/stories/34/a5496834.shtml (accessed 10 July 2016).

33 *Summary Report by the Ministry of Health 1 April 1939–31 March 1941*, p. 33, Exeter City Council, Town Clerk's Papers, Group G, Box 1.

34 Margaret Pryer, BBC People's War website, submitted 25 August 2005. https://www.bbc.co.uk/history/ww2peopleswar/stories/56/a5321756.shtml (accessed 10 July 2016).

35 Jean Gibbins, BBC People's War website, submitted 2 September 2005. http://www.bbc.co.uk/history/ww2peopleswar/stories/34/a5496834.shtml (accessed 10 July 2016).

36 Worcestershire Archives and Archaeological Society Interviews not yet catalogued when assessed in 2013. Margaret Brazier, WW2/105.

37 Joan Twyman, BBC People's War website, submitted 6 May 2004. http://www.bbc.co.uk/history/ww2peopleswar/stories/18/a2607518.shtml (accessed 10 July 2016).

38 IWM document no. 13286. https://www.iwm.org.uk/collections/item/object/1030013137.

39 Gillian Mawson, 'Guernsey Mothers and Children: Forgotten Evacuees' in *The Home Front in Britain* (Basingstoke: Palgrave Macmillan, 2014.), pp. 139–51.

40 For a fuller account, see Gillian Mawson, *Guernsey Evacuees* (Stroud: History Press, 2012).

41 *Guernsey Press Supplement*, June 2000, p. 13.

42 Mass Observation Report, Survey of Public Opinion, File 284. http://www.massobservation.amdigital.co.uk/Documents/Preview-FileReports (accessed 17 July 2017).

43 Mass Observation Report, Survey of Public Opinion, File 284. http://www.massobservation.amdigital.co.uk/Documents/Preview-FileReports (accessed 17 July 2017).

44 Vera Brittain, *Englands Hour: An Autobiography 1939–1941* (London: A&C Black, 2005), p. 62.

45 Sean Longden, *Blitz Kids: The Children's War against Hitler* (London: Hachette UK, 2012), p. 79.

46 James Hayward, *Myths & Legends of the Second World War* (Stroud: History Press, 2009), p. 91.

47 Mass Observation Archives, TCS /2/ C F25 (accessed 12 June 2012).

48 Longden, *Blitz Kids*, p. 526.

49 Jeremy A. Addison, Paul Addison, and Paul Crang, *Listening to Britain: Home Intelligence Reports on Britain's Finest Hour-May to September 1940* (London: Random House, 2011), p. 411.

50 Ruth Inglis, *The Children's War: Evacuation 1939–1945* (London: Fontana Press, 1990), p. 78.

51 Mass Observation Archives, TCS/2/G Investigator on Paddington Station, 9 September 1940 (accessed 12 June 2012).

52 Inglis, *The Children's War*, p. 76.

53 Bryan Cogley, BBC People's War website, submitted 13 June 2005. http://www.bbc.co.uk/history/ww2peopleswar/stories/90/a4185290.shtml (accessed 14 July 2013).

54 John Ray, *The Night Blitz, 1940–1941* (Arms & Armour, 1996), p. 260.

55 *Berrow's Worcester Journal*, 16 November 1940.

56 Brittain, *Englands Hour*, p. 158.

57 Ibid., pp. 160–1.

58 Ibid., p. 165.

59 Mass Observation Archive, Second Evacuation, Box F 35 SXMoA1/2/S/2/A TCS/2/A (accessed 12 July 2012).

60 Susan Hess, 'Civilian Evacuation to Devon in the Second World War', unpublished PhD thesis, University of Exeter, 2006.

61 Stoke-on-Trent archives, D 3766/1/5/2/3.

62 Hess, 'Civilian Evacuation', p. 226.

63 Ibid., p. 258.

64 Staffordshire Archive and Museum Service, On the Move Project, R2010.004.0033.

65 Material for this paragraph comes from Stoke-on-Trent Archive but was as yet uncatalogued when I looked at it in 2010.

66 Martin L. Parsons, *I'll Take That One: Dispelling the Myths of Civilian Evacuation 1939–45* (CNIB, 2009), p. 232.

67 Staffordshire Archives, D 14441/1/89.

68 Mike Brown, *Evacuees: Evacuation in Wartime Britain 1939–1945* (Stroud: History Press, 2005).

69 Mass Observation Evacuation Report 1940, File 11, p. 4. Mass Observation Online, http://www.massobservation.amdigital.co.uk/Documents/Preview-FileReports (accessed 30 July 2017).

70 Hess, 'Civilian Evacuation', p. 222.

71 Wicks and Rider, *The Day They Took the Children*, p. 134.

72 Ibid., p. 126.

73 Sonya O. Rose, *Which People's War?: National Identity and Citizenship in Wartime Britain 1939–1945* (OUP Oxford, 2003).

74 Wicks and Rider, *The Day They Took the Children*, p. 132.

75 Norfolk Record Office, Are We Still in England: The Story of Evacuees in Norfolk (2005), p. 2.

76 Staffordshire Record Office, D 3766/1/5/2/3.

77 Mr White, *HC Deb 04 March 1941, vol 369, cc780-1W780W*.

78 This quote comes from Evacuation Committee Notes in the Stoke-on-Trent Archive, but was as yet uncatalogued when I looked at it in 2010.

79 Parsons, *I'll Take That One* (CNIB, 2009).

80 Stoke-on-Trent archives, D 3766/1/5/2/3.

81 MO Living Conditions Report 1942, p. 17.

82 Wicks and Rider, *The Day They Took the Children*, p. 138.

83 Mass Observation Archives Evacuation, Box 2 SXM0/oA1/2/S/2/A TCS/2/A (accessed 12 July 2012).

84 Brittain, *Englands Hour*, p. 166.

85 Informal Interview, Jill Grundy, Abbots Bromley, 2012.

86 Staffordshire Archives and Museum Service, On the Move Project, R2010.004.0006.

87 Evelyn Ann Hurste, BBC People's War website. http://www.bbc.co.uk/history/ ww2peopleswar/stories/18/a2746118.shtml (accessed 30 July 2016).

88 Mary-Rose Benton, *Family Values: Pillar to Post Evacuee-Early Stages for a Touring Actor* (Thanet, 1998).

89 Carlton Jackson, *Who Will Take Our Children?* (York: Methuen Publishing, 1985), p. 54.

90 Staffordshire Record Office, D 14441/1/89.

91 Staffs Tony Longdon ref: R2010.004.0004.

92 Staffordshire Archives and Museum Service, On the Move Project, R2010.004.0020.

93 Staffordshire Archives and Museum Service, On the Move Project, R2010.004.0020.

94 Jenna Bailey, *Can Any Mother Help Me?* (London: Faber & Faber, 2011).

95 Sally Pincus, BBC People's War website, submitted 12 August 2005. https:// www.bbc.co.uk/history/ww2peopleswar/stories/61/a5022361.shtml (accessed 30 July 2016).

96 Staffordshire Archives and Museum Service, On the Move Project, R2010.004.0010.

97 *Leek Post and Times*, 31 January 1942.

5 The challenges of enforced intimacy: Looking after evacuees

1 Barnett House and Evacuation Survey Committee, *London Children in War-Time Oxford: A Survey of Social and Educational Results of Evacuation: By a Barnett House Study Group* (Oxford: Oxford University Press, 1947), p. 107.

2 Mrs St. Loe Strachey, *Borrowed Children: A Popular Account of Some Evacuation Problems and Their Remedies* (London: John Murray, 1940), p. x.

3   https://www.iwm.org.uk/collections/item/object/19994 (accessed 4 April 2018).

4   Lucy Noakes, *Women in the British Army: War and the Gentle Sex, 1907–1948*
    (London: Routledge, 2006).

5   Dorothy Sheridan, *Wartime Women: An Anthology of Women's Wartime Writing for
    Mass-Observation 1937–45* (London: Vintage, 1991), p. 55.

6   Mass Observation Reports, Evacuation 1939–44 Box 1 TV 5 94 (accessed 12
    July 2012).

7   Worcestershire Archives and Archeological Society, Box of newspaper cuttings on
    evacuation, Ref 10557-491.

8   Staffordshire Archive and Museum Service, On the Move Project, R2010.004.0025.

9   Geoffrey Shakespeare MP, Report on Conditions in Reception Areas 1941 copy
    viewed in Staffordshire Record Office.

10 Ruth Inglis, *The Children's War: Evacuation 1939–1945* (Peterborough: Fontana
    Press, 1990), p. 80.

11 House and Evacuation Survey Committee, *London Children in War-Time
    Oxford*, p. 27.

12 Ibid., p. 15.

13 A further discussion of these ideas of social motherhood can be found in, Eileen
    Janes Yeo, 'The Creation of "Motherhood" and Women's Responses in Britain and
    France, 1750–1914', *Women's History Review* 8.2 (1999), pp. 201–18. Or Eileen Janes
    Yeo, 'Constructing and Contesting Motherhood, 1750–1950', *Hecate* 31.2 (2005),
    p. 4 and in Chapter 8.

14 Clive Dellino interviewed for the BBC Peoples War website, submitted on 13
    November 2003, http://www.bbc.co.uk/history/ww2peopleswar/stories/53/
    a2032453.shtml (accessed 12 September 2017).

15 Staffordshire Archive and Museum Service, On the Move Project, R2010.004.0044.

16 University Department of Social Science, *Our Wartime Guests-Opportunity Or
    Menace? A Psychological Approach to Evacuation* (Liverpool: University Press of
    Liverpool, 1940), p. 9.

17 Mrs St. Loe Strachey, *Borrowed Children*, p. 11.

18 Letter from Mrs Gibbs to Cannock Town Clerk 2/1/ 1941, Staffordshire Record
    Office Papers D 1441/1/91.

19 Pam Hobbs, *Don't Forget to Write: The True Story of an Evacuee and Her Family*
    (London: Random House, 2009), p. 80.

20 Staffordshire Archive and Museum Service, On the Move Project, R2010.004.006.

21 Staffordshire Archive and Museum Service, On the Move Project, R2010.004.00.

22 Geoff Blore, *Dicky Blood's War* (Dreamstar Books, 2005), p. 76.

23 Staffordshire Archive and Museum Service, On the Move Project, R2010.004.0007.

24 Staffordshire Archive and Museum Service, On the Move, R2010.004.0035.

25 Staffordshire Archive and Museum Service, On the Move Project, R2010.004.00025.

26 Staffordshire Archive and Museum Service, On the Move Project, R2010.004.0011.

27 Staffordshire Archive and Museum Service, On the Move Project, R2010.0004.0005.

28 Staffordshire Archive and Museum Service, On the Move Project, R2010.004.001.

29 Hobbs, *Don't Forget to Write*, p. 120.

30 Staffordshire Archive and Museum Service, On the Move Project, R2010.004.0051.

31 Jill Wallis, 'A Welcome in the Hillsides', *The Merseyside and North Wales Experience* (Gwespyr: Avid Publications), p. 48.

32 Staffordshire Archive and Museum Service, On the Move Project, R2010.004.004.

33 Staffordshire Archive and Museum Service, On the Move Project, R2010.004.00.

34 Richard Broad and Suzie Fleming, ed., *Nella Last's War: The Second World War Diaries of Housewife, 49* (Profile Books, 2006),p. 5.

35 Worcestershire Archives and Archaeological Service WW2 oral history transcripts, not catalogued when looked at in 2013, number 105 – pp1–2.

36 Staffordshire Archive and Museum Service, On the Move Project, R2010.004.0032.

37 Letter received by Cannock District council 22/10/1940 Staffordshire Record Office Papers.

38 Staffordshire Archive and Museum Service, On the Move Project, RF2010.004.0036.

39 Hobbs, *Don't Forget to Write*, p. 167.

40 Ben Wicks and David Rider, *The Day They Took the Children* (London: Bloomsbury, 1989), p. 86.

41 Ruth Inglis, *The Children's War: Evacuation 1939–1945* (Petrborough: Fontana Press, 1990), p. 51.

42 Mass Observation File Report, Living Conditions, 1942, p. 15.

43 *Western Morning New*, 6 May, 1940.

44 Mrs St. Loe Strachey, *Borrowed Children*.

45 University Department of Social Science, *Our Wartime Guests-Opportunity*, p. 11.

46 Mrs St. Loe Strachey, *Borrowed Children*, p. 37.

47 Report of Evacuation – From Staffordshire Federation of Women's Institutes November 1939, Women's Library – 5 FWI /H/56 (accessed 12 September 2016).

48 Staffordshire Record Office. D 1425/1/4.

49 Constance Miles, *Mrs Miles's Diary* (London: Simon & Schuster, 2013), p. 224.

50 Ibid.

51 Staffordshire Archive and Museum Service, On the Move Project, R2010.004.0077.

52 Staffordshire Archive and Museum Service, On the Move Project, R2010.004.0034.

53 Quoted in John Welshman, *Churchill's Children: The Evacuee Experience in Wartime Britain* (Oxford: Oxford University Press, 2010), p. 223.

54 Richard Padley and Margaret, eds, *Evacuation Survey: A Report to the Fabian Society* (London: Routledge, 1940), p. 5.

55 Staffordshire Record Office D 1425/1/4.

56 Padley and Cole, *Evacuation Survey*.

57 Staffordshire Archive and Museum Service, On the Move Project, R2010.004.0018.

58 Elizabeth Roberts, *A Woman's Place: An Oral History of Working-Class Women, 1890–1940* (Oxford: B. Blackwell, 1984).

59 Staffordshire Archive and Museum Service, On the Move Project, R0201.004.0032.

60 Miles, *Mrs Miles's Diary*, p. 97.

61 Staffordshire Archive and Museum Service, On the Move Project, R2010.004.0027.

62 Staffordshire Archive and Museum Service, On the Move Project, RO210.004.0013.

63 Staffordshire Archive and Museum Service, On the Move Project, R2010.004.0089.

64 Staffordshire Record Office D 1441/1/88.

65 Staffordshire Record Office D 1441/1/88 Feb 1940.

66 Mrs St. Loe Strachey, *Borrowed Children*, p. 120.

67 Stoke-on-Trent Archives SD1593.

68 University Department of Social Science, *Our Wartime Guests-Opportunity*, p. 10.

69 Eleanor F. Rathbone, *The Disinherited Family* (1924) and Eleanor Florence Rathbone, *The Case for Family Allowances* (London: Edward Arnold, 1940).

70 Staffordshire Record Office, BA 916–493 332.

71 Letter received by Cannock District council 22/10/1940, Archives, Staffordshire Record Office, D 14441/1/89.

72 Report of Evacuation – From Staffordshire Federation of Women's Institutes November 1939, Women's Library – 5 FWI /H/56 (accessed 12 September 2016).

73 Report of Evacuation – From Staffordshire Federation of Women's Institutes November 1939, Women's Library – 5 FWI /H/56 (accessed 12 September 2016).

74 Staffordshire Archive and Museum Service, On the Move Project, R2010.004.0005.

75 Mary F. Williamson and Tom Sharp, eds, *Just a Larger Family: Letters of Marie Williamson from the Canadian Home Front, 1940–1944* (Waterloo, Canada: Wilfrid Laurier University Press, 2011).

76 Inglis, *The Children's War*.

77 Staffordshire Archive and Museum Service, On the Move Project, R2010.004.006.

78 Ibid.

79 Staffordshire Archive and Museum Service, On the Move Project, RF2010.004.0036.

80 Barbara Fox, *When the War Is Over* (London: Sphere, 2016), p. 320.

81 Staffordshire Archive and Museum Service, On the Move Project, R2010.004.0006.

82 Staffordshire Archive and Museum Service, On the Move Project, R2010.004.0003.

83 For example a foster mother from Standon Bridge got special permission to deliver her charges to Kent, Staffordshire Record Offices Papers D 1441/1/91(j).

84 Staffordshire Archive and Museum Service, On the Move Project, R2010.004.0051.

85 Staffordshire Archive and Museum Service, On the Move Project, R2010.004.006.

86 Staffordshire Archive and Museum Service, On the Move Project, R2010.004.0075

87 Staffordshire Archive and Museum Service, On the Move Project, R2010.004.0026.

88 Staffordshire Archive and Museum Service, On the Move Project, R2010.004.0031.

89 Staffordshire Archive and Museum Service, On the Move Project, R02010.004.0016.

90 Staffordshire Archive and Museum Service, On the Move Project, R2010.004.0005.

91 Staffordshire Archive and Museum Service, On the Move Project, R2010.004.00025.

6 Women paid to care: Teachers and welfare workers

1 Clarke A Chambers, 'Women in the Creation of the Profession of Social Work', *Social Service Review* 60.1 (1986), pp. 1–33. Gerry Holloway, *Women and Work in Britain since 1840* (London: Routledge, 2007).

2 See, for example, Eileen Janes Yeo, "Social Motherhood and the Sexual Communion of Labour in British Social Science, 1850–1950', *Women's History Review* 1.1 (1992), pp. 63–87. Elizabeth Darling, 'Womanliness in the Slums: A Free Kindergarten in Early Twentieth-Century Edinburgh', *Gender & History* 29.2 (2017), pp. 359–86.

3 Carol Dyhouse, 'Family Patterns of Social Mobility through Higher Education in England in the 1930s', *Journal of Social History* 34.4 (2001), pp. 817–42. June Purvis, *A History of Women's Education in England* (London: Open University, 1991).

4 Elizabeth Edwards, "'The Culture of Femininity in Women's Teacher Training Colleges 1900–50', *History of Education* 22.3 (1993), pp. 277–88.

5 Carol Dyhouse, 'Signing the Pledge? Women's Investment in University Education and Teacher Training before 1939', *History of Education* 26.2 (1997), pp. 207–23, p. 221.

6 Frances Widdowson, *Going Up into the Next Class: Women and Elementary Teacher Training 1840–1914*, No. 7 (Abingdon: Taylor & Francis, 1983).

7 Jenny Keating, 2012, www.history.ac.uk/projects/digital/history-in-education (accessed 12 June 2018).

8 Peter Gosden, *Education in the Second World War: A Study in Policy and Administration* (London: Routledge, 2013).

9 Staffordshire Archive and Museum Service, On the Move Project, R2010.004.0006.

10 Beatrice Mary (Betty) DUDDELL, BBC People's War website, contributed 18 July 2005, http://www.bbc.co.uk/history/ww2peopleswar/stories/79/a4476279.shtml (accessed 12 September 2016).

11 Sean Longden, *Blitz Kids: The Children's War against Hitler* (London: Hachette UK, 2012), p. 24.

12 Mrs St. Loe Strachey, *Borrowed Children: A Popular Account of Some Evacuation Problems and Their Remedies* (London: John Murray, 1940), p. 46.

13 Jill Wallis, *A Welcome in the Hillsides: The Merseyside and North Wales Experience of Evacuation 1939–1945* (Gwespyr: Avid Publications), p. 32.

14 Dorothy Sheridan, *Wartime Women: An Anthology of Women's Wartime Writing for Mass-Observation 1937–45* (London: Vintage, 1991), p. 51.

15 Staffordshire Record Office CED /1/7/63.

16 Sheridan, *Wartime Women*, pp. 66–7.

17 Derek Ernest Johnson, *The Exodus of Children* (Houston, TX: Pennyfarthing Publications, 1985).

18 Mass Observation TCS/1/C (accessed 13 July 2017).

19 Mass Observation TCS C/1/C 1 Observer KB 31 /8 (accessed 12 July 2017).

20 Staffordshire Archive and Museum Service, On the Move Project, R2010.004.0021.

21 Sheridan, *Wartime Women*, p. 65.

22 Juliet Gardiner, *Daily Mail*, 5 March 2005, Juliet Gardiner, https://search-proquest-com.apollo.worc.ac.uk/docview/321590263?pq-origsite=summon&accountid=15133 (accessed 3 October 2017).

23 Juliet Gardiner, https://search-proquest-com.apollo.worc.ac.uk/docview/321590263?pq-origsite=summon&accountid=15133 (accessed 3 October 2017).

24 Gosden, *Education in the Second World War*, p. 11.

25 Staffordshire Archive and Museum Service, On the Move Project, R2010.004.0007.

26 Irene Mary Watts (nee Gittins), BBC People's War website, Contributed 11 July 2005, http://www.bbc.co.uk/history/ww2peopleswar/stories/72/a4425572.shtml (accessed 2 September 2017).

27 Barnett House and Evacuation Survey Committee, *London Children in War-Time Oxford: A Survey of Social and Educational Results of Evacuation: By a Barnett House Study Group* (Oxford: Oxford University Press, 1947), p. 49.

28 Ibid., p. 48.

29 Vera Brittain, *England's Hour: An Autobiography 1939–1941* (London: A&C Black, 2005).

30 Pamela Lyndon Travers, *I Go by Sea, I Go by Land* (London: Hachette UK, 2015), p. 89.

31 Jessica Mann, *Out of Harm's Way* (London: Headline, 2014), p. 75.

32 Letter to Geoffrey Shakespeare 1 May 1941, quoted in Carlton Jackson, *Who Will Take Our Children?* (York: Methuen, 1985), p. 101.

33 Carlton Jackson, *Who Will Take Our Children?* (York: Methuen, 1985), pp. 102–6.

34 Staffordshire Record Office CED/1/7/2.

35 Longden, *Blitz Kids*, p. 269.

36 Geoff Blore, *Dicky Blood's War* (Dreamstar Books, 2005), p. 31.

37 Staffordshire Archive and Museum Service, On the Move Project, R2010.004.0006.

38 Ruth Inglis, *The Children's War: Evacuation 1939–1945* (Peterborouth: Fontana Press, 1990), p. 59.

39 Jan Pollard, *Evacuee, a Real Life WW2 Story* (Witney: London Scholastic Children's Books, 2015), p. 53.

40 May Smith, *The Wonderful Rumours: A Young Schoolteachers Wartime Diaries 1939–1945* (London: Virago, 2012), p. 42.

41 Ibid., p. 164.

42 Available at https://player.bfi.org.uk/free/film/watch-village-school-1940-online (accessed 4 May 2018).

43 Letter from Ministry of Health, 2 July 1940, Staffordshire Record Office.

44 Ibid.

45 Smith, *Wonderful Rumours*, p. 139.

46 Gosden, *Education in the Second World War*, and Smith, *Wonderful Rumours*.

47 http://www.thornburyroots.co.uk/war/ww2evacuees/ (accessed 4 April 2018).

48 Smith, *Wonderful Rumours*, p. 49.

49 Mass Observation Archive, File Reports Living Condition, p. 17 (accessed 12 July 2012).

50 Private Papers of S. J. Parkes in Imperial War Museum Archives, 146 (accessed 12 August 2016).

51 Susie Fisher. BBC People's War website, Contributed on 12 February 2004, http://www.bbc.co.uk/history/ww2peopleswar/stories/42/a2289242.shtml (accessed 5 September 2017).

52 Richard Padley and Margaret Cole, eds, *Evacuation Survey: A Report to the Fabian Society* (Routledge, 1940), p. 152.

53 See for example Staffordshire Archive and Museum Service, On the Move Project, R2010.004.0023.

54 Staffordshire Record Office CED/1/7/2.

55 Ibid.

56 Ibid.

57 Roy Cartwright. BBC Peoples War website, Contributed 12 October 2005, http://www.bbc.co.uk/history/ww2peopleswar/stories/99/a6111299.shtml (accessed 12 September 2017).

58 Padley and Cole, *Evacuation Survey*, p. 153.

59 Gosden, *Education in the Second World War*, p. 12.

60 Ibid.

61 Wallis, *A Welcome*, p. 135.

62 Pollard, *Evacuee*, p. 83.

63 See Philip Gardner and Peter Cunningham, 'Oral History and Teachers' Professional Practice: A Wartime Turning Point?', *Cambridge Journal of Education* 27.3 (1997), pp. 331–42.

64 Pam Hobbs, *Don't Forget to Write: The True Story of an Evacuee and Her Family* (London: Random House, 2009), p. 99.

65 Mrs St. Loe Strachey, *Borrowed Children*, p. 131.

66 Sheridan, *Wartime Women*, p. 66.

67 Staffordshire Record Office. CED /1/7/83.

68 David Stranack, *Schools at War: A Story of Education, Evacuation and Endurance in the Second World War* (Bognor Regis: Phillimore, 2005), pp. 59–60.

69 Ibid., p. 1.

70 Constance Miles, *Mrs Miles's Diary* (London: Simon & Schuster, 2013), p. 278.

71 Stranack, *Schools at War*, p. 8.

72 Hobbs, *Don't Forget to Write*, p. 162.

73 Staffordshire Record Office, D14441/1/84b.

74 Staffordshire Record Office, CEQ /13/3/10.

75 Sue Wheatcroft, *Worth Saving* (Oxford: Oxford University Press, 2015).

76 Ibid., pp. 46–7.

77 Ibid., p. 49.

78 Ibid., p. 48.

79 Ibid., p. 126.

80 Hostels for Difficult Children: A Survey of Experience under the Evacuation Scheme, HMSO for Ministry of Health. Welcome Institute, GC/ 148/25/1: Box 2.

81 Janie Hampton, *How the Girl Guides Won the War* (Glasgow: HarperCollins UK, 2010), Kindle edition 68%.

82 Ibid., Kindlle edition 69%.

83 Denise Riley, *War in the Nursery: Theories of the Child and Mother* (London: Virago, 1983), pp. 109–49.

84 Miles, *Mrs Miles's Diary*, p. 261.

85 Birmingham Archives and Heritage Pipewood Camp School Log Book BAH:S147/1(110/2244).

86 The Little Book of History of Pipewood, Unpublished pamphlet in the Imperial War Museum Archive 5998, p. 4.

87 Staffordshire Archive and Museum Service, On the Move Project, R2010.004.0092.

88 Staffordshire Archive and Museum Service, On the Move Project, R2010.004.0092.

89 Birmingham Lives – the Carl Chinn Archive: Archive reference 480, http://lives.bgfl.org/carlchinn/search.cfm?mr=&res=y&rt=&media=&area=&phys=&hum=&k1=Birmingham&k2=&k3=&k4=&k5=&k6=&k7=&k8= (accessed 12 July 2017).

90 Staffordshire Archive and Museum Service, On the Move Project, R2010.004.0092.

91 Staffordshire Archive and Museum Service, On the Move Project, R2010.004.008

92 Staffordshire Archive and Museum Service, On the Move Project, R2010.004.0084.

93 Staffordshire Archive and Museum Service, On the Move Project, R2010.004.008.

94 David Limond, 'Only Talk in the Staffroom: "Subversive" Teaching in a Scottish School, 1939–40', *History of Education* 29.3 (2000), pp. 239–52, 240.

95 Sheridan, *Wartime Women*, p. 68.

96 Gardner and Cunningham, 'Oral History', pp. 331–42, 336.

97 Laura Tisdall, 'Education, Parenting and Concepts of Childhood in England, c. 1945 to c. 1979', *Contemporary British History* 31.1 (2017), pp. 24–46, 25.

7 Social motherhood: An army of volunteers

1 Eileen Janes Yeo, 'Social Motherhood and the Sexual Communion of Labour in British Social Science, 1850–1950', *Women's History Review* 1.1 (1992), pp. 63–87 and Eileen Janes Yeo, 'The Creation of "Motherhood" and Women's Responses in Britain and France, 1750–1914', *Women's History Review* 8.2 (1999), pp. 201–18.

2 Ruth Inglis, *The Children's War: Evacuation 1939–1945* (Peterborough: Fontana Press, 1990), p. 20

3 Yeo, Creation of 'Motherhood' and Women's Responses, p. 214.

4 Ibid., p. 202.

5 See Maggie Andrews and Janis Lomas, *Hidden Heroines* (Marlborough: Crowood, 2018).

6 Peter Grant, *Philanthropy and Voluntary Action in the First World War: Mobilizing Charity* (London: Routledge, 2014).

7 See Deborah Dwork, *War Is Good for Babies and Other Young Children: A History of the Infant and Child Welfare Movement in England, 1898–1918* (Abingdon: Taylor & Francis, 1987) and Estelle Sylvia Pankhurst, *The Home Front* (London: Hutchinson, 1932). Maggie Andrews, 'Ideas and Ideals of Domesticity and Home in the First World War', *The Home Front in Britain* (Basingstoke: Palgrave Macmillan, 2014), pp. 6–20.

8 Eileen Janes Yeo, 'Social Motherhood and the Sexual Communion of Labour in British Social Science, 1850–1950', *Women's History Review* 1.1 (1992), pp. 63–8, p. 77.

9 James Hinton, *Women, Social Leadership, and the Second World War: Continuities of Class* (Oxford: Oxford University Press on Demand, 2002), p. 238.

10 The postgraduate work of Elspeth King at the University of Worcester sheds interesting light on this in relation to rationing.

11 Sue Bruley, 'The Politics of Food: Gender, Family, Community and Collective Feeding in South Wales in the General Strike and Miners' Lockout of 1926', *Twentieth Century British History* 18.1 (2007), pp. 54–77 and Rosemary AN Jones, 'Women, Community and Collective Action: The "Ceffyl Pren" Tradition', in Angela Johns, ed., *Our Mothers' Land: Chapters in Welsh Women's History 1830–1939* (Cardiff: University of Wales Press, 2011), pp. 17–42.

12 Nella Last, *Nella Last's War: The Second World War Diaries of 'Housewife, 49'*, Vol. 1 (London: Profile Books, 1981).

13   John Bowlby, 'Psychological Aspects', in Padley and Cole, eds, *Evacuation Survey* (London: Routledge, 1940), pp. 186–96, 192.

14   Staffordshire Archive and Museum Service, On the Move Project, R2010.004.0021.

15   Staffordshire Record Office, CED /1/7/62.

16   Mrs St. Loe Strachey, *Borrowed Children: A Popular Account of Some Evacuation Problems and Their Remedies* (London: John Murray, 1940), p. 8.

17   Staffordshire Archive and Museum Service, On the Move Project, R2010.004.0007.

18   Staffordshire Archive and Museum Service, On the Move Project, R2010.004.0036.

19   Robert Malcolmson and Patricia Malcolmson, *Women at the Ready: The Remarkable Story of the Women's Voluntary Services on the Home Front* (London: Hachette UK, 2013), p. 215.

20   *Tamworth Herald*, 13 September 1941.

21   Inglis, *Children's War*, p. 79.

22   Women's Royal Voluntary Service Archive (WRVS)'WRVSA&HC /WRVS/Q/NR/R9/1939-STFF/RGY (accessed 12 May 2018).

23   WRVSA&HC /WRVS/Q/NR/R9/1939-STFF/RGY (accessed 12 May 2018).

24   WRVSA&HC /WRVS/Q/NR/R9/1939-STFF/RGY (accessed 12 May 2018).

25   WRVSA&HC/WRVS/HQ/NR/R2/1943-YWR/BGL UD (accessed 12 May 2018).

26   WRVSA&HC /WRVS/Q/NR/R9/1939-STFF/RGY (accessed 12 May 2018).

27   Malcolmson and Malcolmson, *Women at the Ready*.

28   *Gloucester Citizen*, 18 August 1944.

29   *Derby Daily Telegraph*, 15 July 1944.

30   Imperial War Museum, Archives, IWM PST 2830, http://www.vads.ac.uk/results.php?cmd=search&words=evacuees&mode=boolean&submit=search (accessed 11 May 2018).

31   Hinton, *Women, Social Leadership*, p. 33.

32   Malcolmson and Malcolmson, *Women at the Ready*.

33   *Leek Post and Times*, 22 February 1941.

34   Worcester WRVS Narrative Report 31/01/1939-31/12/1939, Archives WRVS Devizes, WRVSA&HC/WRVS/HQ/NR/R9/1939-CB/WCT.

35   https://www.royalvoluntaryservice.org.uk/about-us/our-history (accessed 11 April 2018).

36   *Leek Post and Times*, 22 February 1941.

37   Hinton, *Women, Social Leadership*, p. viii.

38   Angus Calder, *The People's War: Britain 1939–1945* (London: Random House, 2012).

39   Malcolmson and Malcolmson, *Women at the Ready*, p. 66.

40   Yeo, Creation of 'Motherhood' and Women's Responses.

41   Inglis, *Children's War*, p. 86.

42 WVS Report of Ten Years Work for the Nation 1938-1948 Royal Voluntary Service Archive & Heritage Collection, https://www.royalvoluntaryservice.org.uk/Uploads/Documents/About%20us/ten_Years_work_020916.pdf (accessed 11 May 2018).

43 Malcolmson and Malcolmson, *Women at the Ready*, p. 232.

44 Ibid., p. 230.

45 Richard M. Titmuss, 'Problems of Social Policy. History of the Second World War', *The Social Worker Speaks* 204 (1950), p. 269.

46 WRVSA&HC/WRVS/HQ/NR/R9/1941-STAF/LEK RD (accessed 13 March 2018).

47 WRVSA&HC/WRVS/HQ/NR/R9/1941-STAF/CHE RD (accessed 13 March 2018).

48 *Northern Whig*, 19 April 1941.

49 WRVSA&HC /WRVS/Q/NR/R9/1939-STFF/RGY (accessed 13 March 2018).

50 Ibid.

51 Jill Wallis, *A Welcome in the Hillsides? The Merseyside and North Wales Experience of Evacuation, 1939–1945* (Gwespyr: Avid Publications, 2000), p. 135.

52 Malcolmson and Malcolmson, *Women at the Ready*, p. 111.

53 WRVSA&HC /WRVS/Q/NR/R9/1939-STFF/RGY (accessed 4 April 2018).

54 WRVSA&HC/WRVS/HQ/NR/R9/1941-STAF/NUL UD (accessed 14 April 2018).

55 WRVSA&HC/WRVS/HQ/NR/R2/1943-YWR/BGL UD (accessed 14 April 2018).

56 WRVSA&HC/WRVS/HQ/NR/R9/1941-STAF/CHE RD (accessed 14 April 2018).

57 WRVSA&HC /WRVS/Q/NR/R9/1939-STFF/RGY (accessed 4 April 2018).

58 WRVSA&HC/WRVS/HQ/NR/R9/1940-STAF/RGY UD (accessed 4 April 2018).

59 WRVSA&HC/WRVS/HQ/NR/R9/1940-STAF/RGY UD (accessed 4 April 2018).

60 Iris Jones Simantel, *Far from the East End* (London: Penguin, 2012), p. 71.

61 Maggie Andrews, *The Acceptable Face of Feminism: The Women's Institute Movement as a Social Movement* (London: Lawrence and Wishart, 1998), second edition, 2015.

62 See for example Eleanor Rathbone, *The Disinherited Family* (London: Edward Arnold, 1924).

63 Hinton, *Women, Social Leadership*, p. 157.

64 Stamper, Anne. Countrywomen in War Time – Women's Institutes 1938–1945. Paper Delivered to the Second International Conference on the History of Voluntary Action, Roehampton Institute September 2003, https://www.thewi.org.uk/__data/assets/pdf_file/0005/11111/countrywomen-in-war-time-womens-institutes-1938–1945-.pdf (accessed 12 February 2017).

65 *Buckingham Advertiser and Free Press*, 12 October 1940.

66 Un-catalogued papers 'Evacuation Report in Centre Leaders Conference on 2 March 1940', Stoke-on-Trent Archives.

67 Richmal Crompton, *Just William and the Evacuees* (London: George Newness, 1940).

68 Staffordshire Archive and Museum Service, On the Move Project, R2010.004.0026.

69 *Buckingham Advertiser and Free Press*, 12 October 1940.

70 WRVSA&HC/WRVS/HQ/NR/R2/1943-YWR/BGL UD (accessed 14 April 2018).

71 WRVSA&HC/WRVS/HQ/NR/R9/1941-STAF/UTT UD (accessed 4 April 2018).

72 National Federations of Women's Institutes. *Town Children through Country Eyes* (London: Published by the NFWI, 1940).

73 The Women's Library NFWI Collections 5WFM/E/2.

74 For further discussion of Towneyism see Andrews, *Acceptable Face of Feminism*.

75 *Home and Country* June 1942, p. 114.

76 See for example Rathbone, *Disinherited Family*.

77 John Welshman, 'Evacuation, Hygiene, and Social Policy: The Our Town's Report of 1943', *The Historical Journal* 42.3 (September 1999), pp. 781–807.

78 St. Loe Strachey, *Borrowed Children: A Popular Account of Some Evacuation Problems and Their Remedies* (Commonwealth Fund, 1940), p. 96.

79 House of Commons Debate, 14 September 1939, vol. 351 cc802–86.

80 Constance Miles, *Mrs Miles's Diary* (London: Simon & Schuster, 2013), p. 43.

81 Ibid., p. 65.

82 *Express and Echo*, 22 September 1939.

83 *Western Morning News*, 1 January 1940.

84 *Dorking and Leatherhead Advertiser*, 15 September 1939.

85 *The Leicester Mercury*, 25 November 1939.

86 *Lincolnshire, Boston and Spalding Free Press*, October 30 1939.

87 Record Office 3/9/2011, 'Evacuation Report' in Centre Leaders Conference on March 2 1940.

88 Ministry of Health Memorandum, 2 July 1940, Staffordshire Record Office Papers.

89 Ibid.

90 Ministry of Health Memorandum, 21 December 1940, Staffordshire Record Office Papers.

91 WRVSA&HC/WRVS/HQ/NR/R9/1941-STAF/UTT UD.

92 Staffordshire Archive and Museum Service, On the Move Project RD 14441/1/89.

93 *Taunton Courier, and Western Advertiser*, 31 May 1941,

94 Malcolmson and Malcolmson, *Women at the Ready*, p. 113.

95 WRVSA&HC /WRVS/Q/NR/R9/1939-STFF/RGY (accessed 4 April 2018).

96 *Coventry Evening Telegraph*, 11 August 1941.

97 *Warwick and Warwickshire Advertiser and Leamington Gazette*, 11 April 1941.

98 *Northams Evening Telegraph*, 22 December 1939.

99 Miles, *Mrs Miles's Diary*, pp. 155–6.

100 Inglis, *Children's War*, p. 19.

101 WRVSA&HC/WRVS/HQ/NR/R9/1941-STAF/UTT UD (accessed 14 April 2018).

102 WRVSA&HC /WRVS/Q/NR/R9/1939-STFF/RGY (accessed 4 April 2018).

103   Miles, *Mrs Miles's Diary*, p. 279.

104   *Mid Sussex Times*, 10 December 1941.

105   WRVSA&HC/WRVS/HQ/NR/R9/1941-STAF/UTT UD (accessed 14 April 2018).

106   *Leek Post and Times*, 11 August 1944.

107   WRVSA&HC/WRVS/HQ/NR/R9/1941-STAF/CHE RD (accessed 14 April 2018).

108   WRVSA&HC /WRVS/Q/NR/R9/1939-STFF/RGY (accessed 4 April 2018).

8   Myths, memories and memorials of evacuation

1   https://www.telegraph.co.uk/culture/tvandradio/doctor-who/8959341/Doctor-Who-Christmas-special-BBC-One-preview.html (accessed 4 February 2018).

2   Angus Calder, *The Myth of the Blitz* (London: Random House, 1992).

3   Olive Shapley, *Broadcasting a Life* (London: Scarlet Press, 1996). Reprinted in Caroline Mitchell, *Women and Radio Airing the Difference* (London: Routledge, 2000), p. 68.

4   Shapley, *Broadcasting a Life*. Reprinted in Mitchell, *Women and Radio*.

5   Jane Waller and Michael Vaughan-Rees, *Women in Wartime: The Role of Women's Magazines 1939–1945* (Osborne Park: Optima, 1987), p. 20.

6   Louise L. Sherman, 'In the Homes of Strangers: The World War II Evacuation of British Children in Children's Literature', *School Library Journal* 35(8) (April 1989), pp. 42–44, 42.

7   Jeffrey Richards, *Happiest Days: The Public Schools in English Fiction* (Manchester: Manchester University Press, 1988).

8   Thomas Hughes, *Tom Brown's Schooldays*. 1857 (reprinted Oxford: Oxford University Press, 1999).

9   J. K. Rowling, *Harry Potter and the Prisoner of Azkaban* (London: Raincoast, 1999).

10   Elinor M. Brent-Dyer, *The Chalet School at War* (London: W.R Chambers, 1941).

11   Enid Blyton, *The Children of St. Kidillin* (London: Bloomsbury, 1997), new edition.

12   Violet Methley, *Vaccies* (Oxford: Oxford University Press, 1940).

13   Clive Staples Lewis, *The Lion, the Witch and the Wardrobe* (New York: HarperCollins, 1950), Kindle edition.

14   Ibid., Kindle edition, 3%.

15   Ibid., Kindle edition, 27%.

16   Methley, *Vaccies*, p. 255.

17   Blyton, *Children of St. Kidillin*, p. 29.

18   Lewis, *Lion, the Witch and the Wardrobe*, Kindle edition 1%.

19   Owen Dudley Edwards, *British Children's Fiction in the Second World War* (Edinburgh: Edinburgh University Press, 2007), p. 133.

20 Blyton, *Children of St. Kidillin*, p. 92.

21 Methley, *Vaccies*, p. 81.

22 Wendy Webster, *Imagining Home: Gender, Race and National Identity, 1945–1964* (London: Routledge, 2005), p. 155.

23 Angela Davis, *Modern Motherhood: Women and Family in England, c. 1945–2000* (Manchester: Manchester University Press, 2013), p. 146.

24 Richard M. Titmuss, 'Problems of Social Policy. History of the Second World War', *Social Worker Speaks* 204 (1950).

25 Arthur Marwick, *Britain in the Century of Total War: War, Peace, and Social Change, 1900–1967* (London: Little, Brown, 1968). Arthur Marwick, *War and Social Change in the Twentieth Century: A Comparative Study of Britain, France, Germany, Russia and the United States* (Basingstoke: Palgrave Macmillan, 1974).

26 John Welshman, 'Evacuation and Social Policy during the Second World War: Myth and Reality', *Twentieth Century British History* 9.1 (1998), pp. 28–53.

27 My thanks go to University of Worcester postgraduate student in English, Rose Miller for pointing out the links between evacuees and Paddington Bear to me.

28 Michael Bond interviewed by BBC local news, http://www.bbc.co.uk/news/uk-england-berkshire-16964890 (accessed 18 July 2017).

29 Michael Bond, *A Bear Called Paddington* (first published William Collins and Sons 1958, reprinted New York: HarperCollins Children's Book, 2017), p. 30.

30 Angus Calder, 'Britain's Good War?', *History Today* 45.5 (1995), p. 55.

31 Edward Palmer Thompson, *The Making of the English Working Class* (first published Victor Gollancz, 1963; reprinted New York: Open Road Media, 2016), p. 12.

32 For further details see http://www.history.ac.uk/makinghistory/themes/history_from_below.html (accessed 10 September 2017).

33 Raphael Samuel, *Theatres of Memory: Past and Present in Contemporary Culture* (London: Verso Books, 2012).

34 There are for example collections of evacuee oral histories at the Imperial War Museum, https://www.iwm.org.uk/collections/search?query=evacuation&page Size=the British Library, https://www.bl.uk/collection-guides/oral-histories-of-war-and-conflict (accessed 4 April 2018) and Reading University https://www.reading.ac.uk/merl/collections/Archives_A_to_Z/merl-D_EVAC.aspx (accessed 2 June 2017).

35 Juliet Mitchell, *Psychoanalysis and Feminism: A Radical Reassessment of Freudian Psychoanalysis* (New York: Basic Books, 2000).

36 Laura Tisdall, 'Education, Parenting and Concepts of Childhood in England, c. 1945 to c. 1979', *Contemporary British History* 31.1 (2017), pp. 24–46, 34.

37 Carol Smart, *Divorce in England 1950–2000: A Moral Tale?* (Centre for Research on Family, Kinship & Childhood, 2000).

38 Nina Bawden, *Carrie's War* (2013), Kindle edition.

39 Michelle Magorian, *Goodnight Mister Tom* (Vancouver: Kestrel, 1981).

40 Bawden, *Carrie's War*, Kindle edition 88%.

41 Ibid., Kindle edition 90%.

42 The book came out only two years after the Hollywood Court drama *Kramer vs. Kramer* (1979) which portrays a father who when his wife leaves him is forced to look after his son, something he portrayed as able to do much better than her.

43 Bawden, *Carrie's War*, Kindle edition 84%.

44 Wendy Wheeler, 'Nostalgia Isn't Nasty: The Postmodernising of Parliamentary Democracy', *Altered states: Postmodernism, Politics, Culture* (London: Lawrence and Wishart, 1994), pp. 94–107.

45 Susan Murray and Laurie Ouellette, eds, *Reality TV: Remaking Television Culture* (New York: NYU Press, 2004).

46 Geoff Blore, *Dicky Blood's War* (Stafford: Dreamstar Books, 2003).

47 Blore, *Dicky Blood's War*, p. 84.

48 Mary Rose Benton, *Family Values* (Margate: Thanet Publications, 1998).

49 https://www.theschooloflife.com/thebookoflife/the-great-psychoanalysts-melanie-klein/ (accessed 1 June 2018).

50 Benton, *Family Values*, p. 35–6.

51 E. Ann Kaplan, *Motherhood and Representation: The Mother in Popular Culture and Melodrama* (London: Routledge, 2013), p. 48.

52 Jay Winter, 'Notes on the Memory Boom', in David Bell, ed., *Memory, Trauma and World Politics* (Basingstoke: Palgrave Macmillan, 2006), pp. 54–73.

53 http://www.bbc.co.uk/history/ww2peopleswar/categories/ (accessed 8 July 2017).

54 Marianne Hirsch, 'The Generation of Postmemory', *Poetics Today* 29.1 (2008), pp. 103–28.

55 Alison Landsberg, *Prosthetic Memory: The Transformation of American Remembrance in the Age of Mass Culture* (New York: Columbia University Press, 2004), Landsberg 2003: 148.

56 Alison Landsberg, *Prosthetic Memory: The Transformation of American Remembrance in the Age of Mass Culture* (New York: Columbia University Press), p. 147.

57 For further discussion of myth and the Second World War see Martin Evans and Kenneth Lunn, *War and Memory in the Twentieth Century* (Berg Publishers, 1997). Penny Summerfield, *Reconstructing Women's Wartime Lives: Discourse and Subjectivity in Oral Histories of the Second World War* (Manchester: Manchester University Press, 1998). Lucy Noakes and Juliette Pattinson, eds, *British Cultural Memory and the Second World War* (London: A&C Black, 2013). Ibid.

58 Benedict Anderson, *Imagined Communities: Reflections on the Origin and Spread of Nationalism* (London: Verso Books, 2006).

59 Calder, *Myth of the Blitz*.

60 Angus Calder, *The People's War: Britain 1939–1945* (London: Random House, 2012). Maggie Andrews and Janis Lomas, eds, *The Home Front in Britain: Images, Myths and Forgotten Experiences Since 1914* (New York: Springer, 2014).

61 See, for example, Calder, *The People's War*. Sonya O. Rose, *Which People's War?: National Identity and Citizenship in Wartime Britain 1939–1945* (Oxford: Oxford University Press, 2003).

62 https://www.gwsr.com/search?q=1940s+weekend (accessed 2 February 2018).

63 Karen J. Burnell, Peter G. Coleman, and Nigel Hunt, 'Coping with Traumatic Memories: Second World War Veterans' Experiences of Social Support in Relation to the Narrative Coherence of War Memories', *Ageing & Society* 30.1 (2010), pp. 57–78.

64 Judith Lewis Herman, 'Complex PTSD: A Syndrome in Survivors of Prolonged and Repeated Trauma', *Journal of Traumatic Stress* 5.3 (1992), pp. 377–91.

65 Ulrich Beck, *Risk Society: Towards a New Modernity*, Vol. 17 (Sage, 1992).

66 Daniel Miller, 'How Infants Grow Mothers in North London', *Theory, Culture & Society* 14.4 (1997), pp. 67–88. Alison J. Clarke, 'Maternity and Materiality', *Consuming Motherhood* (2004), pp. 55–71.

67 Edward M. Bruner, 'Experience and Its Expressions', *The Anthropology of Experience* 3 (1986), pp. 32.

68 Staffordshire Archive and Museum Service, On the Move Project, R2010.004.0043.

69 May Ien Ang, *Watching Dallas: Soap Opera and the Melodramatic Imagination* (London: Routledge, 1985; reprinted 2013).

70 Staffordshire Archive and Museum Service, On the Move Project, R2010.004.00.

71 Burnell, Coleman, and Hunt, 'Coping with Traumatic Memories'.

72 Staffordshire Archive and Museum Service, On the Move Project, R2010.004.00

73 Benton, *Family Values*.

74 Staffordshire Archive and Museum Service, On the Move Project, R2010.004.0040.

75 http://www.thenma.org.uk/about-us/news-stories/memorial-to-wwii-evacuees-dedicated-at-the-arboretum/ (accessed 10 August 2017).

76 http://www.evacuees.org.uk (accessed 5 March 2018).

77 http://www.evacuees.org.uk/memorial.html (accessed 8 January 2018).

78 http://www.svr.co.uk/pdf/Education/2017/Blitz%20and%20%20Evacuation%20 2017%20SVR.pdf (accessed 4 April 2018).

Afterword: Shifting discourses of motherhood

1 Claire Langhamer, 'Love and Courtship in Mid-Twentieth-Century England', *The Historical Journal* 50.1 (2007), pp. 173–96.

2 Denise Riley, *War in the Nursery* (London: Virago, 1983), pp. 109–49.

3 David Kynaston, *Family Britain, 1951–1957* (London: Bloomsbury, 2010).

4 Christine Gledhill and Gillian Swanson, eds, *Nationalising Femininity: Culture, Sexuality and British Cinema in the Second World War* (Manchester: Manchester University Press, 1996), p. 74.

5 H. M. Government *Social Insurance and Allied Services* (The Beveridge report) (London: His Majesty's Stationery Office) p. 52 quoted Angela Davis, *Modern Motherhood: Women and Family in England, c. 1945–2000* (Manchester University Press, 2013). Also see Pat Thane, *The Foundations of the Welfare State* (London: Longman, 1996).

6 See for example Anna Davin, 'Imperialism and Motherhood', *History Workshop*, Editorial Collective, History Workshop, Ruskin College (1978). Ellen Ross, *Love and Toil: Motherhood in Outcast London, 1870–1918* (Oxford: Oxford University Press, 1993).

7 John Bowlby, *Maternal Care and Mental Health*, Vol. 2 (World Health Organization, 1951).

8 J. Bowlby, *Child Care and the Growth of Love* (London: Penguin, 1953). Angela Davis, *Modern Motherhood: Women and Family in England, c. 1945–2000* (Manchester: Manchester University Press, 2013), p. 122.

9 Michal Shapira, 'Psychoanalysts on the Radio: Domestic Citizenship and Motherhood in Postwar Britain', *Women and Gender in Postwar Europe* (London: Routledge, 2012), pp. 81–96.

10 For a further discussion of the popularization of psychologists' writing, see Denise Riley, *War in the Nursery* (Virago, 1983), pp. 81–108. Michal Shapira, *The War Inside*, Vol. 38 (Cambridge: Cambridge University Press, 2013).

11 Angela Davis, *Modern Motherhood*, pp. 146, 124.

12 Gal Gerson, 'Winnicott, Participation and Gender', *Feminism & Psychology* 14.4 (2004), pp. 561–81, 561–2.

13 Donald Woods Winnicott, *Home Is Where We Start from: Essays by a Psychoanalyst* (W.W. Norton, 1990).

Index

Printed in Great Britain
by Amazon